Procedural Programming with PostgreSQL PL/pgSQL

Design Complex Database-Centric Applications with PL/pgSQL

Baji Shaik
Dinesh Kumar Chemuduru

Procedural Programming with PostgreSQL PL/pgSQL: Design Complex Database-Centric Applications with PL/pgSQL

Baji Shaik
Texas, TX, USA

Dinesh Kumar Chemuduru
Andhra Pradesh, India

ISBN-13 (pbk): 978-1-4842-9839-8
https://doi.org/10.1007/978-1-4842-9840-4

ISBN-13 (electronic): 978-1-4842-9840-4

Managing Director, Apress Media LLC: Welmoed Spahr
Acquisitions Editor: Divya Modi
Development Editor: James Markham

Cover designed by eStudioCalamar

Cover image designed by Freepik (www.freepik.com)

Distributed to the book trade worldwide by Apress Media, LLC, 1 New York Plaza, New York, NY 10004, U.S.A. Phone 1-800-SPRINGER, fax (201) 348-4505, e-mail orders-ny@springer-sbm.com, or visit www.springeronline.com. Apress Media, LLC is a California LLC and the sole member (owner) is Springer Science + Business Media Finance Inc (SSBM Finance Inc). SSBM Finance Inc is a **Delaware** corporation.

For information on translations, please e-mail booktranslations@springernature.com; for reprint, paperback, or audio rights, please e-mail bookpermissions@springernature.com.

Apress titles may be purchased in bulk for academic, corporate, or promotional use. eBook versions and licenses are also available for most titles. For more information, reference our Print and eBook Bulk Sales web page at http://www.apress.com/bulk-sales.

Any source code or other supplementary material referenced by the author in this book is available to readers on GitHub (https://github.com/Apress). For more detailed information, please visit https://www.apress.com/gp/services/source-code.

Paper in this product is recyclable

*I extend this dedication to Afrah Razzak, my exceptional wife.
Her enduring support and remarkable patience during the extended
writing sessions have been invaluable to me.*

—*Baji Shaik*

*I lovingly extend this dedication to my dear friend, Baji Shaik.
Your unwavering support and encouragement have been my guiding
light, especially in the most challenging moments. Your belief in me has
been a constant source of inspiration, and I am grateful for your
presence in my journey. This book is as much a tribute to our
friendship as it is a testament to the power of steadfast camaraderie.
Thank you for always being there.*

—*Dinesh Kumar Chemuduru*

Table of Contents

About the Authors.. xiii

About the Technical Reviewer xv

Acknowledgments xvii

Introduction xix

Chapter 1: Introduction to PL/pgSQL 1

  A Closer Look at PL/pgSQL.. 1

  PL/pgSQL Installation 2

  PL/pgSQL Execution Flow 4

  PL/pgSQL Blocks.. 6

    Anonymous or Unnamed Blocks... 6

  Named Blocks 10

  Summary... 12

  What's Next 12

Chapter 2: PL/pgSQL Variables 13

  What Are Variables in PL/pgSQL?... 13

  Declaring Variables 13

  Variable Scope 15

  Constant Variables 17

  Variable Alias 18

    Scalar Variables 19

    Array Variables 21

    Record Variables.. 22

    Cursor Variables 23

Summary..25

What's Next..25

Chapter 3: PL/pgSQL Data Types 27

Data Types..27

Declaring Variables with Data Types...28

Supported Types 30

Base Type...32

Composite Type 33

Domain Type...35

Pseudo-Type 37

Range Type...38

Multirange Types..40

Summary...41

What's Next..41

Chapter 4: Dealing with Strings, Numbers, and Arrays 43

Strings..43

Function Format 45

Dealing with Null String..47

Numbers 50

Arrays...53

Example Use Cases..54

Strings..54

Numbers 55

Arrays 57

Summary...58

What's Next..59

Chapter 5: Control Statements 61

IF/ELSE Statement 62

Cascading IF Statements..65

CASE Statement..66

Iterative Statement 68

    LOOP Statement 69

WHILE Statement 72

FOR Statement 74

Example Use Cases 78

    Example 1 78

    Example 2 81

    Best Practices of Using Control Statements in PL/pgSQL 84

Summary... 85

What's Next... 85

Chapter 6: Handling Arrays **87**

Array Index.. 88

Array Length.. 89

Iterate Array 91

Find Duplicate Elements in Array.. 92

Append Elements to Array... 93

Array Merge 94

Multidimensional Arrays 94

Summary... 96

What's Next... 96

Chapter 7: Handling JSON **97**

What Is JSON? 97

Use Cases 100

Advantages and Disadvantages.. 104

Build PL/pgSQL Functions for JSON.. 105

Indexing JSON Data 109

Other Useful JSON Functions.. 111

Summary... 111

What's Next... 112

Chapter 8: Cursors..**113**

  What Are Cursors? 113

      CURSOR Attributes..115

      ISOPEN Attribute 115

      FOUND Attribute..117

      NOTFOUND Attribute 119

      ROWCOUNT Attribute 120

      Monitor Cursors 122

      SCROLL Cursor 123

      NO SCROLL Cursor...125

      WITH HOLD Cursors 127

      Refcursors 128

  Summary...130

  What's Next..130

Chapter 9: Custom Operators **131**

  Built-In Operators..131

  Creating a Custom Operator...135

      Simple Example...136

      SCENARIO 1: Case-Insensitive Comparison............................140

      SCENARIO 2: Custom Data Type Math.....................................142

      SCENARIO 3: Date Differentiate Operator 144

      SCENARIO 4: Custom Operator for Data Classification 146

  Advantages 148

  Disadvantages...149

  Summary...149

  What's Next..149

Chapter 10: Custom Casting **151**

  Built-In Casts 151

  Custom Casts 160

Creating a Custom Cast 160

Simple Example 161

SCENARIO 1: Converting Custom Data Types 163

SCENARIO 2: Custom Data Type to JSONB 165

Summary 168

What's Next 168

Chapter 11: Dynamic SQL **169**

What Is Dynamic SQL? 169

Syntax of Dynamic SQL in PL/pgSQL 169

Simple Example 170

Use Cases of Dynamic SQL 171

Best Practices and Considerations for Dynamic SQL 178

1. Preventing SQL Injection 179

2. Sanitizing and Validating Inputs 179

3. Security Concerns 180

4. Performance Optimization 180

Summary 181

What's Next 181

Chapter 12: Building Functions and Procedures **183**

Functions 183

Defining Functions 184

Calling Functions 184

Categories 185

Immutable Functions 186

STABLE Functions 188

VOLATILE Functions 191

Procedures 194

Temporary Functions/Procedures 195

VARIADIC Functions/Procedures 196

Best Practices 198

Summary.. 199

What's Next... 199

Chapter 13: Return Values and Parameters... 201

Return Values... 201

Simple Example.. 202

Different Ways to Return Values... 203

RETURNS 203

RETURNS SETOF 204

RETURNS TABLE 204

OUT 205

Simple Difference Matrix... 206

Different Examples for Each RETURN Type... 206

Using SELECT Statements 207

Using RETURNS TABLE.. 208

Using RETURN NEXT 209

Using RETURNS SETOF TABLE 210

Using RETURNS SETOF Data Type.. 210

Using RETURNS RECORD 211

Using RETURNS SETOF RECORD.. 212

Using OUT Parameters.. 214

Using INOUT Parameter 216

Summary.. 216

What's Next... 217

Chapter 14: Handling Exceptions.. 219

Exceptions... 219

GET DIAGNOSTICS.. 219

FOUND 223

Exceptions in PL/pgSQL 225

Different Ways to Handle Exceptions in PL/pgSQL 226

Using the BEGIN and END Statements... 226

Using the RAISE Statement 231

Custom Exceptions 232

Rethrow Exceptions 233

ASSERT 234

Get Call Stack 235

Using the GET STACKED DIAGNOSTICS Statement 237

Advantages of Using Exceptions 238

Disadvantages of Using Exceptions 239

Summary 239

What's Next 240

Chapter 15: Triggers 241

What Are Triggers? 241

Syntax 242

Simple Example 243

Types of Triggers in PostgreSQL 245

Row-Level Triggers 246

INSTEAD OF Triggers 253

Statement-Level Triggers 254

Event Triggers 258

Advantages of Triggers 260

Disadvantages of Triggers 261

DROP Triggers 261

Summary 262

What's Next 262

Chapter 16: Transaction Management 263

Nested Transactions 263

Exception Handling 266

Summary 270

What's Next 270

Chapter 17: Aggregates **271**

Custom Aggregate.. 271

    Simple Example.. 272

    State Transition Function.. 273

    Final Function.. 275

    Creating Custom Aggregate.. 276

    Create Type.. 277

    Create State Transition Function... 277

    Create Aggregate.. 278

    Final Function.. 279

Summary... 281

What's Next... 281

Chapter 18: Listen and Notify **283**

Simple Example 283

Build Polling in psql 285

TCN Extension 290

Summary... 292

What's Next... 292

Chapter 19: PL/pgSQL Essential Extensions **293**

plprofiler Extension.. 293

    Installation... 295

    Usage... 296

plpgsql_check Extension 305

    Installation... 305

    Usage... 306

Summary... 309

Index.. **311**

About the Authors

Baji Shaik, currently serving as a Senior Database Consultant at AWS Professional Services, embarked on his journey into the world of databases in 2011. Since then, his expertise has encompassed an array of database technologies, including Oracle, PostgreSQL, EDB Postgres, Amazon RDS, Amazon Aurora, Amazon Redshift, and Greenplum. Baji's extensive background spans both depth and breadth, showcasing his mastery in SQL/NoSQL database technologies.

Baji stands out as a Database Migration Expert, having successfully developed numerous database solutions that tackle complex business challenges, particularly in migrating databases from on-premises environments to Amazon RDS and Aurora PostgreSQL/MySQL. His prowess also extends to performance optimization, having fine-tuned RDS/Aurora PostgreSQL/MySQL databases to achieve remarkable performance benchmarks.

With a passion for knowledge sharing, Baji has authored several notable books on PostgreSQL, such as *PostgreSQL Configuration*, *Beginning PostgreSQL on the Cloud*, and *PostgreSQL Development Essentials*. His commitment to education and information dissemination is further evident through his contributions to conferences, workshops, and a multitude of insightful blogs within the AWS blog community.

Dinesh Kumar Chemuduru, an accomplished Principal Architect (OSS), brings a wealth of experience to the realm of technology and open source solutions. With a notable background at AWS as a proficient database consultant, Dinesh excelled in orchestrating numerous successful database migrations. His expertise extends to the open source arena, where he has both crafted and augmented solutions around PostgreSQL, showcasing his commitment to collaborative innovation.

A coding enthusiast at heart, Dinesh finds joy in crafting applications using Flutter, Golang, and C++, platforms where his creativity knows no bounds. His proficiency extends to the deployment phase, as he deftly navigates Kubernetes to bring his coding creations to life. In the literary domain, Dinesh stands as a coauthor of the esteemed *PostgreSQL High Performance Cookbook*, a testament to his mastery of the subject matter. Beyond his own works, he actively engages in the appraisal of fellow authors' PostgreSQL books, cementing his status as a valued participant in the exchange of knowledge.

Dinesh's impact reverberates through his open source contributions, which include the inception and enrichment of projects such as PTOR – an ingenious RPO/RTO/SLA calculator tailored for PostgreSQL. Another tool, "hammerpost," sets a benchmark for synthetic parameter evaluation in PostgreSQL, seamlessly integrated with HammerDB.

About the Technical Reviewer

Deepak Ramnandan Mahto works as a PostgreSQL Database Engineer at Google Cloud. He has been working with PostgreSQL since 2018, and he also worked as a database migration consultant at AWS. He is also a keen blogger and loves to publish articles on migration, best practices, and on cloud with PostgreSQL. He loves to code and build database-related utilities using PL/pgSQL and SQL.

Acknowledgments

I would like to express my gratitude to several individuals who have played a crucial role in making this book a reality. A heartfelt thank-you to Apress Media for providing me with this valuable opportunity. I am especially grateful to my coauthor and mentor, Dinesh Kumar Chemuduru, for his exceptional collaboration. I want to express my gratitude to Divya Modi and Nirmal Selvaraj for being understanding of our hectic schedules and providing us with continuous support throughout the entire process. Special thanks to Deepak Mahto for his thorough review of the book. Lastly, I am profoundly thankful to my parents, Lalu Saheb Shaik and Nasar Bee, whose unwavering support has shaped me into the person I am today.

—Baji Shaik

I would like to extend my heartfelt gratitude to a remarkable group of individuals who have been instrumental in making this endeavor a reality. My heartfelt thank-you to Apress Media for providing me with this valuable opportunity. A special note of appreciation to my esteemed coauthor, Baji Shaik. Sincere thanks to Deepak Mahto, whose meticulous review and insightful feedback significantly enhanced the quality and depth of this manuscript. To Divya Modi and Nirmal Selvaraj, our project coordinators, your organizational skills and dedication ensured that every aspect of this project fell seamlessly into place. To my parents Vanamma, Sreenivasulu and my dearest children, Yashvi and Isha, and to the future luminaries, Hema Siri K and Rahul Sonu K – your unwavering love and understanding throughout the demanding phases of this project have served as my steadfast anchor. Your continuous support is my driving force.

Finally, a heartfelt thank-you to my exceptional team at Tessell. Your commitment to excellence and innovation is awe-inspiring. Together, we are shaping the future of DBaaS, and I am privileged to work alongside such talented individuals.

—Dinesh Kumar Chemuduru

Introduction

The PostgreSQL engine comes with its own dedicated procedural language, similar to procedural languages found in other commercial database engines. This language, known as PL/pgSQL, offers a range of powerful features that developers have long desired. For instance, PL/pgSQL includes certain object-oriented programming capabilities like the ability to define custom operators and types, as well as custom aggregates.

In contrast to other programming languages supported by PostgreSQL, PL/pgSQL is intricately linked with the PostgreSQL database engine interface. This tight integration ensures optimal performance and a seamless fit for constructing business logic on the database side. In this book, we not only introduce the fundamentals of PL/pgSQL, but we also dive deep into specific use cases that we've implemented for particular scenarios. Our aim is to comprehensively cover the various features, functionalities, and application scenarios of PL/pgSQL, offering assistance in crafting effective server-side objects with ease.

Through the content of this book, you will gain an understanding of PL/pgSQL's design and dive deep into its transaction model, including how commit and rollback operations function. You'll discover strategies for optimizing PL/pgSQL functions and procedures and explore the mechanics of inline or anonymous server-side code, along with its limitations. Furthermore, you'll acquire insights into debugging and profiling PL/pgSQL code and learn techniques for conducting statistical analyses on the PL/pgSQL code you create.

CHAPTER 1

Introduction to PL/pgSQL

In this chapter, we will start with an introduction of PL/pgSQL, on what is PL/pgSQL and what are the key features of it. We will talk about some common use cases where PL/pgSQL is used. PL/pgSQL comes by default when you install the PostgreSQL server. However, we will provide the steps to install PL/pgSQL. We will explain how PL/pgSQL works with a simple flow diagram. We will show some basic examples of PL/pgSQL code blocks which are called anonymous and named code blocks.

A Closer Look at PL/pgSQL

PostgreSQL uses SQL (Structured Query Language) as a default query language. SQL is a common domain-specific language for relational databases. PostgreSQL uses some extensions and features to implement the standards of SQL. In addition to SQL, PostgreSQL supports many procedural languages like PL/pgSQL, PL/Java, PLV8, PL/Python, PL/Perl, etc. Using these languages, you can create functions, stored procedures, and triggers which will improve the performance by reducing the multiple iterations to the databases.

PL/pgSQL is the most commonly used procedural language in PostgreSQL. It is an extension of SQL. It is similar to Oracle's PL/SQL and supports features like control structures, exception handling, variables, loops, and conditional statements. These features help us to develop complex database applications in an efficient way.

When working on designing a complex business logic inside the database, you would need to develop multiple SQLs which are sometimes interdependent. Results of one SQL will be used by other SQLs. In this case, running multiple SQLs increases the data flow between the database and the client application and will cause performance bottlenecks due to high data transfer through the network. To overcome this, you can use stored procedures or functions.

© Baji Shaik and Dinesh Kumar Chemuduru 2023
B. Shaik and D. K. Chemuduru, *Procedural Programming with PostgreSQL PL/pgSQL*,
https://doi.org/10.1007/978-1-4842-9840-4_1

PL/pgSQL supports stored procedures, functions, and triggers. A stored procedure is a set of precompiled SQL statements which can be executed repeatedly. Stored procedures can help to reduce network traffic and improve performance by reducing the amount of data that needs to be sent between the database and the client application.

The common use cases to use stored procedures or functions using PL/pgSQL are

1. Improve data processing speed by using precompiled code through stored procedures which will be faster than raw SQL queries.

2. Write more complex code using features like control structures, exception handling, variables, loops, conditional statements, etc.

3. Using stored procedures or functions, you can create a reusable code to call from the applications to save time and effort.

4. PL/pgSQL is portable across different operating systems and platforms. This makes it easier to migrate code between different environments.

5. Prevent unauthorized access and data breaches by controlling the user authentication on stored procedures or functions.

6. Use triggers to implement constraints of business processes that cannot be expressed as foreign keys or check constraints.

PL/pgSQL Installation

PL/pgSQL is already included in PostgreSQL, so if you have PostgreSQL installed, you should have PL/pgSQL as well. However, you may need to enable it if it is not already enabled. Here are the steps to enable PL/pgSQL in PostgreSQL:

1. Install PostgreSQL psql client to connect to the database, or you can use the pgAdmin client tool.

   For Ubuntu, the following are the simple steps to install the client:

   # Create the file repository configuration:

   ```
   sudo sh -c 'echo "deb http://apt.postgresql.org/pub/repos/apt
   $(lsb_release -cs)-pgdg main" > /etc/apt/sources.list.d/pgdg.list'
   ```

Import the repository signing key:

```
wget --quiet -O - https://www.postgresql.org/media/keys/
ACCC4CF8.asc | sudo apt-key add -
```

Update the package lists:

```
sudo apt-get update
```

Install the latest version of PostgreSQL. If you want a specific version, use 'postgresql-12' or similar instead of 'postgresql':

```
sudo apt-get -y install postgresql-client-15
```

For Linux (RHEL), you can follow the steps here:
`www.postgresql.org/download/linux/redhat/`

2. Connect to the database and check if PL/pgSQL is already installed:

```
postgres=# \dx
List of installed extensions
Name | Version | Schema | Description
-----+---------+--------+-------------
(0 rows)
postgres=# select * from pg_extension where extname='plpgsql';
oid | extname | extowner | extnamespace | extrelocatable | extversion | extconfig | extcondition
----+---------+----------+--------------+----------------+------------+-----------+--------------
(0 rows)
```

3. Execute the following command to enable PL/pgSQL:

```
postgres=# CREATE EXTENSION plpgsql;
CREATE EXTENSION
```

4. Verify that PL/pgSQL is enabled by executing the following command:

```
postgres=# \dx
List of installed extensions
Name    | Version |   Schema    |          Description
------ -+---------+------------+----------------------------
plpgsql | 1.0     | pg_catalog | PL/pgSQL procedural language
(1 row)
JavaScript
postgres=# select * from pg_extension where extname='plpgsql';
oid    | extname | extowner | extnamespace | extrelocatable | extversion | extconfig | extcondition
------+---------+----------+--------------+----------------+------------+-----------+-------------
16388 | plpgsql |       10 |           11 | f              | 1.0        |           |
(1 row)
```

PL/pgSQL Execution Flow

PL/pgSQL is like every other "loadable, procedural language." PL/pgSQL gets loaded through a function manager called fmgr. The fmgr loads the language handler when a procedural language function or procedure is executed and calls it. The execution flow of PL/pgSQL code is similar to that of other procedural programming languages, with parsing, compilation, execution, and cleanup stages. However, PL/pgSQL code is executed on the server side, which means that it has direct access to the database and can perform database operations more efficiently than client-side code.

On the first call of a PL/pgSQL function or procedure in a session, the server first parses the code to check for syntax errors. The call handler will "compile" a function statement tree once the code is parsed. When the code is compiled, it turns into an internal form that the server can execute more efficiently. SQL queries in the function are just kept as a string at this point, and the expressions like the following are actually SQL queries:

```
my_var := some_param * 10
```

The SQL queries are actually parsed at this point, and parser hooks are used to replace variables/parameters with PARAM nodes in the parse tree. The PL/pgSQL statement tree is very similar to a PostgreSQL execution tree. After the parse and compile, the call handler then executes that statement tree. On the first execution of a statement node that has an SQL query in it, that query is prepared via the Server Programming Interface (SPI). The SPI provides a simple and efficient way to execute SQL commands, retrieve query results, and manipulate the database. The compiled code is then executed by the server. Based on any variable and control structure declaration, the server creates a new execution environment for the PL/pgSQL code. If the PL/pgSQL code is a function or stored procedure that returns a result set, the server will send the result set back to the client. Once the execution of the code is complete, the server will clean up any resources that were used by the PL/pgSQL code, including variables and any temporary tables that were created.

Figure 1-1 represents the flow of execution.

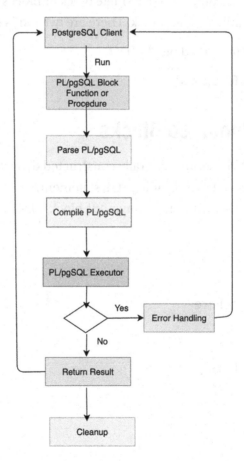

Figure 1-1. *PL/pgSQL execution flow*

This diagram illustrates the high-level steps of the PL/pgSQL execution flow. However, it's important to note that PL/pgSQL code can be quite complex and may include multiple control structures, error handling blocks, and nested and even recursive PL/pgSQL function calls and trigger invocations and database operations. The actual execution flow of a specific PL/pgSQL function or stored procedure will depend on the specific code and logic used. This call hierarchy is not limited to PL/pgSQL. All procedural languages share the common entry point of the fmgr, so they can be mixed and matched in trigger and function call stacks.

PL/pgSQL Blocks

PL/pgSQL is a block-structured language. The basic unit in any PL/pgSQL code is a block. All PL/pgSQL code is composed of a single block or blocks that occur either sequentially or nested within another block. There are two kinds of blocks:

- Anonymous or unnamed blocks (DO)

- Named blocks (functions)

Anonymous or Unnamed Blocks

Anonymous or unnamed blocks are generally constructed dynamically and executed only once by the user. It is sort of a complex SQL statement.

The following is the structure of an anonymous block, for example:

```
DO $$
[ <<label>> ]
[ DECLARE
-- Variable declaration here
]
BEGIN
-- Execute statements here
END [ label ];
$$;
```

Now, let us start with a simple hello world code block, which does not have any name associated with it:

```
postgres=# DO
$$
BEGIN
        RAISE NOTICE 'Hello World';
END;
$$;

NOTICE:  Hello World
DO
```

In the preceding example, the `RAISE NOTICE` command will help us to print the given message on the client console. As you can see here, the block is declared without a name, and if you want to print `Hello World`, then you have to repeat the same set of instructions again.

Now, let us print the `Hello World` line by line rather than in a single line:

```
postgres=# DO
$o$
BEGIN
        RAISE NOTICE $i$
        Hello
        World
        $i$;
END;
$o$;

NOTICE:
        Hello
        World
DO
```

In the preceding example, we used different multiline specifiers. The whole block got enclosed by o, and the inner `Hello World` got enclosed by i. From this example, we can learn that in PL/pgSQL, we can have the nested multiliners, where each multiline should follow its own enclosure.

Now, let us write a nested BEGIN ... END inside a main BEGIN ... END block. Here is an example:

```
postgres=# DO
$$
BEGIN

        BEGIN
                RAISE NOTICE 'Hello World';
        END;
END;
$$;
NOTICE:  Hello World
DO
```

In the preceding example, we print the Hello World message from the nested BEGIN ... END block. It is possible to have multiple nested statements inside a single BEGIN... END block. We will see more of these in the coming chapters, where we discuss exception handling.

Now, let us go a little deeper and print the Hello World message from the nested unnamed code block:

```
postgres=# DO
$o$
BEGIN
        DO
        $i$
                BEGIN
                        RAISE NOTICE 'Hello World';
                END;
        $i$;
END;
$o$;
NOTICE:  Hello World
DO
```

As you can see in the preceding example, we are able to define an unnamed block inside an unnamed block. By defining the nested code blocks, we can segregate a large unnamed block into multiple stand-alone work units. We don't need to write a nested

8

unnamed block; in most of the cases, the nested BEGIN...END block would be sufficient. But in general, we don't keep large unnamed blocks in the database; rather, we store them inside with a name (function/procedure), and we call that object name, whenever it is required.

Here is another example where we can have a nested block inside an exception:

```
postgres=# DO $inline$
BEGIN
        PERFORM 1/0;
        RAISE NOTICE 'Hello World!';

EXCEPTION
        WHEN OTHERS THEN
        DO $$
        BEGIN
                RAISE NOTICE 'Got error';
        END;
        $$;
END;
$inline$;
NOTICE:  Got error
DO
```

PL/pgSQL does not restrict the anonymous blocks as stand-alone objects; we can also embed these inline definitions inside the function or procedure object. We haven't discussed about procedures and functions yet, but showing you an example where you can declare the inline anonymous block inside a function:

```
postgres=# CREATE OR REPLACE FUNCTION test_func()
RETURNS void
LANGUAGE plpgsql
AS $function$
BEGIN
        DO $$ BEGIN RAISE NOTICE 'Hello World!'; END;$$;
END;
$function$;
CREATE FUNCTION
```

```
postgres=# SELECT test_func();
NOTICE:  Hello World!
 test_func
-----------

(1 row)
```

How it works is, unlike other procedural languages, PL/pgSQL gives an inline statement handler `plpgsql_inline_handler`. By using this handler, PL/pgSQL executes the unnamed or inline PL/pgSQL blocks. If there are any nested code blocks, then those will be evaluated recursively by the `plpgsql_inline_handler`.

💡 Note that it is not possible to return any value from the unnamed code blocks. Always use anonymous code blocks to define the business logic, which involves making a set of function or procedure calls. If you want to return any value from anonymous blocks, then we might need to use any session-level variables, which need to be set inside the anonymous block, and access them from the outside of the blocks.

Named Blocks

Named blocks have a name associated with them, are stored in the database, can be executed repeatedly, and can take in parameters.

A named block in PL/pgSQL is defined using the following syntax:

```
<<label>>
DECLARE
-- declare variables here
BEGIN
-- Named block's code here
END;
```

Here, `label` is the name of the block and is enclosed within << >> brackets.It is not just cosmetic, but that nested code blocks can refer to outer variables by using that label instead of finding the innermost match for the variable name.

The **DECLARE** section is used to declare variables that are used within the block, while the **BEGIN** and **END** sections contain the actual code for the block.

Once a named block has been defined, it can be called from within the same function or procedure using the **PERFORM** statement:

```
PERFORM block_name;
```

This will execute the code within the named block. Named blocks can be called multiple times within the same function or procedure, allowing for reusable and modular code.

Here's an example of a PL/pgSQL function that uses named blocks to calculate the factorial of a number:

```
CREATE OR REPLACE FUNCTION factorial(num INTEGER)
RETURNS INTEGER AS $$
DECLARE
    result INTEGER := 1;
BEGIN
    <<factorial_loop>>
    FOR i IN 1..num LOOP
        result := result * i;
    END LOOP factorial_loop;

    RETURN result;
END;
$$ LANGUAGE plpgsql;
```

In this example, the named block **factorial_loop** is used within a **FOR** loop to calculate the factorial of the input number. The **DECLARE** section declares a variable **result** to store the final result, while the **BEGIN** and **END** sections contain the code for the named block.

The named block is called within the **FOR** loop using the **LOOP** statement. This allows the loop to continue until it reaches the specified number of iterations.

Once the **FOR** loop is complete, the final result is returned by the function.

To call the function and calculate the factorial of a number, you would execute the following SQL statement:

```
SELECT factorial(5);
```

This would return the value **120**, which is the factorial of 5.

Summary

In this chapter, we talked about PL/pgSQL use cases, installation, and how it works with a flow diagram. We have also shown how simple PL/pgSQL code blocks look like and how to execute them. These examples will help you to understand and start with PL/pgSQL code. In the next chapter, we will talk about the variables that are used inside PL/pgSQL code blocks. We will start with how to declare those variables and dive deep into different types of methods to use based on the use cases. These will help you to decide which type of variables you should use when building the PL/pgSQL code for the functions or procedures.

What's Next

In the next chapter, we will be covering some key features of PL/pgSQL variables like the following:

- **Variable Types**: Explore the different types of variables and learn how to choose the appropriate variable type for your needs.

- **Variable Scoping Mastery**: Gain a better grasp of variable scoping rules and how to manage variables effectively within different blocks.

- **Variable Naming Conventions**: Learn about naming conventions that can help you write more maintainable and readable code.

- **Advanced Variable Usage**: Extend your knowledge by using variables in more complex scenarios.

CHAPTER 2

PL/pgSQL Variables

In the previous chapter, we talked about what PL/pgSQL is and some use cases where you need it. We also explained the steps to install and the execution flow of PL/pgSQL with a simple diagram. We have discussed some PL/pgSQL anonymous and named code block examples which will help in understanding the basics. In this chapter, we will introduce variables that are used in the PL/pgSQL code. We will provide different types of variables and use cases on when to use them. We will show the declaration and scope of variables and different types of variables with some examples.

What Are Variables in PL/pgSQL?

Similar to other programming languages, PL/pgSQL has variables which are used to store values for later use in the program. These variables can hold different types of data such as integers, floating-point numbers, strings, and boolean values.

Declaring Variables

PL/pgSQL offers to declare variables in its declaration section of the block. Here is an example:

```
postgres=# DO
$$
DECLARE
        v_var1 INT;
        v_var2 INT:=10;
BEGIN
        RAISE NOTICE 'v_var1 %', v_var1;
        RAISE NOTICE 'v_var2 %', v_var2;
```

© Baji Shaik and Dinesh Kumar Chemuduru 2023
B. Shaik and D. K. Chemuduru, *Procedural Programming with PostgreSQL PL/pgSQL*,
https://doi.org/10.1007/978-1-4842-9840-4_2

```
END;
$$;
NOTICE:   v_var1 <NULL>
NOTICE:   v_var2 10
DO
```

In the preceding example, we have declared two variables. The v_var1 variable is declared but not defined with any value to it. The second variable v_var2 is declared but has a value 10 to it. If we try to access a variable which is declared and not defined, then expect that we would get NULL from it. In the preceding output, we can also see that the v_var1 is set to NULL.

From the previous chapter, we learned that we can have nested blocks inside the main PL/pgSQL block. By using that nested block feature, we have multiple declarations and multiple variables in the single PL/pgSQL block. Here is an example:

```
postgres=# DO
$o$
DECLARE
        v_var1 INT:=10;
BEGIN

        RAISE NOTICE 'v_var1 %', v_var1;

        DO
        $i$
        DECLARE
                v_var1 INT:=100;
        BEGIN
                RAISE NOTICE 'v_var1 %', v_var1;
        END;
        $i$;

END;
$o$;
NOTICE:   v_var1 10
NOTICE:   v_var1 100
DO
```

In the preceding example, we have nested unnamed blocks, where we have two variable declarations. The variable v_var1 in the main block is declared with the value 10, and also v_var1 in the inside block is declared with the value 100. Also, the scope of the variable is always local.

Note   In PL/pgSQL, we can't declare variables on the fly. We should always declare them in the DECLARE section, and we have to use them in the block. But, while defining the FOR LOOP, we can have the variables declared on the fly. We will discuss more about this in the coming chapters.

Variable Scope

The scope of the declared variables in PL/pgSQL is always local to its current block. That is, once we declare the variable in a block, we can't access them outside of that block. Here is an example:

```
postgres=# DO
$$
DECLARE
BEGIN
        DECLARE
                v_var1 INT:=10;
        BEGIN
                RAISE NOTICE 'v_var1 %', v_var1;
        END;

        RAISE NOTICE 'v_var1 %', v_var1;
END;
$$;
NOTICE:  v_var1 10
ERROR:  column "v_var1" does not exist
LINE 1: v_var1
        ^
QUERY:  v_var1
CONTEXT:  PL/pgSQL function inline_code_block line 10 at RAISE
```

From the preceding example, as you can see we got an error, column "v_var1" does not exist, when we try to access the variable v_var1 from the outer BEGIN... END block. That is, the scope of variable v_var1 is local to that inner BEGIN...END block, and we can't access them from the outside. If we declare the variable v_var1 in the parent BEGIN...END block, then we can access that variable inside the nested BEGIN... END blocks too. Because the v_var1 is declared at the parent block level, its scope is at the whole block level. Now, you might have questions like what if we declare the same variable v_var1 in parent and nested BEGIN...END blocks and how to access the parent block's v_var1 along with the local declared variable. Here is an example for this use case:

```
postgres=# DO
$$
DECLARE
        v_var1 INT:=1;
BEGIN
        DECLARE
                v_var1 INT:=10;
        BEGIN
                RAISE NOTICE 'v_var1 %', v_var1;
        END;
END;
$$;
NOTICE:  v_var1 10
DO
```

From the preceding example, we were only able to access the variable v_var1, which was declared in the nested BEGIN...END block. To access the parent v_var1 variable, then we should access that variable with the block's label. That is, we have to give a label name to the parent block, and then we should access the v_var1 along with its label name. Here is an example:

```
postgres=# DO
$$
<<parent>>
DECLARE
        v_var1 INT := 1;
```

16

```
BEGIN
        DECLARE
                v_var1 INT := 10;
        BEGIN                                        .
                RAISE NOTICE 'Parent v_var1 %', parent.v_var1;
                RAISE NOTICE 'Local  v_var1 %', v_var1;
        END;
END;
$$;
NOTICE:  Parent v_var1 1
NOTICE:  Local  v_var1 10
DO
```

Constant Variables

We can declare constant variables inside PL/pgSQL, which shouldn't get updated by further instructions. Here is an example:

```
postgres=# DO
$$
DECLARE
    v_c_pi CONSTANT REAL DEFAULT 3.14;
BEGIN
    v_c_pi = 3.15;
END;
$$;
ERROR:  variable "v_c_pi" is declared CONSTANT
LINE 6:     v_c_pi = 3.15;
```

In the preceding example, we declared the variable v_c_pi as CONSTANT and set its DEFAULT value as 3.14. But, in further instructions, when we tried to update its value as 3.15, we got the exception as the variable is declared as CONSTANT, which should not get updated by any of the instructions.

Variable Alias

In PL/pgSQL, we can also create a reference variable which points to another variable or system variables. For example, if we want to create a reference variable or a short-length variable name to another variable, then we can create those short-length variables using ALIAS. Here is an example:

```
DO
$$
DECLARE
    var_earth_sun_distance REAL DEFAULT 149.6;
    v_e_s_d ALIAS FOR var_earth_sun_distance;
BEGIN
    RAISE NOTICE 'Reference       #1 %', v_e_s_d;
    v_e_s_d = 149.5;
    RAISE NOTICE 'Actual Variable   %', var_earth_sun_distance;
END;
$$;
NOTICE:  Reference       #1 149.6
NOTICE:  Actual Variable   149.5
DO
```

In the preceding example, we created a reference variable v_e_s_d to the actual variable var_earth_sun_distance. Also, if we perform any update on the reference variable, then we can see those changes from the actual variable. ALIAS is not limited to creating a reference variable to the actual variable, it will allow creating a reference to another reference. Here is an example:

```
DO
$$
DECLARE
    var_earth_sun_distance REAL DEFAULT 149.6;
    v_e_s_d ALIAS FOR var_earth_sun_distance;
    vd ALIAS FOR v_e_s_d;
BEGIN
    RAISE NOTICE 'Reference       #1 %', v_e_s_d;
    RAISE NOTICE 'Reference       #2 %', vd;
```

```
        RAISE NOTICE 'Update Ref #1';
        v_e_s_d = 149.5;
        RAISE NOTICE 'Actual Variable        %', var_earth_sun_distance;
        RAISE NOTICE 'Update Ref #2';
        vd = 149.4;
        RAISE NOTICE 'Actual Variable        %', var_earth_sun_distance;
END;
$$;
NOTICE:  Reference         #1 149.6
NOTICE:  Reference         #2 149.6
NOTICE:  Update Ref #1
NOTICE:  Actual Variable       149.5
NOTICE:  Update Ref #2
NOTICE:  Actual Variable       149.4
DO
```

In the preceding example, we created an ALIAS variable from another ALIAS variable. That is, we created a new reference variable, which points to another reference variable. Also, if we update the second reference variable, it will reflect those changes on the actual variable via the first reference.

PL/pgSQL supports the following types of variables:

- Scalar Variables

- Array Variables

- Record Variables

- Cursor Variables

Scalar Variables

In all the previous examples, we demonstrated scalar variables. Scalar variables hold a single value of a specific data type, such as an integer or a string. They can be declared and initialized using the DECLARE keyword and can be assigned values using the := assignment operator.

For example, the following code declares each type of scalar variable:

```
postgres=# DO $$
DECLARE
    my_int integer := 1;
    my_text text := 'Hello, world!';
    my_bool boolean := true;
BEGIN
    -- perform operations on the scalar variables
    my_int := my_int + 10;
    my_text := my_text || ' How are you?';
    my_bool := not my_bool;

    -- print the scalar variables
    RAISE NOTICE 'my_int = %', my_int;
    RAISE NOTICE 'my_text = %', my_text;
    RAISE NOTICE 'my_bool = %', my_bool;
END;
$$;
NOTICE:  my_int = 11
NOTICE:  my_text = Hello, world! How are you?
NOTICE:  my_bool = f
DO
```

In the preceding example, we declare three scalar variables: my_int with a value of 1 and a data type of integer, my_text with a value of 'Hello, world!' and a data type of text, and my_bool with a value of true and a data type of boolean. We then perform some operations on these variables using arithmetic, concatenation, and logical negation. Finally, we print the values of the variables using the RAISE NOTICE statement.

Scalar variables are useful for storing temporary values or performing calculations within a stored procedure or function. They can be used in a variety of ways, such as tracking state, performing conditional logic, or holding input or output parameters.

Array Variables

Array variables are variables that can hold multiple values of the same data type. They are declared using a data type followed by the [] syntax, such as integer[] or text[].

For example, the following code declares an array variable:

```
postgres=# DO $$
DECLARE
    my_array integer[] := '{1, 2, 3, 4, 5}';
BEGIN
    -- print the entire array
    RAISE NOTICE 'my_array = %', my_array;

    -- access individual elements of the array
    RAISE NOTICE 'my_array[2] = %', my_array[2];

    -- modify individual elements of the array
    my_array[3] := 10;

    -- print the modified array
    RAISE NOTICE 'my_array = %', my_array;
END;
$$;
NOTICE:  my_array = {1,2,3,4,5}
NOTICE:  my_array[2] = 2
NOTICE:  my_array = {1,2,10,4,5}
DO
```

In the preceding example, we declare an array variable my_array with a data type of integer[] and initialize it with the values {1, 2, 3, 4, 5}. We then print the entire array using the RAISE NOTICE statement, access and print the value of the second element of the array, modify the value of the third element of the array, and print the entire array again.

Array variables are useful for storing and manipulating sets of related data, such as lists of numbers, strings, or boolean values. They can be used in a variety of ways, such as for performing calculations on multiple values at once, storing input or output parameters, or passing data between functions or procedures.

Record Variables

Record variables are used to store a row of data from a table or a query result. They are declared using the %ROWTYPE attribute and can be assigned values using the SELECT INTO statement.

For example, the following code declares a record variable:

```
postgres=# CREATE TABLE emp (emp_id INT, emp_name VARCHAR, emp_salary
NUMERIC);
CREATE TABLE

postgres=# INSERT INTO emp VALUES (100, 'SCOTT', '10000.00');
INSERT 0 1

postgres=# DO $$
DECLARE
    my_record emp%ROWTYPE;
BEGIN
    -- select a row of data into the record variable
    SELECT * INTO my_record FROM emp WHERE emp_id = 100;

    -- print the values of the record variable
    RAISE NOTICE 'emp_id = %', my_record.emp_id;
    RAISE NOTICE 'emp_name = %', my_record.emp_name;
    RAISE NOTICE 'emp_salary = %', my_record.emp_salary;

    -- update the values of the record variable
    my_record.emp_name := 'Smith';
    my_record.emp_salary := 50000;

    -- update the row of data in the table
    UPDATE emp SET emp_name = my_record.emp_name, emp_salary = my_record.
emp_salary WHERE emp_id = 1001;
END;
$$;
NOTICE:  emp_id = 100
NOTICE:  emp_name = SCOTT
NOTICE:  emp_salary = 10000.00
DO
```

In the preceding example, we declare a record variable my_record that holds a row of data from the emp table. We then select a row of data into the record variable using a SELECT statement, print the values of the record variable using the RAISE NOTICE statement, update the values of the record variable, and update the row of data in the table using an UPDATE statement.

Record variables are useful for storing and manipulating rows of data from tables or query results within a stored procedure or function. They can be used in a variety of ways, such as for passing data between functions or procedures, performing calculations on data, or storing input or output parameters.

Cursor Variables

Cursor variables are variables that hold a reference to a cursor, which is a named SQL statement that can be executed repeatedly. They are declared using the CURSOR keyword.

For example, the following code declares a record variable named "my_row" that corresponds to the columns of a table named "my_table":

```
postgres=# CREATE TABLE emp (emp_id INT, emp_name VARCHAR, emp_salary
NUMERIC);
CREATE TABLE

postgres=# INSERT INTO emp VALUES (100, 'SCOTT', '10000.00');
INSERT 0 1

postgres=# INSERT INTO emp VALUES (100, 'ROBERT', '50000.00');
INSERT 0 1

postgres=# DO $$
DECLARE
   my_cursor refcursor;
   my_record emp%ROWTYPE;
BEGIN
   -- open the cursor and fetch the first row of data
   OPEN my_cursor FOR SELECT * FROM emp;
   FETCH my_cursor INTO my_record;

   -- print the values of the first row of data
```

```
    RAISE NOTICE 'emp_id = %', my_record.emp_id;
    RAISE NOTICE 'emp_name = %', my_record.emp_name;
    RAISE NOTICE 'emp_salary = %', my_record.emp_salary;

    -- fetch the next row of data
    FETCH my_cursor INTO my_record;

    -- print the values of the second row of data
    RAISE NOTICE 'emp_id = %', my_record.emp_id;
    RAISE NOTICE 'emp_name = %', my_record.emp_name;
    RAISE NOTICE 'emp_salary = %', my_record.emp_salary;

    -- close the cursor
    CLOSE my_cursor;
END;
$$;
NOTICE:   emp_id = 100
NOTICE:   emp_name = SCOTT
NOTICE:   emp_salary = 10000.00
NOTICE:   emp_id = 100
NOTICE:   emp_name = ROBERT
NOTICE:   emp_salary = 50000.00
DO
```

In the preceding example, we declare a cursor variable my_cursor and a record variable my_record that holds a row of data from the emp table. We then open the cursor using a SELECT statement, fetch the first row of data into the record variable using a FETCH statement, print the values of the first row of data using the RAISE NOTICE statement, fetch the second row of data into the record variable, print the values of the second row of data, and then close the cursor using the CLOSE statement.

Cursor variables are useful for manipulating and iterating through result sets returned by queries. They can be used in a variety of ways, such as for processing large datasets, performing calculations on data, or storing input or output parameters.

Variables can be very useful in PL/pgSQL programs as they allow you to store and manipulate data in a flexible way.

Summary

In this chapter, we learned about the types of variables with nice examples and explanations of how they work. We went through the declaration of variables in the DECLARE section of the code as well as in an independent code block on the fly. The scope of variables is different for each block of PL/pgSQL code. We explained how the scope of variables varies with some examples. Also, we looked at constant variables and how to use aliases for the variables.

What's Next

In the next chapter, we will be covering some key features of PL/pgSQL data types like the following:

- **Advanced Data Type Exploration**: Delve into complex data types like composite and range types to efficiently manage intricate data structures.

- **Custom Domain Types**: Create user-defined domain types with specific constraints to ensure data integrity and validation in your applications.

- **Optimal Type Selection**: Understand how to choose the right data type based on application needs, considering performance, maintainability, and space efficiency.

- **Dynamic Application Building**: Harness PL/pgSQL data types to create adaptable applications that handle diverse data inputs and outputs.

CHAPTER 3

PL/pgSQL Data Types

In the previous chapter, we introduced variables that are used in the PL/pgSQL code. We talked about different types of variables and use cases on when to use them. We have shown the declaration and scope of the variables and different types of variables with some examples. In this chapter, we will introduce the supported data types to use in PL/pgSQL code. We will walk through each data type and use cases with some examples.

Data Types

Choosing the right data type for the data being used is a best practice that developers should follow. Choosing the correct data type can help us avoid many data validation checks and prevent exceptions when incorrect data is entered. The PostgreSQL database engine supports multiple data types for each data kind. By using these data types, we build tables and insert proper data into them. We can use most of the PostgreSQL data types inside PL/pgSQL blocks, besides pseudo-types like any, anyenum, and record. It is not just limited to using existing data types; we can also construct new composite types by using these existing data types.

Understanding data types is crucial for developing efficient and effective database applications. We will cover data types such as integers, floating-point numbers, booleans, and strings, as well as more advanced data types like arrays and composite types. By the end of this chapter, you will have a good understanding of the different data types available in PL/pgSQL and how to use them effectively in your business logic. We will also cover how to declare variables and constants using these data types and how to convert between different data types using type casting. This knowledge is essential for writing robust and error-free PL/pgSQL code that can handle a variety of data inputs and outputs.

27

© Baji Shaik and Dinesh Kumar Chemuduru 2023
B. Shaik and D. K. Chemuduru, *Procedural Programming with PostgreSQL PL/pgSQL*,
https://doi.org/10.1007/978-1-4842-9840-4_3

Note   You can find the list of supported data types here: `www.postgresql.`
`org/docs/current/datatype.html`.

Declaring Variables with Data Types

In the previous chapter, we saw several examples where we declared variables along
with their data types. Now, let us begin with a simple example where we demonstrate the
primitive data types like `int`, `boolean`, and `text`:

```
postgres=# DO
$$
declare
v_int int:=10;
v_text text:='text';
v_boolean boolean:=false;
begin
raise notice 'v_int      %',v_int;
raise notice 'v_text     %',v_text;
raise notice 'v_boolean  %',v_boolean;
end;
$$;

NOTICE:  v_int      10
NOTICE:  v_text     text
NOTICE:  v_boolean  f
DO
```

In the preceding example, we declared three variables along with their data types
and printed the results. Let us rewrite the previous example as follows and see the
results:

```
postgres=# DO
$$
declare
int int:=10;
text text:='text';
```

```
boolean boolean:=false;
begin
raise notice 'int  %',int;
raise notice 'text %',text;
raise notice 'boolean %', boolean;
end;
$$;
NOTICE:  int  10
NOTICE:  text text
NOTICE:  boolean f
DO
```

As you can see in the preceding example, variable names can be declared with the corresponding data type names. As data type names are not reserved keywords, we can also use them as variable names. Here, we are demonstrating the possibility of declaring variable names as data types. However, this kind of variable declaration is not typically used in production.

In the previous example, as well as in the previous chapter, we discussed only the base scalar data types in PostgreSQL. These data types accept only a single value into their declared variable type. To obtain a list of available base scalar types in the current database, we can query the PostgreSQL catalog table pg_type. The following query returns base data types in the database limited to three only:

```
postgres=# SELECT typname FROM pg_type WHERE typtype='b' LIMIT 3;
 typname
---------
 bool
 bytea
 char
(3 rows)
```

Supported Types

PostgreSQL not only supports base types but also composite types, enumerated types, pseudo-types, and range types. To list all the supported type categories in the database, query the pg_type catalog table with the following query:

```
postgres=# SELECT distinct typtype::char FROM pg_type;
 typtype
---------
 r
 m
 p
 d
 c
 b
(6 rows)
```

In the preceding output we see, the return values are m, r, p, d, c, and b. All the types, including the user-defined types, will fall under these category types. Table 3-1 describes each code value.

Table 3-1. Code values

Code	Description	Example
r	Range type	postgres=# SELECT daterange(current_date, current_date+30);daterange------------------------------[2023-03-15,2023-04-14)(1 row)
m	Multirange type	postgres=# SELECT datemultirange(daterange(current_date, current_date+30), daterange(current_date+31, current_date+60));datemultirange-----------------------------------{[2023-03-15,2023-04-14), [2023-04-15,2023-05-14)}(1 row)
p	Pseudo-type	postgres=# SELECT (1,2,3)::anyelement;row------------(1,2,3)(1 row)
d	Domain type	postgres=# SELECT 'YES'::information_schema.yes_or_no;yes_or_no------------YES(1 row)
c	Composite type	Any row type or user defined type postgres=# SELECT ('port', '5432')::record::pg_config;row---------------(port,5432)(1 row)
b	Base type	postgres=# SELECT 1::int;int4------1(1 row)

31

Base Type

Base types are the primitive building blocks for other data types in the database. For example, take the domain type information_schema.yes_or_no which only accepts the text which is of length 3, and the values have to be YES or NO. This domain type is used as a replacement to bool to maintain the information_schema standards. Let us examine the underlying data type of this yes_or_no domain type using the format_type function as follows:

```
postgres=# SELECT format_type(typbasetype, typtypmod), typbasetype FROM
pg_type WHERE typname='yes_or_no';
     format_type       | typbasetype
-----------------------+-------------
 character varying(3)  |        1043
(1 row)
```

From the preceding output, we got the domain's base type as 1043. By using the following query, we see what is the data type which is mapped to 1043:

```
postgres=# SELECT 1043::regtype::text;
       text
-------------------
 character varying
(1 row)
```

By using the following query, see whether this 1043 is a base type or not:

```
postgres=# SELECT typtype,typname FROM pg_type WHERE oid=1043;
 typtype | typname
---------+---------
 b       | varchar
(1 row)
```

As you can see from the preceding results, the base types are the primitive building blocks to the data types which we create. By using these base types, we can build our own composite, domain, and range types.

Composite Type

In PostgreSQL, it is possible to create custom data types using the base data types. Custom data types can be defined using not only the base types but also other custom data types or other data types excluding pseudo-types.

Let us construct a simple composite type with the help of base types:

```
postgres=# CREATE TYPE all_fields_base AS (a int, b text, c date);
CREATE TYPE
postgres=# \d all_fields_base
        Composite type "public.all_fields_base"
 Column |  Type   | Collation | Nullable | Default
--------+---------+-----------+----------+---------
 a      | integer |           |          |
 b      | text    |           |          |
 c      | date    |           |          |
```

Here, we created a type `all_fields_base` as its member fields declared as base data types. Now, write a simple PL/SQL block, which uses this composite as one of its variable's desired data types:

```
postgres=# DO
$$
DECLARE
        v_composite all_fields_base;
BEGIN
        v_composite:= (1, 't', current_date)::all_fields_base;
        RAISE NOTICE '%', v_composite;
END;
$$;
NOTICE:  (1,t,2023-03-18)
DO
```

As you can see in the preceding example, we created the variable `v_composite` with data type `all_fields_base` and assigned multiple values (`1, 't', current_date`) as a single unit. Here, we also used `::` which is a data type casting operator. That is, this `::` operator converts the provided values into the defined data type.

It is not just limited to use only the base types as members inside the composite type. We can also declare a member as a composite, pseudo, or range type. Consider the following example:

```
postgres=# CREATE TYPE mixed_fields_type AS (d real, f all_fields_base);
CREATE TYPE
postgres=# \d mixed_fields_type
          Composite type "public.mixed_fields_type"
 Column |      Type       | Collation | Nullable | Default
--------+-----------------+-----------+----------+---------
 d      | real            |           |          |
 f      | all_fields_base |           |          |
```

Now, let's write a simple example by using the preceding mixed_fields_type data type and assign some value to it:

```
DO
$$
DECLARE
        v_mixed_type mixed_fields_type;
BEGIN
        v_mixed_type:= (3.14, (1, 't', current_date)::all_fields_
        base)::mixed_fields_type;
        RAISE NOTICE '%', v_mixed_type;
        RAISE NOTICE 'Value % Type %', v_mixed_type.d, pg_typeof(v_mixed_type.d);
        RAISE NOTICE 'Value % Type %', v_mixed_type.f, pg_typeof(v_mixed_type.f);
END;
$$;
NOTICE:  (3.14,"(1,t,2023-03-18)")
NOTICE:  Value 3.14 Type real
NOTICE:  Value (1,t,2023-03-18) Type all_fields_base
DO
```

From the preceding example, as you can see we saved a nested composite value into the nested composite variable. Also, by using the object reference notation, we are able to access the required field from this composite type. By using pg_typeof, we displayed the data type of the member variable.

Domain Type

Domain types are used when a particular set of constraints need to be enforced on a base type. They are essentially a user-defined type that is based on an existing type. We can create a domain type using the CREATE DOMAIN statement. A domain type can be used when we need to enforce certain conditions on input values. For example, information_schema.yes_or_no is a domain that only allows YES or NO values. Here is an example:

```
postgres=# SELECT 'YES'::information_schema.yes_or_no;
 yes_or_no
-----------
 YES
(1 row)

postgres=# SELECT 'TRUE'::information_schema.yes_or_no;
ERROR:  value for domain information_schema.yes_or_no violates check
constraint "yes_or_no_check"
```

In the preceding example, the domain type information_schema.yes_or_no only accepts YES and does not recognize TRUE. This is how the domain type is constructed.

Let's build our own custom domain type called tiny_text, which only accepts up to eight characters. If the input size is greater than eight characters, an error should be thrown:

```
postgres=# CREATE DOMAIN tiny_text text CONSTRAINT tiny_text_length_
constraint CHECK (length(VALUE)<=8);
CREATE DOMAIN
postgres=# CREATE TABLE preferences(short_userid tiny_text, short_pass
tiny_text);
CREATE TABLE
postgres=# INSERT INTO preferences VALUES ('a0bef74', 'i89llk');
INSERT 0 1
```

Try inserting text that is more than eight characters and see if the validation is enforced or not:

```
postgres=# INSERT INTO preferences VALUES ('this is big user id', 'this is
big password');
ERROR:  value for domain tiny_text violates check constraint "tiny_text_
length_constraint"
```

In the preceding example, if you attempt to send more than eight characters, the domain check constraint is violated, and an error message will be displayed as shown earlier.

Domain types can also be created on top of composite types. Consider the following example, where we create a common type called products_type and then create a domain type, toys_type, with a constraint. This type will only allow products in the toys category and will throw an error if you try to insert products from another category.

```
postgres=# CREATE TYPE products_type as (id text, category text, sku int,
price real);
CREATE TYPE
```

```
postgres=# CREATE DOMAIN toys_type products_type CHECK ((VALUE).
category='toys');
CREATE DOMAIN
```

```
postgres=# CREATE TABLE toys_products(t toys_type);
CREATE TABLE
```

```
postgres=# INSERT INTO toys_products VALUES (('dfd89', 'toys', 10, 20.2));
INSERT 0 1
```

Now, try to insert another category product and see if the domain constraint got enforced or not:

```
postgres=# INSERT INTO toys_products VALUES (('dfd99', 'books', 15, 15.2));
ERROR:  value for domain toys_type violates check constraint "toys_type_check"
```

Perfect! We can restrict other categories of data from entering the toys_products table. We can achieve this with a plain check constraint on the table, but creating a domain type allows us to not only use toys_type at the table level but also across procedures and functions. This domain type ensures that the toys_type variable always holds toy category data.

Pseudo-Type

PostgreSQL supports several pseudo data types, which have specific uses. We cannot use them directly, but we can use them whenever required. In other words, these types are only for internal use or to give instructions to PostgreSQL whenever it is required. For example, void is a pseudo data type that specifies the return data type of a function. It should only be used as a function return type, and not as a table field type. Here is an example:

```
postgres=# CREATE TABLE test_table(v void);
ERROR:  column "v" has pseudo-type void
```

```
postgres=# DO
$$
DECLARE
t void;
BEGIN
t:='';
END;
$$;
ERROR:  variable "t" has pseudo-type void
CONTEXT:  compilation of PL/pgSQL function "inline_code_block" near line 3
```

PostgreSQL is not allowed to create a composite type with pseudo-type:

```
postgres=# CREATE TYPE test_type AS (t void);
ERROR:  column "t" has pseudo-type void
```

Like void, there are few other pseudo data types as follows:

- The any type can be used to present any function/procedure parameter arguments.

- trigger is a pseudo data type which we only use for the trigger's function return type.

- opaque is a pseudo data type which is used internally or by the external plug-ins.

- record is a pseudo data type which in general is used as a function return type.

Range Type

PostgreSQL supports range types, which are designed to handle range values. You can store and manipulate a range of values in a single column.

This data type is useful in situations where you need to store a range of values rather than a single value, such as

Time Ranges: You can use range data types to store time ranges, such as business hours, meeting times, or shifts.

Numeric Ranges: You can use range data types to store ranges of numeric values, such as temperature, age, or income ranges.

Geographic Ranges: You can use range data types to store geographic ranges, such as latitude and longitude ranges, or ranges of distances.

Text Ranges: You can use range data types to store ranges of text values, such as character or string ranges.

For instance, if you want to store "from" and "to" values as a single unit, you can use a range data type to represent such values. As an example, consider a table called `fleet_mileage` that records the mileage of each vehicle using a different type of gasoline. Each vehicle's odometer reading will be different at the start, and the gasoline will run out at a different odometer reading. We should store both of these values and then calculate the mileage we achieved with the specific type of gasoline we used. Here is an example:

```
postgres=# CREATE TABLE fleet_mileage(gasoline_id int, vehicle_id int,
readings numrange);
CREATE TABLE
postgres=# INSERT INTO fleet_mileage VALUES (1,1,numrange(1455.2,
1567.5,'[]'));
INSERT 0 1
postgres=# INSERT INTO fleet_mileage VALUES (1,2,numrange(1255.2,
1374.5,'[]'));
INSERT 0 1
postgres=# INSERT INTO fleet_mileage VALUES (1,3,numrange(1132.7,
1259.6,'[]'));
INSERT 0 1
```

In the preceding example, we created a table called fleet_mileage, with a readings column of type numrange. This column stores the beginning and end odometer readings as a range, by including both values in that range. The syntax [ ] indicates that the begin and end range values are inclusive within that range.

Query the table to retrieve a list of vehicles sorted in descending order based on their mileage:

```
postgres=# SELECT *,upper(readings)-lower(readings) as mileage FROM fleet_
mileage ORDER BY 4 DESC;
 gasoline_id | vehicle_id |     readings      | mileage
-------------+------------+------------------+---------
          1 |          3 | [1132.7,1259.6] |   126.9
          1 |          2 | [1255.2,1374.5] |   119.3
          1 |          1 | [1455.2,1567.5] |   112.3
(3 rows)
```

In the preceding query, we used range-specific functions like upper and lower. These functions return the beginning and end of the range values.

PostgreSQL also offers the ability to create custom range types, similar to the DOMAIN type. Now, let's consider another use case where we have table reservations in a hotel:

```
postgres=# CREATE TYPE room_reserve_ts_range AS RANGE (SUBTYPE=timestamp);
CREATE TYPE
postgres=# CREATE TABLE room_bookings(id int, guest_name text, booking_
dates room_reserve_ts_range);
CREATE TABLE
postgres=# INSERT INTO room_bookings VALUES (1, 'Scott', '[2023-03-22
00:00, 2023-03-25 10:00)');
INSERT 0 1
postgres=# INSERT INTO room_bookings VALUES (2, 'George', '[2023-03-20
00:00, 2023-03-23 10:00)');
INSERT 0 1
postgres=# INSERT INTO room_bookings VALUES (3, 'Denis', '[2023-03-15
00:00, 2023-03-23 10:00)');
INSERT 0 1
```

In the preceding example, we created a custom type `room_reserve_ts_range` which is a subtype or underlying base type of `timestamp`. The custom type we created is similar to the `tsrange` type natively offered by PostgreSQL. We can also use range operators such as `contains`, `overlap`, and `adjacence` on the `booking_dates` column. For example, to list all the guests who reserved their rooms on `2023-03-21`, we can query this table as follows:

```
postgres=# SELECT guest_name FROM room_bookings WHERE booking_dates @>
'2023-03-21'::timestamp;
 guest_name
-------------
 George
 Denis
(2 rows)
```

Multirange Types

PostgreSQL supports multirange data type which represents a set of nonoverlapping ranges of values of some other data type. For example, you could define a multirange type that represents a set of nonoverlapping ranges of integers.

The multirange data type in PostgreSQL is useful for storing and querying sets of nonoverlapping ranges of values. It can be used in various applications such as time series analysis, event scheduling, and resource allocation.

Consider the same example table `fleet_mileage` that is used for range data types. For multirange data types, you can use the built-in `nummultirange` data type:

```
postgres=# CREATE TABLE fleet_mileage(gasoline_id int, vehicle_id int,
readings nummultirange);
CREATE TABLE
postgres=#  INSERT INTO fleet_mileage VALUES (1,1,nummultirange(numran
ge(1455.2, 1567.5,'[]'),numrange(1655.2, 1767.5,'[]')));
INSERT 0 1
postgres=#  INSERT INTO fleet_mileage VALUES (1,1,nummultirange(numran
ge(1255.2, 1367.5,'[]'),numrange(1455.2, 1667.5,'[]')));
INSERT 0 1
```

```
postgres=#  INSERT INTO fleet_mileage VALUES (1,1,nummultirange(numran
ge(1155.2, 1267.5,'[]'),numrange(1355.2, 1567.5,'[]')));
INSERT 0 1
```

In the preceding example, the reading column has been created as a multirange data type, and you can see a couple of range values.

You can query the table to retrieve a list of vehicles sorted in descending order based on their mileage. However, in multirange, it will pick up the higher and lower values from any range in multirange values.

```
postgres=# SELECT *,upper(readings)-lower(readings) as mileage FROM fleet_
mileage ORDER BY 4 DESC;
 gasoline_id | vehicle_id |              readings              | mileage
-------------+------------+-----------------------------------+---------
          1 |          1 | {[1255.2,1367.5],[1455.2,1667.5]} |   412.3
          1 |          1 | {[1155.2,1267.5],[1355.2,1567.5]} |   412.3
          1 |          1 | {[1455.2,1567.5],[1655.2,1767.5]} |   312.3
(3 rows)
```

Summary

In this chapter, we learned about data types with nice examples and explanations on how they work. We talked about the use cases where you can use a particular data type so that it helps you while designing an application based on the requirements. In the next chapter, we will talk about the control structures that are used in PL/pgSQL programming. We will cover conditional operations and simple loops with use cases and some examples.

What's Next

In the next chapter, we will be covering some key features of PL/pgSQL strings, numbers, and arrays like the following:

- **String Handling**: Understand different string data types (char(n), varchar(n), text) and best practices for selection based on data model design.

- **Numeric Operations**: Utilize various numeric data types (smallint, int, bigint, numeric, float, double precision) to store and process numerical data efficiently.

- **Array Usage**: Leverage arrays to work with lists of data, including declaration, initialization, and accessing array elements.

- **String Formatting**: Explore the format() function for dynamic string creation and manipulation and its usage in constructing SQL statements.

- **Data Transformation**: Discover methods to transform and reshape your data using string and array functions for various use cases.

- **Efficiency Techniques**: Explore optimization techniques to efficiently handle strings, numbers, and arrays in your PL/pgSQL code.

CHAPTER 4

Dealing with Strings, Numbers, and Arrays

In the previous chapter, we talked about the different data types available in PL/pgSQL and how to use them with some examples. In this chapter, we will cover how to work with strings, numbers, and arrays inside PL/pgSQL of PostgreSQL. It will include examples of how to declare variables, perform operations, and manipulate data within these data types. Additionally, it will cover best practices for working with these data types to ensure efficient and effective code. By the end of this chapter, you will have a better understanding of how to work with strings, numbers, and arrays within the context of PL/pgSQL.

Strings

These data types and operators include the concatenation operator (||), which allows you to combine two or more strings into a single string, as well as functions for string manipulation and pattern matching. Additionally, PostgreSQL provides the text data type, which allows for efficient storage and manipulation of large amounts of text data. PostgreSQL supports the following three string data types:

- char(n)

- varchar(n)

- text

Data types should be chosen based on the data model design. There are no performance benefits to using one over the other. If an application needs to store fixed-length characters, such as two-digit capital codes, the char(n) data type should be used.

© Baji Shaik and Dinesh Kumar Chemuduru 2023
B. Shaik and D. K. Chemuduru, *Procedural Programming with PostgreSQL PL/pgSQL*,
https://doi.org/10.1007/978-1-4842-9840-4_4

If an application stores dynamic-length characters that won't exceed a certain length, the varchar(n) data type should be used. If an application is unsure of the length of text that it will store in the database, the text data type should be used.

The char(n) data type always allows fixed-length strings. If an application provides a string of length < n, PostgreSQL fills the remaining length with spaces. Consider the following example:

```
postgres=# CREATE TABLE test(t char(126));
CREATE TABLE
postgres=# INSERT INTO test VALUES ('a');
INSERT 0 1
```

Now, let us find the column size "t" by using the following query:

```
postgres=# SELECT pg_column_size(t) FROM test;
 pg_column_size
----------------
            127
(1 row)
```

Based on the preceding results, we can see that the column size is 127 bytes, despite inserting only one character. This is because, when inserting a single character (1 byte), PostgreSQL automatically pads it with an additional 126 bytes. Scaling this behavior can result in a very large table in the database. This large table can be used for multiple purposes, such as benchmarking disk performance or measuring data transfer between nodes. Consider the following example, which creates a large table with a minimal number of text rows:

```
postgres=# CREATE TABLE big_table(t CHAR(10485760));
CREATE TABLE
postgres=# INSERT INTO big_table VALUES('a');
INSERT 0 1
postgres=# INSERT INTO big_table SELECT * FROM big_table;
INSERT 0 1
postgres=# INSERT INTO big_table SELECT * FROM big_table;
INSERT 0 2
....
....
```

```
postgres=# INSERT INTO big_table SELECT * FROM big_table;
INSERT 0 2048
```

Now, fetch the number of rows from the table which we inserted; that should be 4096:

```
postgres=# SELECT COUNT(*) FROM big_table;
 count
-------
  4096
(1 row)
```

We just inserted 4096 text records; now quickly check the table size:

```
postgres=# \dt+ big_table
                                List of relations
 Schema |    Name    | Type  |  Owner   | Persistence | Access method |
  Size  | Description
--------+------------+-------+----------+-------------+---------------+
--------+-------------
 public | big_table  | table | postgres | permanent   | heap          |
 487 MB |
(1 row)
```

We were able to quickly generate a table of size 480MB with only 4096 records. While it's possible to generate an even bigger table with a small record set and media data, we created this large table using the char(n) data type and inserting a single character into the table. This is a tip we often follow to create large tables in a short amount of time for benchmarking purposes.

Function Format

PostgreSQL provides a set of string operators and functions that help in constructing strings. For example, if we want to generate a dynamic SQL statement for all tables that prints the number of rows from each table, we can use a function called "format." The following is an example:

```
postgres=# DO
```

```
$$
DECLARE
v_stmt TEXT:='';
v_rec RECORD;
BEGIN
FOR v_rec IN (SELECT table_name FROM information_schema.tables WHERE table_
schema != 'pg_catalog' LIMIT 4) LOOP
RAISE NOTICE '%', format('SELECT COUNT(*) FROM %I', v_rec.table_name);
END LOOP;
END;
$$;

NOTICE:    SELECT COUNT(*) FROM test_backup
NOTICE:    SELECT COUNT(*) FROM test
NOTICE:    SELECT COUNT(*) FROM big_table
NOTICE:    SELECT COUNT(*) FROM "a table"
DO
```

In the preceding example, we used the format() function, where the string argument %I is replaced with the table names. Here, %I represents identifiers, such as column names, table names, or any other object names. The "format()" method provides several other options for constructing strings, such as generating fixed-length strings and reusing the arguments. Here is an example, where the format() function will reuse the given arguments in the string:

```
postgres=# DO
$$
DECLARE
v_stmt TEXT:='';
BEGIN
SELECT format('SELECT COUNT(%2$s) FROM %1$s WHERE %2$s=%L', 'table_name',
'column_name', 'literal_value') INTO v_stmt;
RAISE NOTICE '%', v_stmt;
END;
$$;
```

```
NOTICE:  SELECT COUNT(column_name) FROM table_name WHERE column_
name='literal_value'
DO
```

In the preceding example, we reused the argument "column_name" in multiple places and used the third argument as a positional literal (%L).

Dealing with Null String

PostgreSQL treats an empty string (") and NULL differently. An empty string is a string with zero characters, while NULL is not equal to any value including an empty string. In PostgreSQL, NULL and empty (") strings are uncomparable. For example, consider the following example:

```
postgres=# SELECT NULL = '';
 ?column?
----------

(1 row)
```

In the preceding example, you can see that comparing NULL and an empty value leads to unknown results. If you expect the result of the preceding SQL statement to be false, you won't get it – because NULL and empty strings are uncomparable. Not NULL and empty strings are uncomparable. One NULL is also not comparable to another NULL in PostgreSQL. Consider the following example:

```
postgres=# SELECT NULL = NULL;
 ?column?
----------

(1 row)
```

Now, if we have PL/pgSQL code like the following where we have a null check in place, then the code won't work as expected:

```
postgres=# DO
$$
DECLARE
    v_data TEXT;
```

```
BEGIN
-- v_data:= Some_Expression_Which_Returns_Null()
      v_data:= NULL;
      IF v_data = NULL THEN
-- NULL control flow statements
              RAISE NOTICE 'result is null';
      ELSE
-- NOT NULL control flow statements
              RAISE NOTICE 'result is not null';
      END IF;
END;
$$;
NOTICE:   result is not null
DO
```

In the preceding example, even though we included a NULL check in the condition, we still executed NOT NULL control flow statements. This may come as a surprise to developers who are familiar with different database management systems. To modify this behavior in PostgreSQL, you can use the session-level setting transform_null_equals. By setting this value to ON, the preceding behavior will be fixed. Try running the same example with this setting enabled and observe the results.

```
postgres=# DO
$$
DECLARE
        v_data TEXT;
BEGIN

SET transform_null_equals TO ON;
-- v_data:= Some_Expression_Which_Returns_Null()
      v_data:= NULL;
      IF v_data = NULL THEN
-- NULL control flow statements
              RAISE NOTICE 'result is null';
      ELSE
-- NOT NULL control flow statements
              RAISE NOTICE 'result is not null';
```

```
        END IF;
END;
$$;
NOTICE:  result is null
DO
```

Now, let's try the SQL query that compares an empty string with NULL by enabling the transform_null_equals parameter and see the results:

```
postgres=# SELECT NULL='';
 ?column?
----------
 f
(1 row)
```

With the help of the transform_null_equals parameter, PostgreSQL implicitly converts equality expressions containing NULL into expr IS NULL. This produces the desired results instead of an unknown value. This also makes developers feel happy and write more NULL safety code in their PL/pgSQL code.

PostgreSQL provides the IS DISTINCT FROM and IS NOT DISTINCT FROM equality statements, which allow comparison between two values and return a boolean value of true or false.

Consider the following example:

```
postgres=# SELECT NULL IS DISTINCT FROM '';
 ?column?
----------
 t
(1 row)

postgres=# SELECT NULL = '';
 ?column?
----------

(1 row)
```

In the preceding example, IS DISTINCT FROM returns the expected value of false, while the = operator returns NULL. It is recommended to use IS DISTINCT FROM and transform_null_equals as needed to avoid unexpected behavior in the application code.

Numbers

PostgreSQL provides multiple numerical data types. They are as follows:

- smallint (2 bytes)

- int (4 bytes)

- bigint (8 bytes)

- numeric (variable length)

- float/real (4 bytes)

- float/double precision (8 bytes)

The data types smallint, int, and bigint are used to store whole numbers (Z). If the use case is to store small integer values, we should use the smallint data type, which accepts whole numbers in the range of –32,767 to 32,767. Consider the following simple casting example:

```
postgres=# SELECT 32767::smallint;
 int2
-------
 32767
(1 row)

postgres=# SELECT 32768::smallint;
ERROR:  smallint out of range
```

In the preceding example, we are able to cast 32767 to smallint, but the next value 32768 is out of range. This is because the smallint data type only uses 2 bytes of storage, and with 2 bytes, we can only generate numbers in the range of -32767 to 32767. Consider the following example:

```
postgres=# SELECT count(*) from generate_series(-32767, 32767);
 count
-------
 65535
(1 row)
```

With 2 bytes, there would be 16 bits (where 1 byte = 8 bits). With the help of 16 bits, we can generate a maximum number up to 65536. Consider the following example:

```
postgres=# SELECT 1<<16;
 ?column?
----------
    65536
(1 row)
```

In the preceding example, we used the right-shifting bitwise operator to shift bit 1 sixteen times to the right, which is equivalent to 2^16. By comparing the preceding two results, we can confirm that we can generate a maximum of 65535 numbers, with an extra bit used to store the sign of the number (+ or –). The more bytes we choose, the more ranges we store in the database. That is, if we want to store big numbers to the columns, then that column should have a proper data type.

PostgreSQL provides multiple numeric data types that allow for high-precision data storage for financial and scientific calculations. There are several data types in PostgreSQL that support real numbers, each with its own specific use case. For example, the float/real data type can store 4 bytes of moderate precision, whereas the float/ double precision (8 bytes) data type provides greater precision by using 8 bytes of storage. The real data type can provide a maximum of 6-digit precision, whereas double precision can support up to 15-digit precision.

In the case of scientific and complex calculations, if we need to store more digits in the precision, it is recommended to use the numeric data type rather than the float or double precision data types. This is because the numeric data type calculates the number of bytes required to store the data when the user submits the real value. At most, the numeric type can store 16383 digits after the decimal value and 131072 before the decimal value.

💡 Refer to the following PostgreSQL official documentation for more details: www.postgresql.org/docs/current/datatype-numeric.html.

The binary representation of floating-point numbers (i.e., using 0/1 bits to represent a floating-point value) cannot exactly represent values such as 0.1 in binary. This leads to rounding errors. This phenomenon is not specific to PostgreSQL, but rather is related to how computers handle floating-point numbers. For example, consider the following case where we print floating-point numbers from 0.1 to 1 using the generate_series function:

```
postgres=# SELECT 0.1+generate_series(0.0, 0.9, 0.1)::float;
      ?column?
--------------------
                0.1
                0.2
 0.30000000000000004
                0.4
                0.5
                0.6
                0.7
 0.7999999999999999
                0.9
                  1
(10 rows)
```

The preceding results show that the value 0.3 was calculated as 0.30000000000000004, and the value 0.8 was calculated as 0.7999999999999999. Computers typically represent floating-point numbers, including decimal fractions, using a fixed number of binary digits. As a result of this binary representation, some decimal fractions cannot be represented exactly. To resolve this floating-point rounding error problem, we can use the numeric/decimal data type, which treats real numbers as true decimal values and then performs the calculation. For example, let's consider the same example we executed using the numeric data type and see the results:

```
postgres=# SELECT 0.1+generate_series(0.0, 0.9, 0.1)::numeric;
 ?column?
----------
      0.1
      0.2
      0.3
      0.4
      0.5
      0.6
      0.7
```

```
    0.8
    0.9
    1.0
(10 rows)
```

From the preceding output, it is clear that we obtained the desired real number without any surprises. This is because `float` data is stored in binary format, where rounding errors are expected. In contrast, `numeric` data is stored in decimal format, treating digits as normal values and performing arithmetic calculations accordingly.

Arrays

Arrays are a complex data type in PL/pgSQL, but they can be incredibly useful for working with lists of data. To declare an array variable, you can use the ARRAY data type. Here is the syntax:

```
DECLARE
  my_array INTEGER[];
```

You can initialize an array with values using curly braces:

```
DECLARE
  my_array INTEGER[] := '{1, 2, 3}';
```

You can access individual elements of an array using square brackets. The following is a simple example:

```
postgres=# DO
 $$
 DECLARE
   my_array INTEGER[] := '{1, 2, 3}';
   second_element INTEGER;
 BEGIN
   second_element := my_array[2];
   RAISE NOTICE 'second element from my array is: %', second_element;
 END;
 $$;
NOTICE:  second element from my array is: 2
DO
```

You can also loop over the elements of an array using a FOR loop. The following is an example:

```
postgres=# DO
 $$
 DECLARE
   my_array INTEGER[] := '{1, 2, 3}';
   total INTEGER := 0;
 BEGIN
   FOR i IN 1..array_length(my_array, 1) LOOP
     total := total + my_array[i];
   END LOOP;
   RAISE NOTICE 'total of the elements in my array is: %', total;
 END;
 $$;
NOTICE:  total of the elements in my array is: 6
DO
```

By using these techniques, you can effectively work with strings, numbers, and arrays within the context of PL/pgSQL in PostgreSQL.

Example Use Cases

Let us look at some use cases to deal with strings, numbers, and arrays.

Strings

Let's say you want to dynamically generate an SQL statement based on user input. You can use string concatenation to achieve this.

Look at the following example with a simple customers table with some data and a function to explain the use case:

```
CREATE TABLE customers ( id SERIAL PRIMARY KEY, first_name VARCHAR(255) NOT
NULL, last_name VARCHAR(255) NOT NULL, email VARCHAR(255) NOT NULL );
INSERT INTO customers (first_name, last_name, email) VALUES ('Foo', 'Bar',
'foo.bar@example.com'), ('Mike', 'Talor', 'mike.talor@example.com'),
('John', 'Smith', 'john.smith@example.com');
```

```
CREATE OR REPLACE FUNCTION get_customer_data(p_first_name VARCHAR, p_last_
name VARCHAR) RETURNS TABLE (id INTEGER, first_name VARCHAR, last_name
VARCHAR, email VARCHAR) AS $$
BEGIN
    RETURN QUERY EXECUTE 'SELECT id, first_name, last_name, email FROM
customers WHERE first_name = ''' || p_first_name || ''' AND last_name = '''
|| p_last_name || ''';';
END;
$$ LANGUAGE plpgsql;
```

Let us run this function with a sample first_name and last_name:

```
postgres=# SELECT * FROM get_customer_data('Foo', 'Bar');
 id | first_name | last_name |         email
----+------------+-----------+----------------------
  1 | Foo        | Bar       | foo.bar@example.com
(1 row)
```

So the function returned a table of results containing the id, first_name, last_
name, and email of any customers with the first name "John" and last name "Doe" in the customers table.

Numbers

Let's say you want to calculate the average revenue for a particular set of products. You can use numeric values to achieve this.

Let us look at the following example with products and sales tables and a function to calculate the total revenue by category of the product:

```
CREATE TABLE products (
    id INTEGER PRIMARY KEY,
    name VARCHAR(255) NOT NULL,
    category_id INTEGER NOT NULL,
    price NUMERIC(10, 2) NOT NULL
);

CREATE TABLE sales (
    id INTEGER PRIMARY KEY,
```

```
    order_id INTEGER NOT NULL,
    product_id INTEGER NOT NULL,
    quantity INTEGER NOT NULL,
    price NUMERIC(10, 2) NOT NULL,
    CONSTRAINT fk_order FOREIGN KEY (order_id) REFERENCES orders (id),
    CONSTRAINT fk_product FOREIGN KEY (product_id) REFERENCES products (id)
);
INSERT INTO products (id, name, category_id, price) VALUES
    (1, 'Product A', 1, 10.00),
    (2, 'Product B', 1, 15.00),
    (3, 'Product C', 2, 20.00),
    (4, 'Product D', 2, 25.00);

INSERT INTO sales (id, order_id, product_id, quantity, price) VALUES
    (1, 1, 1, 2, 10.00),
    (2, 1, 2, 1, 15.00),
    (3, 2, 3, 2, 20.00),
    (4, 2, 4, 1, 25.00);

CREATE OR REPLACE FUNCTION calculate_total_revenue_by_category(p_category_
id INTEGER) RETURNS NUMERIC AS $$
DECLARE
    total_revenue NUMERIC := 0;
BEGIN
    SELECT SUM(s.price * s.quantity) INTO total_revenue FROM products p JOIN
    sales s ON p.id = s.product_id WHERE p.category_id = p_category_id;
    RETURN total_revenue;
END;
$$ LANGUAGE plpgsql;
```

Let us run this function with product_id as 1:

```
book=# SELECT calculate_total_revenue_by_category(1);
 calculate_total_revenue_by_category
--------------------------------------
                                35.00
(1 row)
```

Arrays

Let's say you want to find the top-selling products for a particular month. You can use arrays to achieve this.

Let us look at an example with products and sales tables with a function to find the top-selling product for a given month:

```
-- Create the 'products' table
CREATE TABLE products (
    id INTEGER PRIMARY KEY,
    name VARCHAR(255) NOT NULL,
    price NUMERIC(10, 2) NOT NULL
);

-- Create the 'sales' table
CREATE TABLE sales (
    id INTEGER PRIMARY KEY,
    sale_date DATE NOT NULL,
    product_id INTEGER NOT NULL REFERENCES products(id),
    quantity INTEGER NOT NULL,
    price NUMERIC(10, 2) NOT NULL
);

-- Insert some sample data into the 'products' table
INSERT INTO products (id, name, price) VALUES
    (1, 'Product A', 10.00),
    (2, 'Product B', 15.00),
    (3, 'Product C', 20.00),
    (4, 'Product D', 25.00);

-- Insert some sample data into the 'sales' table
INSERT INTO sales (id, sale_date, product_id, quantity, price) VALUES
    (1, '2021-01-01', 1, 2, 10.00),
    (2, '2021-01-01', 2, 1, 15.00),
    (3, '2021-02-01', 3, 2, 20.00),
    (4, '2021-02-01', 4, 1, 25.00);

-- Create the function which gives top selling product for a given month
```

```
CREATE OR REPLACE FUNCTION get_top_selling_products(p_month INTEGER)
RETURNS TABLE (product_id INTEGER, total_sales NUMERIC) AS $$
DECLARE
    product_ids INTEGER[] := (SELECT ARRAY_AGG(DISTINCT sales.product_id)
    FROM sales WHERE EXTRACT(MONTH FROM sale_date) = p_month);
BEGIN
    RETURN QUERY SELECT s.product_id, SUM(s.price * s.quantity) AS total_
    sales FROM sales s WHERE s.product_id = ANY(product_ids) GROUP BY
    s.product_id ORDER BY total_sales DESC LIMIT 10;
END;
$$ LANGUAGE plpgsql;
```

Let us run the function for months 1 and 2 and see the results as two rows for each month (1 for January and 2 for February):

```
postgres=# SELECT * FROM get_top_selling_products(1);
 product_id | total_sales
------------+-------------
          1 |       20.00
          2 |       15.00
(2 rows)

Time: 0.548 ms
postgres=# SELECT * FROM get_top_selling_products(2);
 product_id | total_sales
------------+-------------
          3 |       40.00
          4 |       25.00
(2 rows)
```

Summary

In this chapter, we provided an overview of how to work with strings, numbers, and arrays inside PL/pgSQL of PostgreSQL. It covered best practices for working with these data types, including using the appropriate data type for your variables, always declaring your variables before using them, and using descriptive variable names. It also included examples of how to declare variables, perform operations, and manipulate data within these data types, as well as real-world code examples for using strings, numbers, and arrays in PL/pgSQL.

What's Next

In the next chapter, we will be covering some key features of PL/pgSQL control statements like the following:

- **Complex Logic**: Learn to handle intricate program flow using nested IF statements, CASE expressions, and looping constructs.

- **Error Handling**: Explore error handling within control statements, ensuring your code remains robust and resilient.

- **Dynamic Decision Making**: Discover advanced control flow techniques such as dynamic SQL generation and conditional execution.

- **Switching Between Statements**: Explore various control statement structures like LOOP, WHILE, and FOR loops for different scenarios.

- **Code Readability**: Deepen your understanding of writing clear and well-structured control statements to improve code maintainability.

CHAPTER 5

Control Statements

In the previous chapter, we talked about strings, numbers, and arrays and how to use them in PL/pgSQL programming. We walked through the use cases and examples to deal with strings, numbers, and arrays. This chapter provides an in-depth guide to the different types of control statements and their usage in the PL/pgSQL programming language. This chapter covers a range of control statements, including IF, CASE, LOOP, WHILE, FOR, and FOREACH statements. By understanding the differences between these statements, programmers can use the appropriate one for their specific needs. Additionally, the chapter provides information on how to use variables and loops in conjunction with these control statements to create complex programs.

Control statements are essential for controlling the flow of a program and making decisions based on certain conditions. This chapter is a comprehensive resource that covers different types of control statements and their usage in the PL/pgSQL programming language.

The chapter provides information on the following control statements and their usage:

- IF Statement

- CASE Statement

- Iterative Statement

  - LOOP Statement

  - WHILE Statement

  - FOR Statement

  - FOREACH Statement

© Baji Shaik and Dinesh Kumar Chemuduru 2023
B. Shaik and D. K. Chemuduru, *Procedural Programming with PostgreSQL PL/pgSQL*,
https://doi.org/10.1007/978-1-4842-9840-4_5

IF/ELSE Statement

The IF statement is used to execute a block of code if a certain condition is true. Here is the simple syntax of the IF statement:

```
IF condition or expression THEN
    -- Code block to execute when condition is true
END IF;
```

Here is a simple example that demonstrates the conditional flow of statement execution:

```
postgres=# DO
$$
BEGIN
IF 1 = 1 THEN
RAISE NOTICE 'OK';
END IF;
END;
$$;
NOTICE:  OK
DO
```

From the preceding example, we received the message "NOTICE: OK" because the condition "1=1" mentioned in the example is true. PL/pgSQL uses SQL's SPI interface to perform conditional evaluation. This means that internally it forms a SELECT statement around the given condition, executes it, and returns in the form of boolean. That is, the "1=1" will be converted into the SQL statement "SELECT 1=1", and the result will be placed in the IF statement.

Now, consider the following example:

```
postgres=# DO
$$
BEGIN
IF 1 = 1 ORDER BY 1 THEN
RAISE NOTICE 'OK';
END IF;
END;
```

```
$$;
NOTICE:   OK
DO
```

In the preceding example, let's examine the condition we mentioned: "1=1 ORDER BY 1". This condition appears different from a regular condition because we included "ORDER BY 1" along with "1=1". As previously mentioned, PL/pgSQL automatically converts the given expression into SQL form and internally creates SQL such as "SELECT 1=1 ORDER BY 1".

In the preceding example, including an ORDER BY clause in the expression is unnecessary. It is only used to demonstrate the evaluation of expressions behind the scenes. We can make the expression evaluation stricter by enclosing it in parentheses as follows:

```
postgres=# DO
$$
BEGIN
IF (1 = 1 ORDER BY 1) THEN
RAISE NOTICE 'OK';
END IF;
END;
$$;
ERROR:   syntax error at or near "ORDER"
LINE 4: IF (1 = 1 ORDER BY 1) THEN
```

As you can see, once we enclose the expression in parentheses, we receive the proper syntax error. This is because the entire unit is evaluated as a single expression, rather than as individual units. We can also specify an expression as a combination of single expressions or individual units, as follows:

```
postgres=# DO
$$
BEGIN
IF (1 = 1) ORDER BY 1 THEN
RAISE NOTICE 'OK';
END IF;
END;
```

```
$$;
NOTICE:   OK
DO
```

The preceding examples simply demonstrate how expressions are evaluated. There is no specific use case for it.

The IF statement is not limited to using only simple conditional expressions. We can also use a SELECT statement as part of its expressions. Consider the following example:

```
postgres=# CREATE TABLE test(t INT);
CREATE TABLE

postgres=# DO
$$
BEGIN
IF (select count(*) from test) < 1 THEN
RAISE NOTICE 'OK';
END IF;
END;
$$;
NOTICE:   OK
DO
```

In the preceding example, we have included an SQL statement as part of the condition. PL/pgSQL will convert this condition into an SQL query like SELECT (SELECT count(*) FROM test) < 1, and the result will be placed in the IF condition.

Note   If conditional statements are placed inside loop statements, there will be a rapid context switch between the PL/pgSQL and SQL engines. This can result in increased resource utilization. If possible, avoid placing conditional expressions inside a huge number of iterations.

PL/pgSQL conditional statements support EXISTS, IS NULL, and NOT operators. By using these combinations of operators, we can construct the conditional statements like IF NOT EXISTS, IS NOT NULL, and EXISTS. Consider the following example, where we try to find if the table is empty or not:

```
postgres=# DO
$$
BEGIN
IF EXISTS(SELECT * FROM test) THEN
      RAISE NOTICE 'table is not empty';
END IF;
END;
$$;
NOTICE:   table is not empty
DO
```

In the preceding example, we used the EXISTS operator to check the table rows, which is an optimal way of checking the table row count status. We don't need to write the query like SELECT COUNT(*) FROM test!= 0, which scans the entire table and returns the number of rows. The latter check actually takes more resources to confirm whether the table is empty or not, while the former short-circuits (stops returning records from SELECT *) the process whenever it finds any single record in the table.

Cascading IF Statements

PL/pgSQL supports writing cascading IF statements, where we can write chained conditional statements. For example, consider the following use case:

```
postgres=# TRUNCATE test;
TRUNCATE TABLE
postgres=# DO
$$
BEGIN
IF EXISTS(SELECT * FROM test) THEN
      RAISE NOTICE 'table is not empty';
ELSIF NOT EXISTS(SELECT * FROM test) THEN
      RAISE NOTICE 'table is empty';
END IF;
END;
$$;
```

```
NOTICE:   table is empty
DO
postgres=#
```

In the preceding example, we discussed cascaded conditional statements. These statements are simple: if one condition is not met, the program checks the next condition in the chain. We can chain many conditions together in a cascaded IF statement and execute a set of statements based on which condition is satisfied. We can nest IF/ELSE statements inside IF/ELSIF statements. Consider the following example:

```
postgres=# CREATE TABLE test_backup(t INT);
CREATE TABLE
postgres=# INSERT INTO test_backup VALUES(generate_series(1, 10));
INSERT 0 10
postgres=# DO
$$
BEGIN
IF EXISTS(SELECT * FROM test) THEN
      RAISE NOTICE 'table is not empty';
ELSIF NOT EXISTS(SELECT * FROM test) THEN
      IF EXISTS(SELECT * FROM test_backup) THEN
            RAISE NOTICE 'test_backup is not empty';
      ELSE
            RAISE NOTICE 'table is empty';
      END IF;
END IF;
END;
$$;
NOTICE:   test_backup is not empty
DO
```

CASE Statement

One of the user-friendly features offered by PL/pgSQL is the ability to implement complex conditional logic in a concise and readable way. The CASE statement in

PL/pgSQL allows users to specify different actions based on different conditions. For example, consider the following case:

```
postgres=# DO
$$
BEGIN
CASE
    WHEN EXISTS(SELECT * FROM test) THEN
          RAISE NOTICE 'table is not empty';
    WHEN NOT EXISTS(SELECT * FROM test) THEN
          RAISE NOTICE 'table is empty';
END CASE;
END;
$$;
NOTICE:   table is empty
DO
```

The example of cascading if statements that we discussed earlier has been rewritten using CASE statements. If you compare the two examples, the CASE statement example is more declarative and readable than the cascaded if statement. We can simplify the preceding example further by using the following statements. We keep the number of rows in a table in a variable and only evaluate the conditions in the CASE statements:

```
postgres=# DO
$$
DECLARE
v_row_count INT:=0;
BEGIN
SELECT COUNT(*) INTO v_row_count FROM test LIMIT 1;
CASE v_row_count
    WHEN 1 THEN
          RAISE NOTICE 'table is not empty';
    WHEN 0 THEN
          RAISE NOTICE 'table is empty';
    ELSE
        RAISE NOTICE 'not reachable';
END CASE;
```

```
END;
$$;
NOTICE:  table is empty
DO
```

The preceding CASE statement code is more readable than nested if statements. If you have more chained or nested if statements, we would suggest you to implement the code using CASE which gives you more readability to the complex conditional checks. We can also use CASE expressions in variable assignments, as follows:

```
postgres=# DO
$$
DECLARE
      a_int INT:=0;
      b_int INT:=0;
BEGIN
      b_int = CASE a_int WHEN 0 THEN 1 ELSE 2 END CASE;
  RAISE NOTICE 'Value is %', b_int;
END;
$$;
NOTICE:  Value is 1
DO
```

In the preceding example, we used a CASE statement as an expression. The statement returns a value of either 1 or 2, which we then assign to a variable.

Iterative Statement

PL/pgSQL offers several iterative statements, including the LOOP, WHILE, FOR, and FOREACH statements. The LOOP statement is used to repeat a block of code until a certain condition is met, while the WHILE statement is used to execute a block of code repeatedly as long as a certain condition is true. The FOR statement is used to loop through a set of values and execute a block of code for each value. The FOREACH is like a FOR LOOP statement, but it is especially designed to work with arrays or composite value types.

> **Note**   It is not advisable to use too many nested iterative statements in PL/pgSQL code. Doing so not only makes the code harder to read and debug but also leads to performance issues. In the upcoming chapter, we will discuss the PL/Profiler extension, which can help us drill down into performance issues.

LOOP Statement

You can define unconditional iterative statements that can only be controlled by either an EXIT or RETURN statement using a simple LOOP statement. Consider the following example, where we repeatedly execute a statement until the given condition is met:

```
postgres=# DO
$$
DECLARE
      v_count INT:=0;
      v_iteration_count INT:=1;
BEGIN
<<OuterLoop>>
      LOOP
              v_count:=v_count+1;
              EXIT WHEN v_count=10;
              v_iteration_count:= v_iteration_count+1;
      END LOOP OuterLoop;
  RAISE NOTICE 'Iteration Count %', v_iteration_count;
END;
$$;
NOTICE:  Iteration Count 10
DO
```

In the preceding example, we iterate the v_count variable value ten times and exit the loop when the value reaches ten. Without the exit condition, the loop would iterate indefinitely, and we would need to either close the session or kill the indefinite running process. Consider the following example:

```
postgres=# DO
$$
DECLARE
      v_count INT:=0;
      v_iteration_count INT:=0;
BEGIN
<<OuterLoop>>
      LOOP
              v_count:=v_count+1;
              CONTINUE WHEN v_count<10;
              EXIT WHEN v_count=10;
              v_iteration_count:= v_iteration_count+1;
      END LOOP OuterLoop;
  RAISE NOTICE 'Iteration Count %', v_iteration_count;
END;
$$;
NOTICE:   Iteration Count 0
DO
```

In the preceding example, the iteration count result is zero. This is because the line "v_iteration_count:=v_iteration_count+1" is not executed at all. The CONTINUE statement mentioned earlier causes the loop to continue until the v_count value reaches ten. That is, the CONTINUE operation skipped the execution of the loop when the condition was met. The immediate EXIT statement ends the loop when the v_count value reaches ten, so v_iteration_count never has a chance to run even once. In the preceding example, we used the label name OuterLoop to refer to the iterative statements. By using label names like this, we can control the execution flow in certain conditions. Consider the following example:

```
postgres=# DO
$$
DECLARE
      v_count INT:=0;
      v_iteration_count INT:=1;
```

```
BEGIN
<<OuterLoop>>
     LOOP
          <<InnerLoop>>
          LOOP
               v_count:=v_count+1;
               EXIT OuterLoop WHEN v_count=10;
               v_iteration_count:= v_iteration_count+1;
          END LOOP InnerLoop;
     -- Outerloop instructions
     END LOOP OuterLoop;
  RAISE NOTICE 'Iteration Count %', v_iteration_count;
END;
$$;
NOTICE:   Iteration Count 10
DO
```

In the preceding example, we use the "OuterLoop" label to exit the iterative
statement whenever the condition is met. Labels allow us to jump forward whenever
a required condition is met. The usage of labels is not just limited inner/outer iterative
statements, we can also use labels to navigate between the blocks. Consider the
following example:

```
postgres=# DO
$$
<<MainBlock>>
BEGIN
     <<OuterBlock>>
     BEGIN
          <<InnerBlock>>
          BEGIN
               RAISE NOTICE 'InnerBlock Complete';
               EXIT OuterBlock;
          END;
          RAISE NOTICE 'OuterBlock Complete';
     END;
```

```
        RAISE NOTICE 'MainBlock Complete';
END;
$$;
NOTICE:   Inner Block Complete
NOTICE:   Main Block Complete
DO
```

In the preceding example, we did not use any iterative statements. Instead, we were able to navigate the blocks by using label names. As you can see, the execution flow jumped directly from the Inner block to the Main block, by skipping the execution of the Outer block. This type of execution should always move forward; we should not go backward. In other words, while inside the Outer block, we cannot EXIT to the Inner block.

WHILE Statement

The WHILE statement is an iterative statement that can execute a block of code repeatedly as long as a certain condition is true. It is similar to the LOOP statement, which also executes a block of code repeatedly based on an entry condition. The condition in the WHILE statement is a boolean expression that is evaluated before each iteration of the loop. If the condition is true, the loop continues to execute. If the condition is false, the loop exits and execution continues with the next statement after the loop. Consider the following example:

```
postgres=# DO
$$
DECLARE
        v_count INT:=0;
        v_iteration_count INT:=0;
BEGIN
        WHILE v_count!=10 LOOP
                v_count:=v_count+1;
                v_iteration_count:=v_iteration_count+1;
        END LOOP;
        RAISE NOTICE 'Iteration Count %', v_iteration_count;
END;
```

```
$$;
NOTICE:   Iteration Count 10
DO
```

In the preceding example, we set the entry condition for iterative statements. Unlike the plain LOOP statement, where the condition is set as part of the iterative statements, here we set the entry point at the beginning of the SQL statement execution. As we discussed earlier, every expression in PL/pgSQL is evaluated using SQL statements. This means that any expression or condition mentioned in the code will be converted to an SQL expression. Consider the following example:

```
postgres=# DO
$$
DECLARE
     v_count INT:=0;
BEGIN
     WHILE v_count!=3 ORDER BY 1 LOOP
          v_count:=v_count+1;
          RAISE NOTICE 'Count... %', v_count;
     END LOOP;
END;
$$;
NOTICE:   Count... 1
NOTICE:   Count... 2
NOTICE:   Count... 3
DO
```

Note   PL/pgSQL works in the same way as other programming languages that support WHILE loops. However, in other programming languages like C/C++/Go, we have loop controlling statements like BREAK and CONTINUE. PL/pgSQL does not offer a BREAK statement; instead, we must use the EXIT WHEN statement. The CONTINUE statement is like other programming languages.

FOR Statement

PL/pgSQL provides several variants of the FOR loop statement, each designed for a specific use case. Unlike WHILE loop statements, FOR loops make it easy to iterate over SQL results. This is because FOR opens an implicit cursor for the specified SQL query, while in a WHILE loop we must explicitly open the cursor and fetch records until the end of the result set.

The FOR statement is more useful when traversing a sequential set of data, while the WHILE statement is better for controlling iteration based on dynamic or static conditions. In other words, using WHILE allows for more control over the iterative statements, while FOR simplifies the data traversal. Consider the following example:

```
postgres=# CREATE TABLE test(t INT);
CREATE TABLE
postgres=# INSERT INTO test VALUES(generate_series(1, 3));
INSERT 0 3

postgres=# DO
$$
DECLARE
v_rec RECORD;
BEGIN
FOR v_rec IN (SELECT * FROM test) LOOP
    RAISE NOTICE 'Record ... %', v_rec;
END LOOP;
END;
$$;
NOTICE:  Record ... (1)
NOTICE:  Record ... (2)
NOTICE:  Record ... (3)
DO
```

In the preceding example, we did not create any cursors to fetch data from the test table. Instead, we included the SQL query as part of the FOR loop declaration and fetched results until the end of the table. When compared with other formats, such as declaring a cursor, opening the cursor, fetching data, and closing it, the FOR statement iterating SQL query results is the easiest. We will discuss cursors further in the upcoming chapter. To run a parameterized SQL query based on the preceding example, a different format of the FOR statement should be used as follows:

```
postgres=# DO
$$
DECLARE
v_rec RECORD;
BEGIN
FOR v_rec IN EXECUTE 'SELECT * FROM test WHERE t=$1' USING 1 LOOP
      RAISE NOTICE 'Record ... %', v_rec;
END LOOP;
END;
$$;
NOTICE:  Record ... (1)
DO
```

In this code, we have used the FOR EXECUTE USING form to execute a parameterized SQL statement. As you can see, it is very convenient to iterate over the SQL results using FOR statements. PL/pgSQL also offers another form of FOR statement, FOREACH, which is used to iterate over arrays. Consider the following example:

```
postgres=# DO
$$
DECLARE
      v_arr INT[]=ARRAY[1,2,3];
      i INT:=0;
BEGIN
      FOREACH i IN ARRAY v_arr
      LOOP
            RAISE NOTICE '%', i;
      END LOOP;
END;
$$;
NOTICE:  1
NOTICE:  2
NOTICE:  3
DO
```

In the preceding example, we traversed a single-dimensional ARRAY and printed the results one by one. Now, let's see the same example with a two-dimensional ARRAY, as follows:

```
postgres=# DO
$$
DECLARE
      v_arr INT[]=ARRAY[[1,2,3], [4,5,6]];
      i INT:=0;
BEGIN
      FOREACH i IN ARRAY v_arr
      LOOP
            RAISE NOTICE '%', i;
      END LOOP;
END;
$$;
NOTICE:  1
NOTICE:  2
NOTICE:  3
NOTICE:  4
NOTICE:  5
NOTICE:  6
DO
```

By default, the entire two-dimensional ARRAY is traversed, and its results are printed. However, by using the FOREACH-specific SLICE option, we can traverse the ARRAY by each individual array, rather than nested. Consider the following example:

```
postgres=# DO
$$
DECLARE
      v_arr INT[]=ARRAY[[1,2,3], [4,5,6]];
      i INT[];
BEGIN
      FOREACH i SLICE 1 IN ARRAY v_arr
      LOOP
            RAISE NOTICE '%', i;
```

```
        END LOOP;
END;
$$;
NOTICE:  {1,2,3}
NOTICE:  {4,5,6}
DO
```

By using the SLICE option, we can define how to iterate through a given ARRAY.

As of PostgreSQL 15.2, the FOREACH array iteration mode should be protected by a NULL array check. That is, if the iterative ARRAY is NULL, FOREACH will throw an exception. Hence, always guard FOREACH with a NULL check condition as follows:

```
postgres=# DO
$$
DECLARE
        v_arr INT[]=NULL;
        i INT:=0;
BEGIN
        IF v_arr IS NULL THEN
                RAISE NOTICE 'Array is null';
                RETURN;
        END IF;

        FOREACH i IN ARRAY v_arr
        LOOP
                RAISE NOTICE '%', i;
        END LOOP;
END;
$$;
NOTICE:  Array is null
DO
```

Example Use Cases

Let us look at the following examples that demonstrate the use of control statements.

Example 1

Consider two tables like users and transactions:

```
CREATE TABLE users (
    id serial PRIMARY KEY,
    name varchar(50),
    email varchar(100),
    balance numeric
);

CREATE TABLE transactions (
    id serial PRIMARY KEY,
    user_id integer REFERENCES users (id),
    amount numeric
);
```

The users table contains information about each user, including their ID, name, email, and balance. The transactions table contains information about each transaction, including its ID, the ID of the user who made the transaction, and the transaction amount.

Insert some data into the tables:

```
INSERT INTO users (name, email, balance) VALUES
    ('John Doe', 'john.doe@example.com', 100),
    ('Jane Smith', 'jane.smith@example.com', 50);

INSERT INTO transactions (user_id, amount) VALUES
    (1, 10),
    (2, 20);
```

This code inserts two users into the users table and two transactions into the transactions table. The first transaction deducts 10 from the balance of the first user, and the second transaction deducts 20 from the balance of the second user.

Let us create a function which controls the user transaction using a control statement like IF:

```
CREATE OR REPLACE FUNCTION process_payments(user_id integer, transaction_
amount numeric) RETURNS void AS $$
DECLARE
    user_balance numeric;
BEGIN
    -- Get user balance from database
    SELECT balance INTO user_balance FROM users WHERE id = user_id;

    -- Check if user has sufficient funds before processing payment
    IF user_balance >= transaction_amount THEN
        -- Deduct transaction amount from user balance
        UPDATE users SET balance = balance - transaction_amount WHERE id =
        user_id;
        -- Process payment transaction
        INSERT INTO transactions (user_id, amount) VALUES (user_id,
        transaction_amount);
    ELSE
        -- Display error message to user
        RAISE EXCEPTION 'Insufficient funds.';
    END IF;
END;
$$ LANGUAGE plpgsql;
```

This function takes in a user ID and a transaction amount as input parameters and processes a payment transaction if the user has sufficient funds. It uses an IF statement to check if the user has enough balance before deducting the transaction amount and inserting a new row into the transactions table. If the user doesn't have sufficient funds, it raises an exception with an error message.

Let us run the function with 10 as the transaction amount:

```
postgres=# select * from users;
 id |   name    |         email          | balance
----+-----------+------------------------+---------
  1 | John Doe  | john.doe@example.com   |     100
```

```
   2 | Jane Smith | jane.smith@example.com |        50
(2 rows)

Time: 0.259 ms
postgres=#
postgres=# select * from transactions;
 id | user_id | amount
----+---------+--------
  1 |       1 |     10
  2 |       2 |     20
(2 rows)

Time: 0.239 ms
postgres=#
postgres=#
postgres=# select process_payments(1,10);
 process_payments
------------------

(1 row)

Time: 0.773 ms
postgres=#
postgres=#
postgres=# select * from users;
 id |    name    |          email          | balance
----+------------+-------------------------+---------
  2 | Jane Smith | jane.smith@example.com  |      50
  1 | John Doe   | john.doe@example.com    |      90
(2 rows)

Time: 0.335 ms
postgres=#
postgres=#
postgres=# select * from transactions;
 id | user_id | amount
----+---------+--------
```

```
 1 |        1 |        10
 2 |        2 |        20
 3 |        1 |        10
(3 rows)

Time: 0.249 ms
postgres=#
```

You can see the transaction of 10 in the transactions table, and 10 is deducted from the users amount in the users table.

Let us try with 100 as the transaction amount:

```
postgres=# select process_payments(1,100);
ERROR:  Insufficient funds.
CONTEXT:  PL/pgSQL function process_payments(integer,numeric) line 16
at RAISE
Time: 0.351 ms
postgres=#
```

As there are not as many funds as 100, it has thrown an error as expected.

Example 2

Let us look at another example that uses a CASE statement to categorize products based on their price range.

Consider two tables, users and products, and insert some data:

```
-- Create the users table
CREATE TABLE users (
    id serial PRIMARY KEY,
    name varchar(50),
    email varchar(100),
    balance numeric
);

-- Insert some sample data into the users table
INSERT INTO users (name, email, balance) VALUES
    ('John Doe', 'john.doe@example.com', 100),
    ('Jane Smith', 'jane.smith@example.com', 50);
```

```
-- Create the products table
CREATE TABLE products (
    id serial PRIMARY KEY,
    name varchar(50),
    price numeric,
    category varchar(50)
);

-- Insert some sample data into the products table
INSERT INTO products (name, price) VALUES
    ('Product A', 5),
    ('Product B', 15),
    ('Product C', 30),
    ('Product D', 60);
```

Create a function which uses a CASE statement to update the category of each product based on its price:

```
CREATE OR REPLACE FUNCTION categorize_products() RETURNS void AS $$
DECLARE
    product_price numeric;
    product record;
BEGIN
    -- Loop through all products and categorize them based on price range
    FOR product IN SELECT * FROM products LOOP
        product_price := product.price;
        CASE
            WHEN product_price <= 10 THEN
                -- Categorize as 'low-priced'
                UPDATE products SET category = 'low-priced' WHERE id =
                product.id;
            WHEN product_price > 10 AND product_price <= 50 THEN
                -- Categorize as 'medium-priced'
                UPDATE products SET category = 'medium-priced' WHERE id =
                product.id;
            ELSE
                -- Categorize as 'high-priced'
```

```
        UPDATE products SET category = 'high-priced' WHERE id =
        product.id;
    END CASE;
  END LOOP;
END;
$$ LANGUAGE plpgsql;
```

Let us run this function and see what happens:

```
postgres=# select * from products;
id |   name    | price | category
----+-----------+-------+----------
5 | Product A |     5 |
6 | Product B |    15 |
7 | Product C |    30 |
8 | Product D |    60 |
(4 rows)

postgres=# SELECT categorize_products();
 categorize_products
---------------------

(1 row)


Time: 2.095 ms
postgres=#
postgres=# select * from products;
 id |   name    | price |   category
----+-----------+-------+---------------
  5 | Product A |     5 | low-priced
  6 | Product B |    15 | medium-priced
  7 | Product C |    30 | medium-priced
  8 | Product D |    60 | high-priced
(4 rows)

Time: 0.286 ms
postgres=#
```

As you can see, running the function updated the category of each product as mentioned in the function logic.

Best Practices of Using Control Statements in PL/pgSQL

Keep Control Statements Simple

One of the main principles of good programming is to keep things simple. This applies to control statements as well. When using control statements, you should strive to keep them as simple as possible. This means that you should avoid nesting too many control statements within each other, and you should avoid using too many conditions in a single statement. By keeping your control statements simple, you will make your code more readable and easier to understand.

Use Comments to Explain Complex Control Statements

Sometimes, you may need to use complex control statements to achieve your desired result. When this happens, it is a good idea to use comments to explain what the control statement is doing. This will help other programmers who read your code to understand what is going on in the control statement. It will also help you to remember what you were trying to achieve when you come back to your code later.

Test Your Control Statements Thoroughly

Control statements can be tricky to get right, especially if you are using complex conditions or loops. For this reason, it is essential to test your control statements thoroughly. Make sure that you test your control statements with a variety of inputs, including inputs that are outside of the expected range. This will help you to catch any bugs or errors in your code before they cause problems in production.

Use Meaningful Variable Names

When writing control statements, it is essential to use meaningful variable names. This will help you to understand what the variable is used for when you come back to your code later. It will also make your code more readable for other programmers who read your code. Avoid using single-letter variable names or abbreviations that are not widely understood.

Don't Overuse Control Statements

Finally, it is important to remember that control statements should not be overused. While they are a powerful tool for controlling the flow of your program, they can also make your code more difficult to read and understand. If you find yourself using too many control statements in a single function, it may be a sign that your code is too complex and needs to be refactored.

Summary

In this chapter, we learned the different types of control statements available in PL/pgSQL, including IF, CASE, LOOP, WHILE, FOR, and FOREACH statements. The programmers can choose the appropriate one for their specific needs. This chapter provides a comprehensive guide to these control statements, covering their usage and providing real-world examples. By following best practices, such as keeping control statements simple, using meaningful variable names, and testing control statements thoroughly, programmers can ensure their control statements are effective, efficient, and optimized. Overall, this chapter is an excellent resource for anyone looking to understand the different types of control statements available in PL/pgSQL and use them effectively to create powerful programs.

What's Next

In the next chapter, we will be covering some key features of PL/pgSQL arrays like the following:

- **Advanced Array Functions**: Dive into more complex array operations and explore functions for transforming, filtering, and aggregating arrays.

- **Array Performance**: Learn optimization strategies for working with arrays, including avoiding unnecessary loops and array manipulation.

- **Nested Arrays**: Explore techniques for working with arrays within arrays, opening up possibilities for complex data structures.

- **Array Manipulation**: Learn how to manipulate arrays for advanced data storage and retrieval.

- **Practical Use Cases**: Discover real-world applications of array manipulation within PL/pgSQL for data analysis, reporting, and more.

CHAPTER 6

Handling Arrays

In the previous chapter, we talked about control statements in PL/pgSQL of PostgreSQL. We covered some examples of IF ELSE, CASE statements and some iterative statements like LOOP, WHILE, FOR and FOREACH. In this chapter, we will dive deep into arrays. We will cover array index and array length, use foreach to iterate over the arrays, and convert arrays to a set of rows. It will also include finding duplicate elements in an array, appending elements to an array, and merging two arrays. By the end of this chapter, you will have a better understanding of how to use arrays in the context of PL/pgSQL.

PostgreSQL provides the ability to store a series of homogeneous data within a single object, by using single- and multidimensional arrays. ARRAY data type columns can be created in a relation, and ARRAY custom data type members can be defined as well as ARRAY variables and parameters in procedures/functions. By using arrays, we can store, retrieve, and process large amounts of data at once. For example, an ARRAY can represent a series of ecommerce items under a specific category, a series of order line items in a specific order, or a series of unit recordings in time series data. In other words, by using ARRAY, we group a certain set of values as a single unit and process all those values at once. Consider the following example, where we demonstrate the ARRAY feature by taking an example of an order line, which has multiple items inside an order:

```
postgres=# DO
$$
DECLARE
V_order_line TEXT ='ord-line-1';
v_items_id TEXT[]= ARRAY['item1', 'item2', 'item3'];
BEGIN
RAISE NOTICE 'Received order line %', v_order_line;
RAISE NOTICE 'Order line items %', v_items_id;
END;
$$;
```

© Baji Shaik and Dinesh Kumar Chemuduru 2023
B. Shaik and D. K. Chemuduru, *Procedural Programming with PostgreSQL PL/pgSQL*,
https://doi.org/10.1007/978-1-4842-9840-4_6

```
NOTICE: Received order line ord-line-1
NOTICE: Order line items {item1,item2,item3}
DO
```

Array Index

PostgreSQL arrays use a one-based index rather than a zero-based index. This means that to access the first element in an array, we have to use an index of one instead of zero. Unlike most of the other programming languages where arrays are zero-based indexes, in PostgreSQL it's a one-based index. Consider the following example, which demonstrates this behavior:

```
postgres=# DO
$$
DECLARE
V_arr TEXT[]:=ARRAY['ONE', 'TWO', 'THREE'];

BEGIN
RAISE NOTICE '0-Based index %', v_arr[0];
RAISE NOTICE '1-Based index %', v_arr[1];
END; $$;

NOTICE: 0-Based index <NULL>
NOTICE: 1-Based index ONE
DO
```

From the preceding output, it can be seen that PostgreSQL follows a default one-based index. Now, let's try setting the array index zero explicitly and then try accessing the element from zero:

```
postgres=# DO
$$
DECLARE
v_arr TEXT[]:=ARRAY['ONE', 'TWO', 'THREE'];

BEGIN
v_arr[0]='ZERO';
RAISE NOTICE '0 index %', v_arr[0];
```

```
END;
$$;

NOTICE: 0 index ZERO
DO
```

As seen previously, PostgreSQL arrays do not restrict us from setting the zero-index value, even though it uses a one-based index. Now, let's try setting a negative index value and accessing it using a negative index number:

```
postgres=# DO
$$
DECLARE
v_arr TEXT[]:=ARRAY['ONE', 'TWO', 'THREE'];

BEGIN
v_arr[-1]='NEGATIVE';
RAISE NOTICE '-1 index %', v_arr[-1];
END;
$$;

NOTICE: -1 index NEGATIVE
DO
```

As seen previously, in PostgreSQL, we can assign any index number to an array, which is not necessarily a positive integer.

Array Length

To find the length of an array, we can use the `array_length` function. The function takes two parameters, the array column and the dimension of the array whose length we want to find. If we want to find the length of the entire array, we can set the second parameter to 1. If we want to find the length of a specific dimension, we can set the second parameter to the dimension number. Consider the following example, which demonstrates the use of the `array_length` function to find the length of an array:

```
postgres=# DO
$$
DECLARE
v_arr TEXT[]:=ARRAY['ONE', 'TWO', 'THREE'];
```

```
BEGIN
v_arr[0] = 'ZERO';
RAISE NOTICE 'Length of array is %', array_length(v_arr, 1);
END;
$$;

NOTICE: Length of array is 4
DO
```

From the preceding output, it can be seen that the array_length function returns the length of the array. In this case, the length of the array is four.

Now, let's try by adding a few more random indexes to the preceding array and then calculate the array length:

```
postgres=# DO
$$
DECLARE
v_arr TEXT[]:=ARRAY['ONE', 'TWO', 'THREE'];

BEGIN
v_arr[0] = 'ZERO';
v_arr[10] = 'TEN';
RAISE NOTICE 'Length of array is %', array_length(v_arr, 1);
END;
$$;

NOTICE: Length of array is 11
DO
```

In the preceding output, the length of an array is reported as 11, while the number of elements in the array is actually 5. This behavior is due to the fact that in PostgreSQL, the length of an array is calculated based on the upper and lower bounds of the array. In this case, the upper bound (index) of the v_arr array is 10, the lower bound (index) is 0, and the number of elements between these indices is 11. When working with indexes in PL/pgSQL, it's important to note that we should not update the values of ARRAY indexes. This is because array indexes in PostgreSQL can be updated to any number, and any gaps between the indexes will be filled with NULL values. Consider the following example, where we got the array length as 11.

```
postgres=# DO
$$
DECLARE
v_arr TEXT[]:=ARRAY['ONE', 'TWO', 'THREE'];

BEGIN
v_arr[0] = 'ZERO';
v_arr[10] = 'TEN';
RAISE NOTICE 'Length of array is %', array_length(v_arr, 1);
RAISE NOTICE 'Array values are %', v_arr;
END;
$$;

NOTICE: Length of array is 11
NOTICE: Array values are [0:10]={ZERO,ONE,TWO,THREE,NULL,NULL,NULL,NULL,
NULL,NULL,TEN}
DO
```

As you can see in the preceding result, there are six NULL values between indexes 4 and 10.

Iterate Array

To iterate over an array in PostgreSQL, we can use the FOREACH loop. This loop allows us to iterate over each element of an array and perform some operation on each element. Consider the following example, which demonstrates how to iterate over an array and print each element:

```
postgres=# DO
$$
DECLARE
v_arr TEXT[]:=ARRAY['ONE', 'TWO', 'THREE'];
v_element TEXT;
BEGIN
FOREACH v_element IN ARRAY v_arr LOOP
RAISE NOTICE 'Element is %', v_element;
END LOOP;
```

```
END;
$$;
NOTICE: Element is ONE
NOTICE: Element is TWO
NOTICE: Element is THREE
DO
```

From the preceding output, it can be seen that we have iterated over the v_arr array and printed each element of the array.

In PostgreSQL, we can also use the unnest function to convert an array into a set of rows. This function returns a set of rows, with each row containing a single element of the array. Consider the following example:

```
postgres=# SELECT * FROM unnest(ARRAY['ONE', 'TWO', 'THREE']) AS arr_
element;
-----------
ONE
TWO
THREE
(3 rows)
```

In the preceding output, we have used the unnest function to convert the array ['ONE', 'TWO', 'THREE'] into a set of rows. Each row contains a single element of the array. We have then selected all the elements from the set of rows using the SELECT statement.

Find Duplicate Elements in Array

While building applications, sometimes we may need to remove duplicate elements from an array. In PostgreSQL, there are a few ways to achieve this by using unnest, group by, and distinct. The following is one of the use cases to remove duplicate elements from the ARRAY:

```
postgres=# DO
$$
DECLARE
v_arr TEXT[]:=ARRAY['ONE', 'TWO', 'THREE', 'TWO', 'FOUR', 'ONE'];
```

```
v_dup TEXT[];
BEGIN
FOR idx IN 1..array_length(v_arr, 1) LOOP
IF v_arr[idx] = ANY(v_dup) THEN
RAISE NOTICE 'Found duplicate %', v_arr[idx];
ELSE v_dup:= v_dup||v_arr[idx];
END IF;
END LOOP;

END;
$$;

NOTICE: Found duplicate TWO
NOTICE: Found duplicate ONE
DO
```

In the preceding example, we have not declared the idx variable in the declaration which is optional while iterating over ARRAY in PL/pgSQL. And also, we used the operator || which actually appends elements to an array.

Append Elements to Array

In PostgreSQL, we can append elements to an array using the array_append function. This function takes two parameters, the array column and the value that we want to append to the array. Consider the following example:

```
postgres=# DO
$$
DECLARE
v_arr TEXT[]:=ARRAY['ONE', 'TWO', 'THREE'];
BEGIN
v_arr:= array_append(v_arr, 'FOUR');
RAISE NOTICE 'Array after appending element is %', v_arr;
END;
$$;
NOTICE: Array after appending element is {ONE,TWO,THREE,FOUR}
DO
```

In the preceding output, we have appended the value `'FOUR'` to the `v_arr` array using the `array_append` function. We can also use the array operator | | to append elements to an array.

Array Merge

To merge two or more arrays in PostgreSQL, we can use the `array_cat` function. This function takes two or more arrays as parameters and concatenates them into a single array. Consider the following example:

```
postgres=# DO
$$
DECLARE
v_arr1 TEXT[]:=ARRAY['ONE', 'TWO', 'THREE'];
v_arr2 TEXT[]:=ARRAY['FOUR', 'FIVE', 'SIX'];
BEGIN
RAISE NOTICE 'Merged array is %', array_cat(v_arr1, v_arr2);
END;
$$;

NOTICE: Merged array is {ONE,TWO,THREE,FOUR,FIVE,SIX}
DO
```

In the preceding output, we have merged two arrays `v_arr1` and `v_arr2` using the `array_cat` function. We have then printed the merged array.

Multidimensional Arrays

Multidimensional arrays are arrays with more than one level of nesting. They can be created in PostgreSQL by using the [ ] [ ] notation to specify the number of dimensions. For example, a two-dimensional array can be created using TEXT[ ][ ]. To access the elements of a multidimensional array, we need to use multiple indexes. The first index specifies the row, and the second index specifies the column. Consider the following example:

```
postgres=#
DO
$$
```

```
DECLARE
v_arr TEXT[][]:=ARRAY[['ONE', 'TWO', 'THREE'], ['FOUR', 'FIVE', 'SIX']];

BEGIN
RAISE NOTICE 'Element at row 1 and column 2 is %', v_arr[1][2];
END;
$$;

NOTICE: Element at row 1 and column 2 is TWO
DO
```

In the preceding output, we can see that we have created a two-dimensional array with two rows and three columns. We have then accessed the element in the first row and second column, which is 'TWO'. We can also use the array_dims function to find the dimensions of an array. This function returns a string that specifies the dimensions of the array. Consider the following example:

```
postgres=# DO
$$
DECLARE
v_arr TEXT[][]:=ARRAY[['ONE', 'TWO', 'THREE'], ['FOUR', 'FIVE', 'SIX']];

BEGIN
RAISE NOTICE 'Array dimensions are %', array_dims(v_arr);
END;
$$;

NOTICE: Array dimensions are [1:2][1:3]
DO
```

In the preceding output, we can see that the array_dims function returns [1:2][1:3], which specifies that the array has two rows and three columns. By using array_ndims(), we can print the number of dimensions we have in that ARRAY. For example, consider the following case:

```
postgres=# DO
$$
DECLARE
v_arr TEXT[][]:=ARRAY[['ONE', 'TWO', 'THREE'], ['FOUR', 'FIVE', 'SIX']];
```

```
BEGIN
RAISE NOTICE 'Array dimensions are %', array_ndims(v_arr);
END;
$$;

NOTICE: Array dimensions are 2
DO
```

Summary

In this chapter, we started with an introduction to arrays, followed by a discussion of array index, length, iteration, and manipulation. The chapter also covered how to convert an array into a set of rows using the unnest function, find duplicate elements in an array, append elements to an array using the array_append function, and merge two or more arrays using the array_cat function. Additionally, the chapter provided guidance on creating and accessing elements of multidimensional arrays.

What's Next

In the next chapter, we will be covering some key features of JSON strings like the following:

- **Advanced JSON Functions**: Explore deeper into JSON manipulation functions and techniques, including nested object extraction and modification.

- **JSON Aggregation**: Learn how to aggregate and process JSON data within PL/pgSQL for reporting and analysis purposes.

- **Working with Large JSON Documents**: Explore strategies for efficiently handling and processing large JSON documents.

- **JSON Performance Optimization**: Dive into performance considerations when working with JSON data, including indexing and storage optimization.

CHAPTER 7

Handling JSON

In the previous chapter, we talked about arrays and how to use them in PL/pgSQL with some examples. In this chapter, we will discuss about JSON data and how to use it in PostgreSQL. We will cover different use cases where JSON data is useful and built-in operators and functions which are used to load and query JSON data. We will go through a few examples of JSON with PL/pgSQL programming.

What Is JSON?

JSON stands for JavaScript Object Notation, and it is a lightweight data interchange format that is easy for humans to read and write and easy for machines to parse and generate.

PostgreSQL has built-in support for JSON, which allows users to store JSON data in a column of a table. This can be useful when working with semi-structured data or when the schema of the data is not known in advance.

Here is an example of creating a table with a JSON column:

```
CREATE TABLE test_table (
  id SERIAL PRIMARY KEY,
  data JSON
);
```

We can then insert data into the table using the INSERT statement:

```
INSERT INTO test_table (data) VALUES ('{"name": "my_name", "age": 30}');
```

© Baji Shaik and Dinesh Kumar Chemuduru 2023
B. Shaik and D. K. Chemuduru, *Procedural Programming with PostgreSQL PL/pgSQL*,
https://doi.org/10.1007/978-1-4842-9840-4_7

To retrieve the data, we can use the SELECT statement and the -> operator to access specific fields:

```
postgres=# SELECT data->'name' as name, data->'age' as age FROM test_table;
   name    | age
-----------+-----
 "my_name" | 30
(1 row)
```

This will return a result set with the name and age fields from the JSON data. The -> operator gets the object field by key. So, if you check the data type of the result, you get JSON:

```
postgres=# SELECT pg_typeof(data->'name') as name, pg_typeof(data->'age')
as age FROM test_table;
 name | age
------+------
 json | json
(1 row)
```

If you want to use the result to type cast to any other data type like INT for further purposes, it does not allow with the -> operator as it returns a key:

```
postgres=# SELECT (data->'name')::varchar as name, (data->'age')::int as
age FROM test_table;
ERROR:  cannot cast type json to integer
LINE 1: ...ECT (data->'name')::varchar as name, (data->'age')::int as a...
```

You can use the ->> operator when you have a use case like this. This operator gets the field in text format so that you can type cast to an allowed type as required:

```
postgres=# SELECT (data->>'name')::varchar as name, (data->>'age')::int as
age FROM test_table;
   name   | age
----------+-----
 my_name  |  30
(1 row)
```

In addition to the -> and ->> operators, PostgreSQL provides several other operators for working with JSON data, including #>, #>>, and @>. These operators allow users to extract specific fields, navigate nested JSON structures, and perform comparisons.

   #> and #>> operators are used to get the fields from any array of values in a JSON string. For example, insert the following data into the `test_table`:

```
postgres=# INSERT INTO test_table(data) VALUES ('{"name":["foo","bar"],
"age":[40,50]}');
INSERT 0 1
Time: 1.468 ms
postgres=# SELECT * FROM test_table;
 id |                data
----+-------------------------------------
  1 | {"name": "my_name", "age": 30}
  2 | {"name":["foo","bar"],"age":[40,50]}
(2 rows)
```

   If you want to get a particular value from the array, you can use the #> or #>> operator. The difference is #> results in a JSON type, and #>> results in TEXT so that you can cast further.

```
postgres=# SELECT data#>'{name,0}' as name, data#>'{age,0}' as age FROM
test_table WHERE id=2;
 name  | age
-------+-----
 "foo" | 40
(1 row)

postgres=# SELECT pg_typeof(data#>'{name,0}') as name, pg_
typeof(data#>'{age,0}') as age FROM test_table WHERE id=2;
 name | age
------+------
 json | json
(1 row)

postgres=# SELECT data#>>'{name,0}' as name, data#>>'{age,0}' as age FROM
test_table WHERE id=2;
 name | age
------+-----
 foo  | 40
(1 row)
```

```
postgres=# SELECT pg_typeof(data#>>'{name,0}') as name, pg_
typeof(data#>>'{age,0}') as age FROM test_table WHERE id=2;
 name | age
------+------
 text | text
(1 row)
```

Use Cases

There are several use cases for using JSON data in PostgreSQL:

1. **Storing Flexible Schema Data**: JSON is a good fit for storing
   data with flexible schema, where the data structure can vary. For
   example, a survey application that collects answers from users
   could store the answers in JSON format, as each user's answers
   may not be the same. The following is a simple example:

   ```
   CREATE TABLE survey (
     id SERIAL PRIMARY KEY,
     answers JSONB
   );

   INSERT INTO survey (answers)
   VALUES ('{"question1": "answer1", "question2": "answer2"}');
   ```

   To retrieve the data, we can use the ->> operator to access
   specific fields:

   ```
   postgres=# SELECT answers->>'question1' as answer1, answers->>
   'question2' as answer2 FROM survey;
    answer1 | answer2
   ---------+---------
    answer1 | answer2
   (1 row)
   ```

   This will return a result set with the answer1 and answer2 fields
   from the JSON data.

2. **Storing Metadata**: JSON can be used to store metadata for objects, such as images or files. For example, an image gallery application could store metadata for each image in JSON format, including information about the image's resolution, size, and creation date. The following is a simple example:

```
CREATE TABLE images (
  id SERIAL PRIMARY KEY,
  metadata JSONB
);

INSERT INTO images (metadata)
VALUES ('{"resolution": "1920x1080", "size": "2MB",
"created_at": "2022-01-01"}');
```

To retrieve the metadata, we can use the ->> operator to access specific fields:

```
postgres=# SELECT metadata->>'resolution' as resolution,
metadata->>'size' as size FROM images;
 resolution | size
------------+------
 1920x1080  | 2MB
(1 row)
```

This will return a result set with the resolution and size fields from the JSON data.

3. **Storing Configuration Data**: JSON can be used to store configuration data for applications. For example, a web application could store configuration data for different environments (development, staging, production) in JSON format. The following is a simple example:

```
CREATE TABLE configurations (
  id SERIAL PRIMARY KEY,
  data JSONB
);

INSERT INTO configurations (data)
```

```
VALUES ('{"development": {"database": {"host": "localhost",
"port": 5432}}, "production": {"database": {"host": "example.com",
"port": 5432}}}');
```

To retrieve the configuration data, we can use the ->> and #>> operators to access specific fields:

```
postgres=# SELECT data->'development'->'database'->'host' as dev_
host, data->'production'->'database'->'host' as prod_host
FROM configurations;
   dev_host    |    prod_host
---------------+----------------
 "localhost"   | "example.com"
(1 row)
```

This will return a result set with the development and production database host fields from the JSON data.

4. **Storing User Preferences**: JSON can be used to store user preferences for applications. For example, a social media application could store each user's preferences for news feed content and notification settings in JSON format. The following is a simple example:

```
CREATE TABLE user_preferences (
  id SERIAL PRIMARY KEY,
  preferences JSONB
);
```

```
INSERT INTO user_preferences (preferences)
VALUES ('{"news_feed": {"show_images": true, "show_videos":
true}, "notifications": {"email": true, "push": false}}');
```

To retrieve the user preferences, we can use the ->> and -> operators to access specific fields:

```
postgres=# SELECT preferences->'news_feed'->'show_images' as
show_images, preferences->'notifications'->'email' as email FROM
user_preferences;
```

```
show_images | email
-------------+-------
 true        | true
(1 row)
```

This will return a result set with the show_images and email fields from the JSON data.

5. **Storing NoSQL-like Data**: JSON can be used to store NoSQL-like data in PostgreSQL. For example, a document-oriented database could use JSON to store data in a document format while still taking advantage of PostgreSQL's powerful indexing and querying capabilities. The following is a simple example:

```
CREATE TABLE documents (
  id SERIAL PRIMARY KEY,
  content JSONB
);

INSERT INTO documents (content)
VALUES ('{"title": "My document", "content": "This is my document text", "metadata": {"tags": ["postgresql", "json"], "views": 100}}');
```

To retrieve the document data, we can use the ->> and #> operators to access specific fields:

```
postgres=# SELECT content->>'title' as title, content->>
'content' as content, content#>'{metadata,tags}' as tags,
content#>>'{metadata,views}' as views FROM documents;
    title    |        content        |         tags          |
  views
-------------+-----------------------+-----------------------+
-------
 My document | This is my document text | ["postgresql", "json"] |
 100
(1 row)
```

This will return a result set with the title, content, tags, and views fields from the JSON data.

103

These are just a few examples of the many use cases for JSON in PostgreSQL. By using JSON, users can store and query semi-structured data in a flexible and efficient manner.

Advantages and Disadvantages

Based on the inherent characteristics of the JSON data format and how it interacts with the features and capabilities of a relational database like PostgreSQL, there are some advantages and disadvantages.

Advantages of using JSON in PostgreSQL

- **Flexibility**: JSON is a flexible data format that allows for the storage of semi-structured data. This can be useful when working with data that does not have a fixed schema or when the schema is not known in advance.

- **Simplified Data Storage**: JSON allows for the storage of complex data structures in a single column, making it easier to store and query data.

- **Improved Performance**: Because JSON data can be stored and queried using a single column, it can lead to improved performance and reduced storage costs.

- **Better Integration with Web Applications**: JSON is a widely used data format in web development, so using JSON in PostgreSQL can make it easier to integrate with web applications.

Disadvantages of using JSON in PostgreSQL

- **Limited Query Capabilities**: While PostgreSQL provides several operators for working with JSON data, these operators are not as powerful as those available for traditional relational data. This can make it more difficult to perform complex queries on JSON data.

- **Increased Complexity**: Storing data in a JSON format can add complexity to the data model, making it more difficult to manage and maintain.

- **Limited Type Safety**: Because JSON is a loosely typed format, it can be more difficult to ensure that data is stored and retrieved in the correct format. This can lead to errors and data inconsistencies if proper care is not taken.

- **Limited Support for Indexing**: While PostgreSQL does provide some indexing capabilities for JSON data, these capabilities are not as robust as those available for traditional relational data. This can lead to slower query performance when working with large amounts of JSON data.

Build PL/pgSQL Functions for JSON

JSON queries can be used in a PL/pgSQL function to return the required output using JSON operators or built-in functions. This will simplify the way you query the tables for JSON data and increase the flexibility. Let's go through a few examples in this section.

Get a member from a document.

Let's consider an example of a table with profile information for certain jobs based on their past experience, companies that they worked for, languages that they can speak where you need to find the candidates with certain experience. Let's create the table and data:

```
CREATE TABLE profiles_json (
        id serial primary key,
        emp_data JSONB
        );
```

```
INSERT INTO profiles_json (emp_data) VALUES ('{"exp": 10, "name": "foo",
"past_exp": ["company1", "company2", "company3"], "languages": ["English",
"French"]}'), ('{"exp": 20, "name": "bar", "past_exp": ["company1",
"company2", "company3", "company4", "company5"], "languages": ["English",
"Spanish", "Hindi", "Chinese"]}');
```

Now, create the PL/pgSQL function which returns the candidate details based on the required experience:

```
CREATE OR REPLACE FUNCTION get_profiles_with_experience(exp INT)
RETURNS TABLE (
    profile_id INT,
    name text,
```

```
        experience INT
)
AS $$
BEGIN
    RETURN QUERY
    SELECT
        id as profile_id,
        emp_data->>'name' as name,
        (emp_data->>'exp')::INT as experience
    FROM profiles_json
    WHERE (emp_data->>'exp')::INT > exp;
END;
$$ LANGUAGE plpgsql;
```

Let's run the function to get the details with ten years of experience:

```
postgres=# SELECT * FROM get_profiles_with_experience(10);
 profile_id | name | experience
------------+------+------------
          2 | bar  |         20
(1 row)
```

As you can see, it returned the candidate details as required.

Check for an array member value.

With the same example, let's check the member value from an array. Languages are defined as an array of values. Let's create the function:

```
CREATE OR REPLACE FUNCTION get_profiles_with_language(lang VARCHAR)
RETURNS TABLE (
    profile_id INT,
    name TEXT
)
AS $$
BEGIN
    RETURN QUERY
    SELECT
        id as profile_id,
        emp_data->>'name' as name
```

```
    FROM profiles_json
    WHERE emp_data->'languages' ? lang;
END;
$$ LANGUAGE plpgsql;
```

Let's run the function to get the candidate details based on the "Spanish" language:

```
postgres=# SELECT * FROM get_profiles_with_language('Spanish');
 profile_id | name
------------+------
          2 | bar
(1 row)
```

As you can see, it returned the candidate details with Spanish language skills.

Check for multiple keys' presence.

Let's create a function to check with multiple key values. Insert some data to verify this:

```
INSERT INTO profiles_json VALUES(5, '{"name": "Bob", "past_exp":
["company1"], "exp": 4, "languages": ["English", "Japanese",
{"special":["brailey", "some_other_special_langugae"]} ], "visa_us": true,
"visa_uk": true, "aws_certified": true}'::JSONB);
```

Create the function that returns the results based on multiple keys:

```
CREATE OR REPLACE FUNCTION get_profiles_with_multi_keys(keys anyarray)
RETURNS TABLE (
    profile_id INT,
    name TEXT
)
AS $$
BEGIN
    RETURN QUERY
    SELECT
        id,
        emp_data->>'name' as name
    FROM profiles_json
    WHERE emp_data ?| keys;
END;
$$ LANGUAGE plpgsql;
```

Let's run the function:

```
postgres=# SELECT * FROM get_profiles_with_multi_keys(array['visa_us',
'visa_uk']);
 profile_id | name
------------+------
          5 | Bob
(1 row)
```

As you can see, it returned the value for multiple keys.

Print pretty-formatted JSON

Here is a simple function to return a formatted JSON:

```
CREATE OR REPLACE FUNCTION get_profiles_formatted_json(profile_id int)
RETURNS TABLE (v_emp_data text)
AS $$
BEGIN
    RETURN QUERY
    SELECT
        jsonb_pretty(emp_data)
    FROM profiles_json
    WHERE id = profile_id;
END;
$$ LANGUAGE plpgsql;
```

Let's run the function for a particular id:

```
postgres=# SELECT * FROM get_profiles_formatted_json(5);
                 v_emp_data
-------------------------------------------------
 {                                              +
     "exp": 4,                                  +
     "name": "Bob",                             +
     "visa_uk": true,                           +
     "visa_us": true,                           +
     "past_exp": [                              +
         "company1"                             +
     ],                                         +
```

```
      "languages": [                              +
          "English",                              +
          "Japanese",                             +
          {                                       +
              "special": [                        +
                  "brailey",                      +
                  "some_other_special_langugae"+
              ]                                   +
          }                                       +
      ],                                          +
      "aws_certified": true                       +
}
(1 row)
```

As you can see, it returned data in formatted JSON.

Indexing JSON Data

Indexing JSON data in PostgreSQL can improve query performance and make it easier to search and filter data. You can use the following index types for JSON data:

1. **GIN (Generalized Inverted Index)**: This index is used to index the keys and values of JSON data. It can be used for simple lookups, as well as for more complex queries that involve nested JSON structures.

2. **GIST (Generalized Search Tree)**: This index is used to index the entire JSON data object. It can be used for more complex queries that involve searching for specific values within the JSON data.

Let's try with an example index:

```
postgres=# CREATE INDEX profile_data_idx ON profiles_json USING
gin(emp_data);
CREATE INDEX
```

Now run the query to see the index scan. Note that as data is less in the table, seq scan is disabled to check the index scan:

```
postgres=# set enable_seqscan to off;
SET
Time: 1.443 ms
postgres=# EXPLAIN ANALYZE SELECT * FROM profiles_json WHERE emp_data ?
'visa_usa';
                                                              QUERY PLAN
-----------------------------------------------------------------------------
-----------------------------------------------
 Bitmap Heap Scan on profiles_json  (cost=8.00..12.01 rows=1 width=36)
(actual time=0.698..0.699 rows=0 loops=1)
    Recheck Cond: (emp_data ? 'visa_usa'::text)
    ->  Bitmap Index Scan on profile_data_idx  (cost=0.00..8.00 rows=1
width=0) (actual time=0.386..0.386 rows=0 loops=1)
          Index Cond: (emp_data ? 'visa_usa'::text)
 Planning Time: 0.055 ms
 Execution Time: 1.176 ms
(6 rows)
```

You can also create the index on JSON members instead of the keys:

```
postgres=# CREATE INDEX profile_data_name_idx2 ON profiles_json ( (emp_
data->>'name') );
CREATE INDEX

postgres=# EXPLAIN ANALYZE SELECT * FROM profiles_json WHERE emp_data ->>
'name' = 'foo';
                                                              QUERY PLAN
-----------------------------------------------------------------------------
 Index Scan using profile_data_name_idx2 on profiles_json  (cost=0.13..8.15
 rows=1 width=36) (actual time=0.180..0.181 rows=1 loops=1)
    Index Cond: ((emp_data ->> 'name'::text) = 'foo'::text)
 Planning Time: 0.064 ms
 Execution Time: 0.194 ms
(4 rows)
```

As you can see, the index on members has been picked up.

Other Useful JSON Functions

Let's look at a few JSON built-in functions that are useful to deal with JSON data. All the available functions are listed in the JSON Functions and Operators (`https://www.postgresql.org/docs/current/functions-json.html`) document. Here are a couple of examples:

JSON query path

You can use json_path_query to retrieve all JSON items returned by the JSON path corresponding to the provided JSON value:

```
postgres=# SELECT jsonb_path_query(emp_data, '$.languages.special') FROM
profiles_json;
            jsonb_path_query
---------------------------------------------
 ["brailey", "some_other_special_langugae"]
(1 row)
```

Building JSON

You can use json_object to build the json string using a text array:

```
postgres=# SELECT json_object('{"id", "1", "name", "foo", "exp", "4"}');
               json_object
---------------------------------------------
 {"id" : "1", "name" : "foo", "exp" : "4"}
(1 row)
```

Summary

In this chapter, we talked about JSON data in PostgreSQL and its supported built-in operators to query the data. We covered different use cases to use JSON data with examples. Also, we have shown simple functions to use JSON queries which simplify retrieving JSON data in our required format. We also covered indexing JSON data to improve performance. There are different built-in functions which are very useful when dealing with JSON data. We had a look into a couple of functions.

What's Next

In the next chapter, we will be covering some key features of PL/pgSQL cursors like the following:

- **Advanced Cursor Manipulation**: Learn about scrollable cursors, dynamic cursors, and techniques for optimizing cursor operations.

- **Cursor Error Handling**: Explore best practices for handling errors when working with cursors, ensuring your code is robust and reliable.

- **Multiple Cursors**: Discover strategies for efficiently managing multiple cursors within your PL/pgSQL code.

- **Cursor Performance**: Deepen your understanding of cursor performance considerations and optimization techniques.

- **Cursor Use Cases**: Explore real-world scenarios where cursors are essential for processing and navigating large result sets.

CHAPTER 8

Cursors

In the previous chapter, we talked about JSON data and how to use it in PostgreSQL. In this chapter, we will discuss the basics of cursors in PL/pgSQL, their advantages, and how they can be used to optimize database performance. The chapter begins with an overview of cursors and their benefits, followed by a comparison of the response time between executing an SQL query on the SQL interface and using cursors. Next, we will delve into the different types of cursors available in PL/pgSQL, such as SCROLL, NO SCROLL, and WITH HOLD cursors. Finally, we will introduce reference cursors, which allow you to create a cursor, open it, and then pass or return the cursor to another function as an input argument.

What Are Cursors?

PL/pgSQL supports cursors, which are a mechanism for traversing through the records of a result set. Cursors are particularly useful when dealing with large datasets, where it is impractical to extract all the records at once. They allow you to fetch a small, manageable number of records at a time, process them, and then fetch the next set of records.

Consider the following example: the table contains a large number of records. Compare the response time of executing the SQL query on the SQL interface vs. using cursors:

```
postgres=# CREATE TABLE many_rows_table(t INT);
CREATE TABLE
postgres=# INSERT INTO many_rows_table VALUES (generate_series(1, 10000000));
INSERT 0 10000000
postgres=# \timing
Timing is on.
```

© Baji Shaik and Dinesh Kumar Chemuduru 2023
B. Shaik and D. K. Chemuduru, *Procedural Programming with PostgreSQL PL/pgSQL*,
https://doi.org/10.1007/978-1-4842-9840-4_8

Execute the SQL query that fetches all records from the preceding table and prints the total time it takes to fetch and return the response to the client:

```
postgres=# SELECT * FROM many_rows_table;
t
_____

1
2
...
...
Time: 2854.458 ms (00:02.854)
```

Based on the preceding output, the SQL query executed on the table "many_rows_table" fetched all records and returned the response within 02.854 seconds. Execute the same SQL statement through a PL/pgSQL code block to fetch the result. Exit the code as soon as the first record is read from the table.

```
postgres=# DO
$$
DECLARE
v_rec RECORD;
BEGIN
FOR v_rec IN (SELECT * FROM many_rows_table) LOOP
IF v_rec IS NOT NULL THEN
RAISE NOTICE 'Found record %', v_rec;
EXIT;
END IF;
END LOOP;
END;
$$;
NOTICE:   Found record (1)
DO
Time: 1.540 ms
```

In the preceding example, we used a FOR LOOP to iterate over the SQL statement, which creates an implicit cursor in PostgreSQL and iterates over the result set. We exit the loop when we find a NOT NULL record, which determines the response time of getting a single record from the table. As seen in the preceding output, we were able to retrieve the first record in just 1.5 milliseconds using this method, unlike the traditional SQL way where the entire result set is returned to the client, which took time around 2 seconds.

Using cursors can help reduce the response time when dealing with large datasets, as it allows the user to fetch a small, manageable number of records at a time. This is particularly useful when rendering data in a dashboard with pagination, where only a certain number of records are displayed at once. Cursors also allow for processing of the data as needed, rather than returning the entire result set at once to the client.

CURSOR Attributes

PL/pgSQL does not directly provide cursor attributes such as ISOPEN, FOUND, NOTFOUND, and ROWCOUNT. However, you can use alternative workarounds for each attribute.

ISOPEN Attribute

The ISOPEN attribute returns true if the cursor is currently open and false otherwise. You can use a boolean variable in PL/pgSQL to achieve this.

Consider the following example:

```
DO
$$
DECLARE
  v_cur CURSOR FOR SELECT * FROM many_rows_table;
  row_data many_rows_table%ROWTYPE;
  cursor_open BOOLEAN := FALSE;
BEGIN
  -- Open the cursor if not already open
  IF NOT cursor_open THEN
    OPEN v_cur;
    cursor_open := TRUE;
  END IF;
```

```
RAISE NOTICE 'Status of the cursor: %' , CASE WHEN cursor_open='t' THEN
'OPEN' ELSE 'CLOSE' END;
  -- Fetch rows using the cursor
  FETCH v_cur INTO row_data;

  -- Close the cursor if it was opened
  IF cursor_open THEN
    CLOSE v_cur;
    RAISE NOTICE 'Cursor is closed.';
    cursor_open := FALSE;
  END IF;
  RAISE NOTICE 'Status of the cursor: %' , CASE WHEN cursor_open='t' THEN
'OPEN' ELSE 'CLOSE' END;
END;
$$;
```

In the preceding example, we declare a cursor named "v_cur" and a boolean variable cursor_open to hold the status of the cursor. We defined the cursor_open variable as FALSE by default. Inside the code, we check the variable value; if it is false, it opens the cursor. And at the end, we are closing the cursor and updating the variable back to FALSE.

Let's run the function:

```
postgres=# DO
 $$
 DECLARE
   v_cur CURSOR FOR SELECT * FROM many_rows_table;
   row_data many_rows_table%ROWTYPE;
   cursor_open BOOLEAN := FALSE;
 BEGIN
   -- Open the cursor if not already open
   IF NOT cursor_open THEN
     OPEN v_cur;
     cursor_open := TRUE;
   END IF;
```

```
RAISE NOTICE 'Status of the cursor: %' , CASE WHEN cursor_open='t' THEN
'OPEN' ELSE 'CLOSE' END;
    -- Fetch rows using the cursor
    FETCH v_cur INTO row_data;

    -- Close the cursor if it was opened
    IF cursor_open THEN
      CLOSE v_cur;
      RAISE NOTICE 'Cursor is closed.';
      cursor_open := FALSE;
    END IF;
    RAISE NOTICE 'Status of the cursor: %', CASE WHEN cursor_open='t' THEN
'OPEN' ELSE 'CLOSE' END;
 END;
 $$;
NOTICE:  Status of the cursor: OPEN
NOTICE:  Cursor is closed.
NOTICE:  Status of the cursor: CLOSE
DO
```

As you can see, it shows the status of the cursor accordingly.

FOUND Attribute

The FOUND attribute returns true if the last operation on the cursor found a row,
and false otherwise. You can use the FOUND variable as an alternative in PL/
pgSQL. Consider the following example:

```
DO
$$
DECLARE
  v_cur CURSOR FOR SELECT * FROM many_rows_table;
  v_rec many_rows_table%ROWTYPE;
BEGIN
  OPEN v_cur;
  FETCH v_cur INTO v_rec;
  IF FOUND THEN
```

```
    RAISE NOTICE 'Row found.';
  ELSE
    RAISE NOTICE 'No rows found.';
  END IF;

  CLOSE v_cur;
END;
$$;
```

In the preceding example, we declare and open a cursor named "v_cur". We then fetch the first record into the v_rec variable and use the FOUND attribute to determine if a record was found. If a record was found, we print the record to the console using the RAISE NOTICE statement. If no records were found, we print a message saying so.

Let's run the function:

```
postgres=# DO
 $$
 DECLARE
   v_cur CURSOR FOR SELECT * FROM many_rows_table;
   v_rec many_rows_table%ROWTYPE;
 BEGIN
   OPEN v_cur;
   FETCH v_cur INTO v_rec;
   IF FOUND THEN
     RAISE NOTICE 'Row found.';
   ELSE
     RAISE NOTICE 'No rows found.';
   END IF;

   CLOSE v_cur;
 END;
 $$;
NOTICE:  Row found.
DO
```

As you can see, it shows "Row found" as there are records in the table.

NOTFOUND Attribute

The NOTFOUND attribute returns the opposite of the FOUND attribute, true if the last operation on the cursor did not find a row and false otherwise. As an alternative, you can use NOT FOUND in PL/pgSQL.

Consider the following example:

```
DO
$$
DECLARE
  v_cur CURSOR FOR SELECT * FROM no_rows_table;
  v_rec no_rows_table%ROWTYPE;
BEGIN
  OPEN v_cur;
  FETCH v_cur INTO v_rec;
  IF NOT FOUND THEN
    RAISE NOTICE 'No rows found.';
  ELSE
    RAISE NOTICE 'Row found.';
  END IF;

  CLOSE v_cur;
END;
$$;
```

In the preceding example, we declare and open a cursor named "v_cur". We then fetch the first record into the v_rec variable and use the NOT FOUND attribute to determine if a record was not found. If no records were found, we print a message saying so. If a record was found, we print the record to the console using the RAISE NOTICE statement.

Let's run the function by creating the table no_rows_table with empty rows:

```
postgres=# CREATE TABLE no_rows_table(id int);
CREATE TABLE
postgres=# DO
 $$
 DECLARE
   v_cur CURSOR FOR SELECT * FROM no_rows_table;
```

119

```
   v_rec no_rows_table%ROWTYPE;
 BEGIN
   OPEN v_cur;
   FETCH v_cur INTO v_rec;
   IF NOT FOUND THEN
     RAISE NOTICE 'No rows found.';
   ELSE
     RAISE NOTICE 'Row found.';
   END IF;

   CLOSE v_cur;
 END;
 $$;
NOTICE:   No rows found.
DO
```

As you can see, it shows "No rows found" as the table is empty.

ROWCOUNT Attribute

The ROWCOUNT attribute returns the number of rows processed by the last FETCH or MOVE statement. You can use the GET DIAGNOSTICS command's ROW_COUNT item as an alternative for this. Consider the following example:

```
DO
$$
DECLARE
  v_cur CURSOR FOR SELECT * FROM many_rows_table;
  v_rec many_rows_table%ROWTYPE;
  num_rows int;
BEGIN
  OPEN v_cur;
  MOVE FORWARD ALL FROM v_cur;
  GET DIAGNOSTICS num_rows = ROW_COUNT;

  RAISE NOTICE 'Number of rows fetched: %', num_rows;
```

```
    CLOSE v_cur;
END;
$$;
```

In the preceding example, we declare and open a cursor named "v_cur". We used MOVE FORWARD to hold all the rows and GET DIAGNOSTICS to get the ROW_COUNT.

Let's run the function and see if it displays the rows:

```
postgres=# SELECT COUNT(1) FROM many_rows_table ;
 count
-------
 10000
(1 row)

postgres=# DO
 $$
 DECLARE
   v_cur CURSOR FOR SELECT * FROM many_rows_table;
   v_rec many_rows_table%ROWTYPE;
   num_rows int;
 BEGIN
   OPEN v_cur;
   MOVE FORWARD ALL FROM v_cur;
   GET DIAGNOSTICS num_rows = ROW_COUNT;

   RAISE NOTICE 'Number of rows fetched: %', num_rows;

   CLOSE v_cur;
 END;
 $$;
NOTICE:  Number of rows fetched: 10000
DO
```

As you can see, it shows the rows from the table.

Monitor Cursors

Unlike other database engines where cursors have to be explicitly closed, in PL/pgSQL cursors will be automatically closed when the transaction ends or when there is an exception in the current execution block. The implicit transactions will also be closed when their task is done. To monitor the current active transaction in PostgreSQL, we can use the PostgreSQL system catalog table "pg_cursors", which provides insight into the details of opened cursors:

```
postgres=# \d pg_cursors
View "pg_catalog.pg_cursors"
Column         |          Type          | Collation | Nullable | Default
---------------+------------------------+-----------+----------+---------
name           | text                   |           |          |
statement      | text                   |           |          |
is_holdable    | boolean                |           |          |
is_binary      | boolean                |           |          |
is_scrollable  | boolean                |           |          |
creation_time  | timestamp with time zone |         |          |
```

PL/pgSQL provides holdable cursors, as well as scrollable cursors that must be explicitly set when creating external triggers. We will discuss these cursors further in this chapter.

As we mentioned in the previous example, a FOR LOOP creates an implicit cursor to fetch data from underlying tables. Now, let's track those implicit cursors created by the FOR LOOP. Execute the same previous example, and while the FOR LOOP is active, query the "pg_cursors" catalog table and display the results:

```
postgres=# DO
$$
DECLARE
        v_rec RECORD;
        v_rec2 RECORD;
BEGIN
        FOR v_rec IN (SELECT * FROM many_rows_table) LOOP
                SELECT name, creation_time FROM pg_cursors INTO v_rec2;
                RAISE NOTICE 'Open cursor details %', v_rec2;
```

```
                IF v_rec IS NOT NULL THEN
                        RAISE NOTICE 'Found record %', v_rec;
                        EXIT;
                END IF;
        END LOOP;
END;
$$;
NOTICE:  Open cursor details ("<unnamed portal 1>","2023-07-23
15:27:26.025685+05:30")
NOTICE:  Found record (1)
DO
```

In the preceding output, you can see an unnamed cursor named "<unnamed portal 1>". Typically, portals are named as system-generated pointers to query result sets. By using these pointers, we can manage fetching data from the cursors.

If you want to use a user-defined or explicit cursor in a PL/pgSQL function, you must first define it using the DECLARE statement and then open it using the OPEN statement. Once the cursor is open, you can fetch rows from it using the FETCH statement. In the case of implicit cursors, such as the one shown earlier, there is no need to create a cursor, open it, and fetch data. This is handled automatically by the database engine.

SCROLL Cursor

PL/pgSQL provides the option to use scrollable cursors, which allow you to move back and forth through the result set. This is particularly useful for applications that require random access to the results, such as when implementing search functionality. To use a scrollable cursor, you must declare it with the SCROLL keyword and then open it with the OPEN statement. Once the cursor is open, you can fetch rows using the FETCH statement and then move forward or backward through the result set using the MOVE statement. Finally, you must close the cursor using the CLOSE statement.

Consider the following example, which demonstrates the behavior of a SCROLL cursor. As we discussed earlier, the scope of the cursor is a transaction by default, so we should try to move the scroll within the transaction rather than from a session:

```
postgres=# CREATE TABLE scroll_test(t INT);
CREATE TABLE
```

```
postgres=# INSERT INTO scroll_test VALUES (generate_series(1, 10));
INSERT 0 10

postgres=# BEGIN WORK;
BEGIN
postgres=*# DO
$$
DECLARE
v_cur SCROLL CURSOR FOR SELECT * FROM scroll_test;
BEGIN
OPEN v_cur;
END;
$$;
DO
postgres=*# FETCH NEXT FROM v_cur;
 t
 _
 1
(1 row)

postgres=*# FETCH NEXT FROM v_cur;
 t
 --
 2
(1 row)

postgres=*# MOVE BACKWARD 1 IN v_cur;
MOVE 1
postgres=*# MOVE BACKWARD 1 IN v_cur;
MOVE 0
postgres=*# FETCH NEXT FROM v_cur;
 t
 —
 1
(1 row)
```

To understand cursors better, let's divide the preceding actions into two phases.

Phase 1

In the preceding example, we started the transaction using BEGIN WORK and created an anonymous PL/pgSQL block that explicitly declares the cursor "v_cur" on the table "scroll_test". We also used an explicit cursor OPEN call on "v_cur", which executes the given SQL statement and points the cursor "v_cur" to the result set.

Phase 2

After executing the anonymous code block, we fetch the cursor "v_cur" using the "FETCH NEXT" statement. This retrieves the data row by row, resulting in a result set of 1 and 2. We used the "MOVE BACKWARD" cursor control statement, which sets the cursor pointer to its previous record. We did this twice to ensure that the cursor pointer is reset to the beginning of the result set as a counterpart to the "FETCH NEXT" statement.

This is a simple way to create a SCROLL cursor, and by using FETCH NEXT or MOVE BACKWARD, we can control the amount of result sets, which we retrieve from the cursor. When building a dashboard with a paginated table, you can use FETCH NEXT calls to retrieve the next page of data while keeping the cursor open in the transaction. If it is not possible to keep the transaction open for pagination, then we should use "WITH HOLD" cursors. These cursors hold the cursor data pointer even after the transaction is closed.

NO SCROLL Cursor

The NO SCROLL cursor behavior is the opposite of the SCROLL behavior.

With the NO SCROLL cursor, the data pointer cannot be moved backward.

Consider the following example, with a NO SCROLL option:

```
postgres=# BEGIN WORK;
BEGIN
postgres=*# DO
$$
DECLARE
v_cur NO SCROLL CURSOR FOR SELECT * FROM scroll_test;
BEGIN
OPEN v_cur;
END;
```

```
$$;
DO
postgres=*# FETCH NEXT FROM v_cur;
t
—
1
(1 row)

postgres=*# MOVE BACKWARD 1 IN v_cur;
ERROR:  cursor can only scan forward
HINT:  Declare it with SCROLL option to enable backward scan.
```

As shown in the preceding example, moving the cursor backward led to an error because the cursor "v_cur" was declared as a "NO SCROLL" cursor. "NO SCROLL" cursors are useful when holding the result set not only for reading data but also for performing UPDATE operations. If you need to traverse a result set with a cursor and perform update operations, it is recommended to use a "NO SCROLL" cursor.

Consider the following example:

```
postgres=# BEGIN WORK;
BEGIN
postgres=*# DO
$$
DECLARE
v_cur NO SCROLL CURSOR FOR SELECT * FROM scroll_test FOR UPDATE;
BEGIN
OPEN v_cur;
END;
$$;
DO

postgres=*# FETCH NEXT FROM v_cur;
t
—
1
(1 row)

postgres=*# DELETE FROM scroll_test WHERE CURRENT OF v_cur;
```

```
DELETE 1
postgres=*# FETCH NEXT FROM v_cur;
t
_
2
(1 row)

postgres=*# END;
COMMIT
```

In the preceding example, we declared a NO SCROLL cursor. The SQL query mentioned in the cursor is used for the FOR UPDATE operation. This means that the cursor not only traverses the rows but also allows the traversed rows to be updated/deleted using DML statements like UPDATE/DELETE.

If the application requires the behavior mentioned earlier, then a "NO SCROLL" cursor should be used. "SCROLL" cursors should only be used for read-only operations. If the SCROLL behavior of the cursor is not defined, PL/pgSQL will determine whether it should be SCROLL or NO SCROLL.

If the SQL is executing FOR UPDATE, then the cursor will be set to "NO SCROLL." If the SQL is read-only, then the cursor will automatically be set to "SCROLL."

WITH HOLD Cursors

PL/pgSQL provides the option to use "WITH HOLD" cursors, which allow the cursor data and pointer to be held even after the transaction is closed. This is useful when dealing with pagination or when you need to preserve the cursor state across multiple transactions. To use a "WITH HOLD" cursor, you must declare it with the "WITH HOLD" keyword and then open it with the OPEN statement. Once the cursor is open, you can fetch rows using the FETCH statement and then close the cursor using the CLOSE statement.

For example, let's say you have a dashboard that displays data from a PostgreSQL database. The dashboard has pagination, and you want to ensure that the cursor state is preserved across multiple page loads. You can use a "WITH HOLD" cursor to achieve this. Consider the following example, which demonstrates the "WITH HOLD" cursor:

```
postgres=# DO
$$
BEGIN
```

```
        EXECUTE 'DECLARE cur CURSOR WITH HOLD FOR select * from
scroll_test;';
END;
$$;
DO

postgres=# FETCH NEXT FROM cur;
t

—

2
(1 row)

postgres=# FETCH NEXT FROM cur;
t

—

3
(1 row)
```

In the preceding example, we declared "WITH HOLD" cursors within a transaction that was also closed. Despite the transaction being closed, we are still able to fetch records from the "cur" cursor from outside the cursor. However, we need to be careful with "WITH HOLD" cursors because they won't close automatically until we close the session.

Currently, PL/pgSQL anonymous blocks do not support the creation of "WITH HOLD" cursors, unlike SCROLL and NO SCROLL cursors. To create these cursors, you must use named functions or procedures. Alternatively, you can create "WITH HOLD" cursors using a dynamic SQL statement approach, as shown earlier.

Refcursors

PL/pgSQL supports reference cursors, which allow you to create a cursor and open it and then pass or return the cursor to another function as an input argument. This means that you can easily pass the cursor data pointer between multiple function calls, which improves code reusability and maintainability. These cursors can be created, opened, and passed or returned as input arguments to other functions. Consider the following example:

```
postgres=# CREATE OR REPLACE FUNCTION test_refcursor(rf REFCURSOR)
RETURNS VOID
AS
$$
DECLARE
v_rec RECORD;
BEGIN
LOOP
FETCH rf INTO v_rec;
RAISE NOTICE 'Record %', v_rec;
-- print only one record and exit the loop
EXIT WHEN FOUND;
END LOOP;
END;
$$ LANGUAGE PLPGSQL;
CREATE FUNCTION
```

In the preceding function, we pass the REFCURSOR as a parameter to the test_
refcursor() function. Unlike regular CURSORS where we declare, open, and fetch the
records, in the preceding function, we do not perform any of those actions. Instead, we
directly fetch the records from the cursor. Consider the following anonymous block,
where we declare and open a cursor and also call the preceding function to print the
results:

```
postgres=# DO
$$
 DECLARE
 v_cur REFCURSOR;
 BEGIN
        OPEN v_cur FOR SELECT * FROM scroll_test;
        PERFORM test_refcursor(v_cur);
END;
$$;
NOTICE:  Record (2)
DO
```

Summary

In this chapter, we started with the basics of cursors in PL/pgSQL and how to use them to optimize performance. We talked about the different types of cursors and their use cases with different examples. Cursors allow for more efficient data retrieval, processing, and manipulation, resulting in better database performance and faster response times. By using different types of cursors, cursor attributes, and reference cursors, developers can optimize their PL/pgSQL code and improve the overall efficiency of their applications.

What's Next

In the next chapter, we will be covering some key features of custom operators like the following:

- **Complex Operator Design**: Delve into advanced operator overloading and customization to create powerful and intuitive custom operators.

- **Operator Performance**: Explore optimization techniques to ensure that custom operators perform efficiently in different scenarios.

- **Operator Consistency**: Learn about the importance of consistent operator behavior and how to design operators that align with PostgreSQL's standards.

- **Practical Operator Use**: Discover real-world use cases where custom operators simplify complex operations within PL/pgSQL code.

CHAPTER 9

Custom Operators

In the previous chapter, we talked about cursors and how to use them in PL/pgSQL with some examples. In this chapter, we will start with what are different types of built-in operators available in PostgreSQL. We will cover custom operators and their purpose. We will walk through the use cases to create custom operators with simple examples. We will also explain the advantages and disadvantages of having custom operators. By the end of this chapter, you will have a better understanding of custom operators and where to use them effectively.

In PostgreSQL, custom operators can be defined and used just like built-in operators. In this chapter, we will explore how to create custom operators in PostgreSQL with PL/pgSQL examples and discuss different use cases and pros and cons of using custom operators.

Built-In Operators

We all know that an operator is a symbol or keyword to perform specific operations on the data. There are several types of operators available in PostgreSQL, and the documentation has all details available already: `www.postgresql.org/docs/current/functions.html`.

You can look at the pg_catalog.pg_operator table to see available operators from the database. For example, if you look at "||" operator availability, you can see what left and right operands can be used with this operator:

```
postgres=# select oprname, oprleft::regtype, oprright::regtype from  pg_
operator where oprname='||';
 oprname |     oprleft      |      oprright
---------+------------------+-------------------
 ||      |  bytea           |  bytea
 ||      |  text            |  text
```

© Baji Shaik and Dinesh Kumar Chemuduru 2023
B. Shaik and D. K. Chemuduru, *Procedural Programming with PostgreSQL PL/pgSQL*,
https://doi.org/10.1007/978-1-4842-9840-4_9

```
||      | text                | anynonarray
||      | bit varying         | bit varying
||      | anynonarray         | text
||      | tsvector            | tsvector
||      | tsquery             | tsquery
||      | jsonb               | jsonb
||      | anycompatible       | anycompatiblearray
||      | anycompatiblearray  | anycompatible
||      | anycompatiblearray  | anycompatiblearray
(11 rows)
```

Or we can use the following command:

```
postgres=# \do ||
                              List of operators
  Schema    | Name |  Left arg type     |   Right arg type    |    Result type      |       Description
------------+------+--------------------+---------------------+---------------------+--------------------
 pg_catalog | ||   | anycompatible      | anycompatiblearray  | anycompatiblearray  | prepend element
            |      |                    |                     |                     | onto front of array
 pg_catalog | ||   | anycompatiblearray | anycompatible       | anycompatiblearray  | append element onto
            |      |                    |                     |                     | end of array
 pg_catalog | ||   | anycompatiblearray | anycompatiblearray  | anycompatiblearray  | concatenate
 pg_catalog | ||   | anynonarray        | text                | text                | concatenate
 pg_catalog | ||   | bit varying        | bit varying         | bit varying         | concatenate
 pg_catalog | ||   | bytea              | bytea               | bytea               | concatenate
 pg_catalog | ||   | jsonb              | jsonb               | jsonb               | concatenate
 pg_catalog | ||   | text               | anynonarray         | text                | concatenate
 pg_catalog | ||   | text               | text                | text                | concatenate
 pg_catalog | ||   | tsquery            | tsquery             | tsquery             | OR-concatenate
 pg_catalog | ||   | tsvector           | tsvector            | tsvector            | concatenate
(11 rows)
```

Mostly, this operator works with strings. For example:

```
postgres=# select 'add '||'strings';
  ?column?
--------------
 add strings
(1 row)
```

However, if you try to use this operator with integers, you will see an error:

```
postgres=# select 1||2;
ERROR:  operator does not exist: integer || integer
LINE 1: select 1||2;
                ^
HINT:  No operator matches the given name and argument types. You might
need to add explicit type casts.
```

It says the operator does not exist, which is true as this operator with left and right operands as int does not exist. So, this is where you can create custom operators.

Let's look at some simple examples of these operators before we start with custom operators. Note that it will not cover a complete list of operators but a few operators which are commonly used.

- **Arithmetic Operators**: + (addition), - (subtraction), * (multiplication), / (division), % (remainder), ^ (exponentiation)

  A simple example is

  ```
  postgres=# select (1+2) as "+", (2-1) as "-", (1*2) as "*",
  (2/1) as "/", (2%1) as "%", (2^1) as "^";
   + | - | * | / | % | ^
  ---+---+---+---+---+---
   3 | 1 | 2 | 2 | 0 | 2
  (1 row)
  ```

- **Comparison Operators**: =, <> or !=, <, <=, >, >=, IS DISTINCT FROM, IS NOT DISTINCT FROM

  A simple example is

  ```
  postgres=# select 1=1 as "=", 1<>1 as "<> or !=", 1<2 as "<", 1>2 as ">", 1<=1 as
  "<=", 1>=1 as ">=", 1 IS DISTINCT FROM 1 as "IS DISTINCT FROM", 1 IS NOT DISTINCT
  FROM 1 as "IS NOT DISTINCT FROM";
   = | <> or != | < | > | <= | >= | IS DISTINCT FROM | IS NOT DISTINCT FROM
  ---+----------+---+---+----+----+------------------+---------------------
   t | f        | t | f | t  | f  |                  | t
  (1 row)
  ```

- **Logical Operators**: AND, OR, NOT

  A simple example is

  ```
  postgres=# select true AND true as "AND", true OR true  as "OR",
  NOT false as "NOT";
   AND | OR | NOT
  -----+----+-----
   t   | t  | t
  (1 row)
  ```

- **Bitwise Operators**: & (bitwise AND), | (bitwise OR), # (bitwise XOR),
  ~ (bitwise NOT)

  A simple example is

  ```
  postgres=# select B'111' & B'011' as "Bitwise AND", B'111' |
  B'011' as "Bitwise OR";
   Bitwise AND | Bitwise OR
  -------------+------------
   011         | 111
  (1 row)
  ```

- **Text Operators**: || (concatenation), LIKE, ILIKE, SIMILAR TO, NOT
  LIKE, NOT ILIKE, NOT SIMILAR TO

  A simple example is

  ```
  postgres=# select 'con'||'cat' as "||", '1111' like '11' as
  "LIKE", '1111' ILIKE '%11' as "ILIKE";
    ||   | LIKE | ILIKE
  -------+------+-------
   concat | f    | t
  (1 row)
  ```

- **Set Operators**: UNION, INTERSECT, EXCEPT

  A simple example is

  ```
  postgres=# select '1' as "UNION" UNION select '2';
   UNION
  -------
  ```

```
 1
 2
(2 rows)

Time: 0.285 ms
postgres=# select '1' as "INTERSECT" INTERSECT select '1';
 INTERSECT
-----------
 1
(1 row)

Time: 0.190 ms
postgres=# select '1' as "EXCEPT" EXCEPT select '2';
 EXCEPT
--------
 1
(1 row)
```

Creating a Custom Operator

We can create custom operators in PostgreSQL to extend the functionality of the database. They are useful when the standard set of operators may not be sufficient to express the desired functionality. To create a custom operator, we need to use the CREATE OPERATOR command. However, you need to use a built-in or custom function to implement the functionality of the custom operator.

Here is the basic syntax:

```
CREATE OPERATOR operator_name (
  PROCEDURE = function_name,
  LEFTARG  = left_type,
  RIGHTARG = right_type
);
```

- operator_name: The name of the operator to be created

- function_name: The name of the PL/pgSQL function that implements the operator

- `left_type`: The data type of the left operand

- `right_type`: The data type of the right operand

Simple Example

Let's start with a simple example to check if a string is empty or not. If the string is empty, we should return true; otherwise, return false. By default, we use PostgreSQL's equality or inequality operators to check for string emptiness, as follows:

```
postgres=# SELECT ''='not empty';
 ?column?
----------
f
(1 row)

postgres=# SELECT ''='';
?column?
----------
t
(1 row)
```

What if we had a unary operator to perform the same action? For example, if we wanted to check whether a string was empty or not, we could just put a "?" in front of it. For instance, "?not empty" would return false. PostgreSQL is developer-friendly and allows us to create custom operators to achieve this. Creating an operator has to be in two steps.

Step 1: Create an operator function.

```
postgres=# CREATE OR REPLACE FUNCTION isempty(text) RETURNS BOOL AS
$$
BEGIN RETURN $1='';
END;
$$ LANGUAGE PLPGSQL;
CREATE FUNCTION
```

Step 2: Create an operator.

```
postgres=# CREATE OPERATOR ?(FUNCTION=isempty, RIGHTARG=text);
CREATE OPERATOR
```

Now, let us execute the desired behavior and see the results:

```
postgres=# SELECT ?'not empty';
?column?
----------
f
(1 row)

postgres=# SELECT ?'';
?column?
----------
t
(1 row)
```

Here is another example where we add a custom operator for the string concat. The built-in operator "+" is for arithmetic operations, which is basically to add two numbers or dates. However, you have an application code where two strings are added using the "+" operator. Usually, adding two strings is nothing but concatenation. You can simply use the "||" operator or concat functions as follows:

```
postgres=# select 'con'||'cat';
 ?column?
----------
 concat
(1 row)

Time: 0.131 ms
postgres=# select concat('', 'con','cat');
 concat
--------
 concat
(1 row)

Time: 0.483 ms
postgres=# select concat_ws('', 'con','cat');
 concat_ws
-----------
 concat
(1 row)
```

However, if you are migrating your database from different database engines which support the "+" operator to add two strings to the PostgreSQL database, you would need to change your application code with the "||" operator or concat function. To avoid the code update, you can create a custom operator "+" which supports the concatenation of two strings. The following are the steps:

1. Create a new schema to create a custom operator and grant privileges to the PUBLIC role so that every user can use the custom operator:

```
CREATE SCHEMA cust_opr;

GRANT USAGE ON SCHEMA cust_opr TO PUBLIC;
```

2. Create a function to use in the custom operator and grant privileges to the PUBLIC role. You can create a PL/pgSQL function or a simple SQL function:

```
CREATE OR REPLACE FUNCTION cust_opr.add_strings(varchar, varchar)
RETURNS varchar LANGUAGE sql immutable as $$
  SELECT $1 operator(pg_catalog.||) $2
$$;
```

or

```
CREATE OR REPLACE FUNCTION cust_opr.add_strings(varchar, varchar)
RETURNS varchar AS $$
  BEGIN
    RETURN $1 || $2;
  END;
$$ LANGUAGE plpgsql
IMMUTABLE;
GRANT EXECUTE ON FUNCTION cust_opr.add_strings(varchar, varchar)
TO PUBLIC;
```

3. Create the custom operator using the custom function created
    in step 2:

```
CREATE OPERATOR cust_opr.+ (
LEFTARG=VARCHAR,
RIGHTARG=VARCHAR,
PROCEDURE = cust_opr.add_strings);
```

4. Make sure to set search_path to use the cust_opr schema before
    pg_catalog. Otherwise, the "+" operator in pg_catalog will be
    used instead of the newly created cust_opr schema:

```
postgres=# select 'con'+'cat';
ERROR:  operator is not unique: unknown + unknown
LINE 1: select 'con'+'cat';
                    ^
HINT:  Could not choose a best candidate operator. You might need
to add explicit type casts.
Time: 1.385 ms
postgres=#
postgres=#
postgres=#
postgres=# set search_path to cust_opr, pg_catalog;
SET
Time: 1.162 ms
postgres=#
postgres=# select 'con'+'cat';
 ?column?
----------
 concat
(1 row)
```

As you can see, without setting the search_path thrown the error as it was using the
operator in the pg_catalog schema.

This is a simple example based on requirements of how the application was built. You can work around the application behavior without changing the application code and efforts by creating a custom operator. There will be several use cases where you would need custom operators which will save your time and efforts of changing the application code or PL/pgSQL code inside the database.

We will cover a few scenarios where custom operators will be useful.

SCENARIO 1: Case-Insensitive Comparison

Many application user interfaces provide an option to search the user details as required. The users like to search the data irrespective of the case-sensitivity. You can use LOWER/ UPPER database functions to implement this functionality. However, some applications need data search to be case-insensitive and case-sensitive based on the requirements without changing the application code. We can implement the solution at the database level so that application changes can be avoided. We can create a custom operator to execute a function which makes data case-sensitive or case-insensitive when required without changing the application SQL code.

The following are the steps:

1. Create a new schema to define the operator and grant necessary privileges on the schema to public:

   ```
   CREATE SCHEMA cust_opr;
   GRANT USAGE ON SCHEMA cust_opr TO PUBLIC;
   ```

2. Create a function to define the functionality of the operator. This function basically changes the case of right and left operands to lowercase so that comparison will be done without modifying the query to use any built-in functions like lower or upper. Grant the necessary privileges on the function to public:

   ```
   CREATE OR REPLACE FUNCTION cust_opr.case_ins_cmp(text, text)
   RETURNS BOOLEAN LANGUAGE sql immutable as $$
      select lower($1) operator(pg_catalog.=) lower($2)
   $$;
   ```

or

```
CREATE OR REPLACE FUNCTION cust_opr.case_ins_cmp(text, text)
RETURNS text AS $$
  BEGIN
    RETURN $1 || $2;
  END;
$$ LANGUAGE plpgsql
IMMUTABLE;

GRANT EXECUTE ON FUNCTION cust_opr.case_ins_cmp(text,text)
TO PUBLIC;
```

3. Create the operator using the new function:

```
CREATE OPERATOR cust_opr.= (
LEFTARG=TEXT,
RIGHTARG=TEXT,
PROCEDURE = cust_opr.case_ins_cmp);
```

4. Test the new operator, for example:

```
CREATE TABLE public.case_test_opt (
  id SERIAL PRIMARY KEY,
  first_name TEXT NOT NULL,
  last_name TEXT NOT NULL,
  email TEXT NOT NULL
);

INSERT INTO public.case_test_opt (first_name, last_name, email)
VALUES ('foo', 'bar', 'foo.bar@example.com'),('foo', 'BAR', 'foo.
BAR@EXAMPLE.COM'),('foo', 'BaR', 'foo.BaR@EXAMPLE.COM');
```

5. Query the data with last_name and review the results:

```
postgres=# select * from public.case_test_opt where last_name='bar';
 id | first_name | last_name |           email
----+------------+-----------+--------------------
  1 | foo        | bar       | foo.bar@example.com
(1 row)
```

You can see only one row based on the case.

6. Set the search_path to use the cust_opr schema before pg_
    catalog and check the results:

```
postgres=# set search_path to cust_opr, pg_catalog;
SET
postgres=# select * from public.case_test_opt where
last_name='bar';
 id | first_name | last_name |             email
----+------------+-----------+--------------------
  1 | foo        | bar       | foo.bar@example.com
  2 | foo        | BAR       | foo.BAR@EXAMPLE.COM
  3 | foo        | BaR       | foo.BaR@EXAMPLE.COM
(3 rows)
```

You can see all three rows irrespective of the case.

Benefits

One benefit of this option is that you don't need to change the application queries
to add any built-in functions like lower and upper or add any operators like ~~* or
ILIKE. Additionally, you can set the search_path as a switch to make the data case-
insensitive if you want only part of your application to behave like case-insensitive
without making any changes to the application.

SCENARIO 2: Custom Data Type Math

Let us consider a custom data type representing complex numbers. We can define
custom operators for addition, subtraction, and multiplication on these complex
numbers. The following is an example.

Let us use the same schema cust_opr created in previous scenarios:

1. Create the custom data type:

```
CREATE TYPE multi_number AS (
  first_part double precision,
  last_part double precision
);
```

2. Create the custom function for the operator:

```
CREATE FUNCTION numbers_add(multi_number, multi_number) RETURNS
multi_number AS $$
  BEGIN
    RETURN ROW($1.first_part + $2.first_part, $1.last_part +
    $2.last_part)::multi_number;
  END;
$$ LANGUAGE plpgsql
IMMUTABLE;
```

3. Create the custom operator using the custom function:

```
CREATE OPERATOR + (
  LEFTARG = multi_number,
  RIGHTARG = multi_number,
  PROCEDURE = numbers_add
);
```

4. Let us test the operator with the following query:

```
postgres=# SELECT (0,5)::multi_number + (5,10)::multi_number;
 ?column?
-----------
 (5,15)
(1 row)
```

As you can see, it added multiple numbers. So, custom operators are helpful when you have specific properties of interest in your complex numbers that you want to compare. This could be the real or imaginary parts, specific combinations of these parts, or any other property relevant to your application. Defining custom operators allows you to create comparisons based on these properties, enabling you to sort or filter complex numbers accordingly.

SCENARIO 3: Date Differentiate Operator

In PostgreSQL, the difference between two dates is an integer. However, the difference between a date and a timestamp or a timestamp and a timestamp is an interval. So, if you try to find the difference between these, you will get an interval as output.

For example, let us find out the difference between two dates and the output data type of it:

```
postgres=# select (now()::date-(now()-'2 days'::interval)::date);
 ?column?
----------
        2
(1 row)

postgres=# select pg_typeof((now()::date-(now()-'2
days'::interval)::date));
 pg_typeof
-----------
 integer
(1 row)
```

As you can see, the difference shows an integer value.

However, if you look at the difference between two timestamps or a timestamp and a date, it's not integer:

```
postgres=# select (now()::date - (now()-'2 days'::interval));
       ?column?
-----------------------
 1 day 01:16:38.129895
(1 row)

postgres=# select pg_typeof(now()::date - (now()-'2 days'::interval));
 pg_typeof
-----------
 interval
(1 row)
```

```
postgres=# select now() - (now()-'2 days'::interval);
 ?column?
----------
 2 days
(1 row)

postgres=# select pg_typeof(now() - (now()-'2 days'::interval));
 pg_typeof
----------
 interval
(1 row)

postgres=#
```

As you can see, the difference is an interval data type.

However, if you are migrating from a database engine where the difference between two timestamps is also an integer, then you need to change a lot of code to add a date type casting to your timestamp values so that it returns an integer. But if your code is huge, then making these changes will take months based on the amount of code. It needs a lot of efforts.

Another solution is to create a custom operator and use it. The following is an example:

1. Create the custom function which converts two arguments to date data types before it finds the difference:

```
CREATE FUNCTION cust_opr.date_diff_days(timestamp with time zone,
timestamp with time zone) RETURNS integer AS $$
BEGIN
RETURN $1::date - $2::date;
END;
$$ LANGUAGE plpgsql;
```

2. Define the custom operator using the created function:

```
CREATE OPERATOR cust_opr.-(
PROCEDURE = date_diff_days,
LEFTARG = timestamp with time zone,
RIGHTARG = timestamp with time zone
);
```

3. You can use the custom operator as follows:

```
postgres=# select (now()::date - (now()-'2 days'::interval));
 ?column?
----------
        2
(1 row)

postgres=# select pg_typeof(now()::date - (now()-'2
days'::interval));
 pg_typeof
-----------
 integer
(1 row)

postgres=# select now() - (now()-'2 days'::interval);
 ?column?
----------
        2
(1 row)

postgres=# select pg_typeof(now() - (now()-'2 days'::interval));
 pg_typeof
-----------
 integer
(1 row)
```

Now, you will see the desired result.

SCENARIO 4: Custom Operator for Data Classification

In certain applications, you may need to classify data based on specific criteria or rules. Creating a custom operator can provide a convenient way to perform the classification operation and simplify your queries.

Let's consider a scenario where you have a table called "employees" that stores information about employees, including their age and job titles. You want to classify employees as "Junior" or "Senior" based on their age, with a custom operator called @>.

1. Create a function to classify employees based on age:

```
CREATE FUNCTION cust_opr.classify_employee(integer, integer)
RETURNS text AS $$
BEGIN
  IF $1 >= $2 THEN
    RETURN 'Senior';
  ELSE
    RETURN 'Junior';
  END IF;
END;
$$ LANGUAGE plpgsql
IMMUTABLE;
```

2. Define the custom operator using the created function:

```
CREATE OPERATOR @> (
  PROCEDURE = cust_opr.classify_employee,
  LEFTARG = integer,
  RIGHTARG = integer
);
```

3. Usage of the custom operator in a query:

```
-- Table Definition
CREATE TABLE employees (
  employee_name VARCHAR(100),
  age INTEGER,
  salary NUMERIC(10, 2)
);

-- Sample Data
INSERT INTO employees (employee_name, age, salary) VALUES
  ('John Smith', 35, 4000.00),
  ('Jane Doe', 45, 5500.00),
  ('Mike Johnson', 28, 3200.00),
  ('Sarah Thompson', 52, 6000.00),
  ('Robert Wilson', 31, 2500.00),
```

```
    ('Emily Brown', 39, 4800.00),
    ('David Lee', 42, 5200.00),
    ('Lisa Davis', 36, 3700.00);

postgres=# SELECT employee_name, age @> 40 AS classification
FROM employees order by 2;
 employee_name  | classification
----------------+----------------
 Lisa Davis     | Junior
 Robert Wilson  | Junior
 Emily Brown    | Junior
 John Smith     | Junior
 Mike Johnson   | Junior
 Jane Doe       | Senior
 David Lee      | Senior
 Sarah Thompson | Senior
(8 rows)
```

As you can see, the data has been classified based on their ages as defined in the custom operator function.

This example shows how you can create a custom operator in PostgreSQL to simplify data classification operations. It allows you to encapsulate the logic for classification in a reusable operator, making your queries more expressive and easier to understand.

Advantages

- Custom operators can make our code more expressive and easier to read, especially when working with domain-specific languages.

- Custom operators can facilitate complex operations and make code more reusable.

- Developers can design custom operators that align with specific business logic, potentially leading to more optimized query plans and better performance compared to using standard operators.

- By defining custom operators for domain-specific operations, you can enforce consistent usage and behavior across queries, reducing the chances of errors due to inconsistent logic.

Disadvantages

- Custom operators can be less portable and may not be compatible with other database systems.

- Custom operators can be harder to debug and maintain, especially if the codebase becomes large and complex.

- Overuse or misuse of custom operators can lead to confusion among team members, especially if the operators are not well documented or if their behavior differs from standard operators.

- While custom operators can potentially optimize certain queries, they can also complicate the query optimizer's job. Complex custom operators might result in less predictable query plans, affecting overall performance.

Summary

In this chapter, we have learned that custom operators in PostgreSQL provide a powerful tool for extending the functionality of the database and making our code more expressive and easier to read. With PL/pgSQL examples, we created custom operators that match the requirements and allow us to perform operations that are not possible with the built-in operators. By carefully designing and implementing custom operators, we can leverage the full power of PostgreSQL to meet the needs of our applications and users.

What's Next

In the next chapter, we will be covering some key features of custom casting like the following:

- **Complex Data Conversion**: Learn to design and implement custom type casts to seamlessly convert between different data types.

- **Casting Consistency**: Explore strategies for maintaining consistent casting behavior and avoiding unexpected conversion outcomes.

- **Casting Performance**: Dive into casting performance considerations and optimization techniques for efficient data conversion.

- **Advanced Type Casting**: Discover techniques for casting complex data types and handling edge cases within your PL/pgSQL code.

Custom Casting

In the previous chapter, we talked about operators in PostgreSQL and how built-in operators work. We also covered how to create custom operators based on the requirements. In this chapter, we will explore custom casting in PostgreSQL and how to define our own custom casting functions. We will also discuss use cases for custom casting and how to create them accordingly. Custom casting can improve the flexibility and expressiveness of our database queries and data manipulation. By the end of this chapter, you will have a better understanding of how to work with custom casting using PL/pgSQL of PostgreSQL.

In PostgreSQL, casting allows you to convert data from one data type to another. There will be implicit and explicit type casting available in PostgreSQL. We can learn more about implicit and explicit casting in the next section.

Built-In Casts

To better understand the features of CAST objects, let's start with a simple example. PostgreSQL provides a set of object identifier types such as regclass, regrole, regproc, regoper, etc. You may have seen one of these while querying SQL queries on the catalog tables. For instance, consider the `regclass` example shown as follows:

```
postgres=#SELECT 805563::regclass;
regclass
----------
test

(1 row)

postgres=#SELECT CAST(805563 AS regclass);
regclass
```

© Baji Shaik and Dinesh Kumar Chemuduru 2023
B. Shaik and D. K. Chemuduru, *Procedural Programming with PostgreSQL PL/pgSQL*,
https://doi.org/10.1007/978-1-4842-9840-4_10

```
----------
test

(1 row)
```

In the preceding example, the number 805563 is being converted into the string test. The purpose of the CAST type is to convert from one data type to another. In this example, the number 805563 is an object ID (oid) of the table named test. Let's query the pg_class table to see the results:

```
postgres=#SELECT oid FROM pg_class WHERE relname='test';
oid
--------
805563

(1 row)
```

Note that the OID value will vary for different environments.

We can leverage the same behavior with user object ids as well. Consider the following example:

```
postgres=# SELECT oid FROM pg_roles WHERE rolname='postgres'; oid
-----
10

(1 row)

postgres=# SELECT 10::regrole;
regrole
----------
postgres

(1 row)

postgres=# SELECT CAST(10 AS regrole);
regrole
----------
postgres

(1 row)
```

In PostgreSQL, there are a lot of built-in casts available which help you with most of the requirements from your application. You can use the `pg_cast` catalog table to check the available castings. Here is an example command:

```
postgres=# select castsource::regtype, casttarget::regtype,
castfunc::regproc, castcontext, castmethod from pg_cast where
castsource='int4'::regtype;
 castsource |    casttarget     |       castfunc        | castcontext | castmethod
------------+-------------------+-----------------------+-------------+-----------
 integer    | bigint            | pg_catalog.int8       | i           | f
 integer    | smallint          | pg_catalog.int2       | a           | f
 integer    | real              | pg_catalog.float4     | i           | f
 integer    | double precision  | pg_catalog.float8     | i           | f
 integer    | numeric           | pg_catalog."numeric"  | i           | f
 integer    | money             | pg_catalog.money      | a           | f
 integer    | boolean           | pg_catalog.bool       | e           | f
 integer    | oid               | -                     | i           | b
 integer    | regproc           | -                     | i           | b
 integer    | regprocedure      | -                     | i           | b
 integer    | regoper           | -                     | i           | b
 integer    | regoperator       | -                     | i           | b
 integer    | regclass          | -                     | i           | b
 integer    | regcollation      | -                     | i           | b
 integer    | regtype           | -                     | i           | b
 integer    | regconfig         | -                     | i           | b
 integer    | regdictionary     | -                     | i           | b
 integer    | regrole           | -                     | i           | b
 integer    | regnamespace      | -                     | i           | b
 integer    | "char"            | pg_catalog."char"     | e           | f
 integer    | bit               | pg_catalog."bit"      | e           | f
(21 rows)
```

The preceding example is to check the casts available for int (int4). Let's look at what these columns represent. This output example is used to explain each column of the following output:

castsource: It represents the source of the cast. In the example, our source is int.

casttarget: It represents the target of the cast. In the example, it shows different types of targets (which are mostly related to numbers) that the source int can cast to. If any cast is not part of it, then we cannot use it. For example, the target column does not have an xml type, but if you try to type cast int to xml, you will see an error:

```
postgres=# select 1::int::xml;
ERROR:  cannot cast type integer to xml
LINE 1: select 1::int::xml;
                  ^
```

castfunc: It represents the function used for type casting. There are functions available for small, int, bigint, etc. In the preceding output where it shows the casts available for integers as source, you can see smallint as the target, and the function is int2. The cast functions listed in pg_cast must always take the cast source type as their first argument type and return the cast destination type as their result type.

The purpose of int2 being used is you cannot cast int values which are out of the smallint range. For example:

```
postgres=# select '1234567'::int::smallint;
ERROR:  smallint out of range
postgres=#
```

Hence, the int2 function is used. You can see the int2 function result is always smallint:

```
postgres=# \df int2
                    List of functions
   Schema    | Name | Result data type | Argument data types | Type
-------------+------+------------------+---------------------+------
 pg_catalog | int2 | smallint         | bigint              | func
 pg_catalog | int2 | smallint         | double precision    | func
 pg_catalog | int2 | smallint         | integer             | func
 pg_catalog | int2 | smallint         | jsonb               | func
 pg_catalog | int2 | smallint         | numeric             | func
 pg_catalog | int2 | smallint         | real                | func
(6 rows)
```

castcontext: It represents the way casting happened which is implicit or explicit or both. The "i" represents implicit, "e" represents explicit, and "a" represents implicit and explicit.

Implicit type casting: This occurs when PostgreSQL automatically converts a value from one data type to another data type without the need for explicit instruction from the user. This can happen when the user attempts to perform an operation on two values of different data types. In such cases, PostgreSQL will attempt to automatically convert one of the values to the data type of the other value. From our example output (queried through the preceding pg_cast for int4), int to bigint is "i" which is implicit. You don't need to use any type casting to convert.

The following is not explicit because you cannot type cast a value which is not allowed in int to bigint – so technically, it should not allow such type of conversion explicitly. For example:

```
postgres=# select '123456799999'::int::bigint;
ERROR:  value "123456799999" is out of range for type integer
LINE 1: select '123456799999'::int::bigint;
                ^

postgres=#
```

As bigint value is not allowed in int, there is no point of having bigint conversion explicitly.

Explicit type casting: Explicit type casting occurs when the user explicitly instructs PostgreSQL to convert a value from one data type to another data type. This can be done using the CAST or :: operator.

For example, to convert the string '123' to an integer, the user can use the CAST operator as follows:

```
postgres=# select cast('123' as integer);
 int4
------
  123
(1 row)
```

Alternatively, the user can use the :: operator as follows:

```
postgres=# select '123'::int;
 int4
------
  123
(1 row)
```

Explicit type casting can also be used to convert values to custom data types or to perform more complex type conversions, which we will be discussing more in this chapter.

In our example output of int, there is an explicit conversion, which is int to boolean. So, inserting int into a boolean field requires an explicit conversion. Here is an example:

```
postgres=# create table bool_test(id boolean);
CREATE TABLE
postgres=# insert into bool_test values(1);
ERROR:  column "id" is of type boolean but expression is of type integer
LINE 1: insert into bool_test values(1);
                                     ^
HINT:  You will need to rewrite or cast the expression.
```

In the preceding error, HINT clearly says you need an explicit cast. So, you can use the following:

```
postgres=# insert into bool_test values(1::boolean);
INSERT 0 1
postgres=# select * from bool_test ;
 id
----
 t
(1 row)

postgres=#
```

It's important to note that while implicit casting is performed automatically by PostgreSQL, explicit casting requires you to explicitly indicate the desired data type. This can help make the intentions of your code clearer and less reliant on the implicit behavior of the database system.

It's recommended to use explicit casting when you want to ensure the expected data type conversions and to handle potential data inconsistencies more explicitly in your SQL statements.

castmethod: This indicates how the cast is performed. f means that the function specified in the castfunc field is used. i means that the input/output functions are used. b means that the types are binary-coercible; thus, no conversion is required. From our example, conversion from int to regclass requires no function for type casting. The following is an example:

```
postgres=#  select 1259::int::regclass;
 regclass
----------
 pg_class
(1 row)
```

pg_cast provides metadata about the available type conversions and can be useful for understanding and managing type casting operations in the database. It can be useful to

- Retrieve a list of all available type casts in the database. You can simply use

```
postgres=# select castsource::regtype, casttarget::regtype,
castfunc::regproc, castcontext, castmethod from pg_cast where
castsource='<source/target data type>'::regtype;
```

Or you can use the following psql shortcut:

```
postgres=# \dC int4
                            List of casts
    Source type      |    Target type     |      Function       |  Implicit?
-------------------+------------------+--------------------+----------
  "char"           | integer          | int4               | no
  bigint           | integer          | int4               | in
assignment
  bit              | integer          | int4               | no
  boolean          | integer          | int4               | no
  double precision | integer          | int4               | in
assignment
  integer          | "char"           | char               | no
  .
  .
```

- It contains information about the source and target data types for each cast entry. It allows you to determine the direction of the cast, that is, whether it is a cast from one type to another or a reverse cast from the target type to the source type. If you look at the following example, the cast from int to money is allowed but not the reverse:

```
postgres=# select castsource::regtype, casttarget::regtype,
castfunc, castcontext, castmethod from pg_cast where
castsource='int'::regtype and casttarget='money'::regtype;
 castsource | casttarget | castfunc | castcontext | castmethod
------------+------------+----------+-------------+-----------
 integer    | money      |     3811 | a           | f
(1 row)

postgres=# select castsource::regtype, casttarget::regtype,
castfunc, castcontext, castmethod from pg_cast where
castsource='money'::regtype and casttarget='int'::regtype;
 castsource | casttarget | castfunc | castcontext | castmethod
------------+------------+----------+-------------+-----------
(0 rows)
```

Hence, if you try to convert money to int, it will throw an error that the cast does not exist:

```
postgres=# select '1'::money;
 money
-------
 $1.00
(1 row)

postgres=# select '1'::money::int;
ERROR:  cannot cast type money to integer
LINE 1: select '1'::money::int;
                        ^
```

- It provides information about the cast method used for each cast entry. Cast methods can include explicit casting functions, implicit casting rules, and more. If you take the following example, inserting an int integer value to a bit data type column is not allowed implicitly:

```
postgres=# create table bit_test(id bit);
CREATE TABLE
Time: 20.101 ms
postgres=# insert into bit_test values(1);
ERROR:  column "id" is of type bit but expression is of
type integer
LINE 1: insert into bit_test values(1);
                                    ^
HINT:  You will need to rewrite or cast the expression.
Time: 1.269 ms
```

You can check the type casting of these types from pg_cast catalog:

```
postgres=# select castsource::regtype, casttarget::regtype,
castfunc, castcontext, castmethod from pg_cast where
castsource='int'::regtype and casttarget='bit'::regtype;
 castsource | casttarget | castfunc | castcontext | castmethod
------------+------------+----------+-------------+------------
 integer    | bit        |     1683 | e           | f
(1 row)
```

As you can see, the castcontext value is e, which represents an explicit type casting. So, you can avoid errors by casting it explicitly as follows:

```
postgres=# insert into bit_test values(1::bit);
INSERT 0 1
postgres=# select * from bit_test ;
 id
----
 1
(1 row)
```

- It is useful when creating custom casts. If you need to define your own type conversions or override the default behavior, you can examine existing cast entries in the pg_cast table and create new cast entries to implement your custom casting rules.

It's important to note that directly manipulating the pg_cast table is not recommended, as it is an internal system catalog table. Modifying the entries without proper knowledge and understanding of the database internals can lead to data inconsistencies and unexpected behavior. Instead, use the appropriate SQL syntax, such as the CAST keyword or the :: operator, to perform type casting operations in a safe and controlled manner.

The pg_cast table is an important part of PostgreSQL's type casting system, allowing for flexible and customizable data type conversions. By understanding how to use the pg_cast table, developers can create more powerful and expressive queries and operators in their PostgreSQL databases.

Custom Casts

PostgreSQL allows you to define custom casting rules to convert data from one type to another. Custom casting can be useful when working with domain-specific data types, where the standard set of casting rules may not be sufficient to express the desired functionality.

Creating a Custom Cast

To create a custom cast, use the CREATE CAST command. Here is the basic syntax:

```
CREATE CAST (source_type AS target_type) WITH FUNCTION function_name;
```

- source_type: The data type to be cast from
- target_type: The data type to be cast to
- function_name: The name of the function that performs the casting

Simple Example

Let us consider you have a requirement of converting temperature values from Celsius to Fahrenheit. The following is your application table with some values:

```
postgres=# CREATE TABLE temperature_table (
          id SERIAL PRIMARY KEY,
          temperature NUMERIC(5, 2)
       );
CREATE TABLE
postgres=#
postgres=# INSERT INTO temperature_table (temperature) VALUES (20.0),
(25.0), (30.0);
INSERT 0 3
postgres=# select * from temperature_table;
 id | temperature
----+-------------
  1 |       20.00
  2 |       25.00
  3 |       30.00
(3 rows)
```

These statements create a table called temperature_table with two columns, id and temperature, and insert three rows with temperature values in Celsius.

Usually, if you have to convert the values in the table to Fahrenheit, you will write a query something like the following:

```
postgres=# select id, (temperature*9/5+32)::numeric(10,2) from
temperature_table;
 id | numeric
----+---------
  1 |   68.00
  2 |   77.00
  3 |   86.00
(3 rows)
```

So, you can use the `Celsius*9/5 + 32` formula to convert Celsius to Fahrenheit.

However, you can create a custom cast function using PL/pgSQL that converts Celsius to Fahrenheit using the same formula. The following are the steps to do it:

1. Create a custom data type as follows:

   ```
   CREATE TYPE fahrenheit AS (value numeric);
   ```

2. Create the cast function using PL/pgSQL. You can have the formula defined inside the function logic:

   ```
   CREATE OR REPLACE FUNCTION celsius_to_fahrenheit(celsius
   numeric) RETURNS fahrenheit AS $$
   BEGIN
     RETURN row(Celsius*9/5 + 32)::fahrenheit;
   END;
   $$ LANGUAGE plpgsql;
   ```

3. Create the cast using the function created in Step 1:

   ```
   CREATE CAST (numeric AS fahrenheit) WITH FUNCTION
   celsius_to_fahrenheit(numeric) AS IMPLICIT;
   ```

   This creates a custom cast from the `numeric` data type to `fahrenheit`, using the `celsius_to_fahrenheit` function.

4. Now you can use the custom cast to convert Celsius temperatures to Fahrenheit automatically:

   ```
   postgres=# SELECT temperature::fahrenheit FROM temperature_table;
    temperature
   -------------
    (68.00)
    (77.00)
    (86.00)
   (3 rows)
   ```

The preceding query automatically converted the `temperature` column from Celsius to Fahrenheit using the custom cast function by just using the explicit type casting to `fahrenheit`.

This is a simple example on how you can use a custom cast by creating PL/pgSQL functions based on your requirements from the application. There are several use cases where you can use the custom cast to fulfill your requirements. We will cover a few scenarios in this chapter which help you to understand and build your own custom casts based on the needs.

SCENARIO 1: Converting Custom Data Types

Let's consider a user-defined data type called `type_phone_number`, which represents a custom format for storing telephone numbers. You can create a custom cast that allows us to convert the `type_phone_number` value into a TEXT value. The following are the steps:

1. Create the user-defined data type with required data types:

```
CREATE TYPE type_phone_number AS (
  country_code INTEGER,
  area_code INTEGER,
  number INTEGER
);
```

2. Create the conversion function:

```
CREATE OR REPLACE FUNCTION convert_type_to_text(value
type_phone_number)
  RETURNS TEXT AS
$$
BEGIN
  -- Convert the type_phone_number value to TEXT format
  RETURN '+' || value.country_code || ' (' || value.area_code ||
') ' || value.number;
END;
$$
LANGUAGE plpgsql;
```

In the preceding example, we define a user-defined data type type_phone_number to represent telephone numbers. Then, we create a conversion function convert_type_to_text that takes a type_phone_number value as input and returns a TEXT value. The function concatenates the various components of the telephone number and formats them into a text representation.

3. Create the custom cast using the CREATE CAST statement:

```
CREATE CAST (type_phone_number AS TEXT)
  WITH FUNCTION convert_type_to_text (type_phone_number)
AS IMPLICIT;
```

In this example, we use the CREATE CAST statement to define a custom cast from type_phone_number to TEXT. We specify the conversion function convert_type_to_text as the function to perform the casting. The IMPLICIT keyword indicates that the cast should be performed implicitly without the need for explicit casting syntax.

4. You can use a custom cast in your queries and expressions like any other cast operation:

```
postgres=# CREATE TABLE my_customers(id int, name varchar,
phone_number type_phone_number);
CREATE TABLE

postgres=# INSERT INTO my_customers VALUES (1, 'customer1',
'(1,912,123456)');
INSERT 0 1

postgres=# SELECT phone_number::TEXT FROM my_customers ;
  phone_number
-----------------
 +1 (912) 123456
(1 row)
```

In the preceding query, phone_number is a column of type type_ phone_number, anvd we are using the custom cast ::TEXT to convert it into a TEXT value.

Note that this is a simplified example to show. However, in practice, you may need to consider additional factors such as error handling, validation, and more complex data transformations depending on your specific requirements.

SCENARIO 2: Custom Data Type to JSONB

This is an example of converting a user-defined data type into JSON and vice versa. The example creates a custom data type, assigns a value to it, and attempts to type cast the object into a JSON string.

First, create a custom type that holds a person's details using the following SQL statement:

```
postgres=# CREATE TYPE person AS ( id INT, name TEXT, age INT,
address TEXT );
CREATE TYPE
```

Then, assign the person type details to a person custom data type as follows:

```
postgres=# SELECT (1, 'Sai Prasanna Kidambi', '35',
'NTR Nagar,  Nellore, India')::person;
                              row
-------------------------------------------------------------
(1,"Sai Prasanna Kidambi",35,"NTR Nagar, Nellore, India")

(1 row)
```

Next, try to convert the custom data type into JSONB using the following SQL statement:

```
postgres=# SELECT (1, 'Sai Prasanna Kidambi', '35', 'NTR Nagar, Nellore,
India')::person::jsonb;
ERROR: cannot cast type person to jsonb LINE 1: ...Kidambi', '35', 'NTR
Nagar, Nellore, India')::person::jsonb;
```

As expected, there is no implicit conversion between the custom type and JSONB, resulting in an error. To fix this, create the required casting functions and operators as follows.

To convert the `person` data type into JSONB, create the following PL/pgSQL function:

```
postgres=# CREATE OR REPLACE FUNCTION public.public_person_to_jsonb(a
public.person) RETURNS JSONB AS $q$
BEGIN
    RETURN  jsonb_build_object('id', a.id,'name', a.name,'age',
    a.age,'address', a.address);
END;
$q$ LANGUAGE PLPGSQL;
CREATE FUNCTION
```

Then, create the CAST object as follows:

```
postgres=# CREATE CAST (public.person AS jsonb) WITH FUNCTION public.
public_person_to_jsonb(public.person) AS ASSIGNMENT;
CREATE CAST
```

To convert JSONB data to the person type, create the following PL/pgSQL function:

```
postgres=# CREATE OR REPLACE FUNCTION public.jsonb_to_public_person(a
jsonb) RETURNS public.person
 AS $q$
DECLARE
typeAttrNames text:='';
inputJsonbKeys text:='';
BEGIN

--Do not try to convert the null JSONB to the custom type.
--Rather return null from here.
    IF a = 'null'::JSONB THEN
        RETURN NULL;
    END IF;
    RETURN  ((a->>'id')::integer,(a->>'name')::text,(a->>
    'age')::integer,(a->>'address')::text)::public.person;
```

```
END;
$q$ LANGUAGE PLPGSQL;
CREATE FUNCTION
```

Now, create the CAST object as follows, which converts JSONB to the person type:

```
postgres=# CREATE CAST (jsonb AS public.person) WITH FUNCTION public.jsonb_
to_public_person(jsonb) AS ASSIGNMENT;
CREATE CAST
```

Finally, try the same SQL query that failed earlier, and verify that it now works as expected:

```
postgres=# SELECT (1, 'Sai Prasanna Kidambi', '35', 'NTR Nagar, Nellore,
India')::person::jsonb;
                                    row
-----------------------------------------------------------------------------
-------------------
{"id": 1, "age": 35, "name": "Sai Prasanna Kidambi", "address": "NTR Nagar,
Nellore, India"}
(1 row)
```

Now, try the conversion from JSONB to the person type and verify the results:

```
postgres=# SELECT '{"id": 1, "age": 35, "name": "Sai Prasanna Kidambi",
"address": "NTR Nagar, Nellore, India"}'::JSONB::person;
                                person
------------------------------------------------------------
(1,"Sai Prasanna Kidambi",35,"NTR Nagar, Nellore, India")

(1 row)
```

From the preceding exercise, we have successfully created the PostgreSQL casting object that converts a custom data type into JSONB and vice versa.

Summary

In this chapter, we have learned custom casting in PostgreSQL which allows you to create more expressive and concise queries when working with domain-specific data types. By defining custom casts, you can represent your data in a way that matches its semantics, making your queries more intuitive and easier to read. With the examples provided in this chapter, you should be able to create your own custom casts to suit your specific needs.

Custom casting allows you to define your own rules for converting data between different types, providing flexibility and customization in how your data is interpreted and manipulated in PostgreSQL.

What's Next

In the next chapter, we will be covering some key features of dynamic SQL in PL/pgSQL like the following:

- **Advanced Dynamic Query Generation**: Dive deeper into constructing dynamic SQL statements for complex scenarios and dynamic conditions.

- **Parameterized Queries**: Learn how to securely pass parameters to dynamic SQL queries and prevent SQL injection vulnerabilities.

- **Query Execution and Performance**: Explore strategies to optimize the execution and performance of dynamically generated SQL queries.

- **Dynamic SQL in Functions**: Discover how to integrate dynamic SQL within stored procedures to build flexible and powerful routines.

CHAPTER 11

Dynamic SQL

In the previous chapter, we talked about custom casting in PostgreSQL and how to define our own custom casting functions. We have also discussed the use cases for custom casting and how to create them accordingly. In this chapter, we will cover the core concepts of dynamic SQL within PostgreSQL's plpgsql environment. We will provide a comprehensive overview of the syntax and its practical implementation. Additionally, we will cover some real-world scenarios and share best practices for harnessing the power of dynamic SQL effectively. By the end of this chapter, readers will have gained a solid grasp of dynamic SQL's intricacies, enabling them to confidently utilize this feature in PostgreSQL for various use cases.

What Is Dynamic SQL?

Dynamic SQL in PostgreSQL is like crafting custom-made instructions for your database as you go. Imagine you are writing a program and you don't know the exact question you will ask the database until it's running. That's where dynamic SQL comes in. In PostgreSQL's PL/pgSQL, you use the EXECUTE statement to create these on-the-spot instructions. You give it a string that holds the SQL command you want to use. If you need, you can also throw in some variables that hold the results or any extra information you need for the command. Think of it as telling the database what to do when you're not sure what you'll need until you're in the middle of doing it. Dynamic SQL via the EXECUTE statement is your toolkit for flexible, adaptable database interactions that change based on what's happening in your program.

Syntax of Dynamic SQL in PL/pgSQL

Dynamic SQL in plpgsql is written using the EXECUTE statement. The basic syntax of the EXECUTE statement is as follows:

```
EXECUTE statement_name [ INTO target ] [ USING expression [, ...] ];
```

169

© Baji Shaik and Dinesh Kumar Chemuduru 2023
B. Shaik and D. K. Chemuduru, *Procedural Programming with PostgreSQL PL/pgSQL*,
https://doi.org/10.1007/978-1-4842-9840-4_11

Here, `statement_name` is a string that contains the SQL statement to be executed. The `INTO` clause is used to specify the target variable or variables for the result of the query. The `USING` clause is used to supply values for any parameters used in the SQL statement.

Simple Example

Dynamic SQL is especially useful when you need to create SQL statements at runtime, based on the data being processed. For example, you might need to create a query that selects data from a different table depending on the input data, or you might need to construct a complex query with many conditions based on user input. Let's go through an example:

- Create a test table and insert some data:

```
CREATE TABLE test_dynamic_sql (id int, name varchar);
INSERT INTO test_dynamic_sql VALUES(1, 'test1');
```

- Create a function that uses dynamic SQL:

```
CREATE OR REPLACE FUNCTION test_func_dynamic_sql(input_table_
name text)
RETURNS TABLE(id integer, name text)
AS $$
BEGIN
  EXECUTE 'SELECT id, name FROM ' || input_table_name INTO
  id, name;
  RETURN NEXT;
END;
$$ LANGUAGE plpgsql;
```

In this example, the name of the table to be queried is passed as an input parameter to the function. The `EXECUTE` statement then constructs an SQL statement by concatenating the input parameter with a string containing the `SELECT` statement. The `INTO` clause is used to store the results of the query into the `id` and `name` variables.

Let's run the function:

```
postgres=# SELECT * FROM test_func_dynamic_sql('test_dynamic_sql');
 id | name
----+-------
  1 | test1
(1 row)
```

As you can see, it executed the SQL as expected.

Use Cases of Dynamic SQL

In this section, we will delve into real-world scenarios that showcase the practical applications of dynamic SQL within PostgreSQL's PL/pgSQL. These use cases include creating tables dynamically, building queries as needed, generating indexes on the go, choosing columns based on circumstances, and executing queries dynamically. This part serves as a practical guide to grasp how dynamic SQL can be practically used in PostgreSQL's world to address various scenarios.

Dynamic Table Creation

Dynamic SQL can be used to create tables dynamically, based on runtime conditions. For example, you might need to create a table with a different name or structure depending on the data being processed.

Let's take a simple example:

```
CREATE OR REPLACE FUNCTION create_dynamic_table(table_name text,
columns jsonb)
RETURNS void AS $$
DECLARE
    column_rec record;
    column_def text;
    sql_stmt text;
BEGIN
    -- Create column definitions
    FOR column_rec IN SELECT * FROM jsonb_each_text(columns)
    LOOP
```

```
        column_def := column_rec.key || ' ' || column_rec.value;
        IF sql_stmt IS NULL THEN
            sql_stmt := column_def;
        ELSE
            sql_stmt := sql_stmt || ', ' || column_def;
        END IF;
    END LOOP;

    -- Execute dynamic SQL to create the table
    EXECUTE 'CREATE TABLE ' || table_name || '(' || sql_stmt || ')';
END;
$$ LANGUAGE plpgsql;
```

In this example, we created a function named create_dynamic_table that accepts two parameters: table_name (the desired table name) and columns (a JSON object specifying column names and types).

The function iterates through the JSON object using a loop and constructs the column definitions dynamically. It then builds the CREATE TABLE statement using the gathered column definitions and executes the SQL statement to create the table with the specified columns.

This function offers an advanced illustration of how dynamic SQL can cater to versatile scenarios. Whether you're handling datasets with varying attributes or accommodating diverse requirements, this approach empowers you to design tables that adapt harmoniously to the unique circumstances at hand.

Let's say you want to create a table named "customer_data" with columns "name" (text) and "age" (integer). You can execute the function like this:

```
postgres=# SELECT create_dynamic_table('customer_data', '{"name": "text",
"age": "integer"}');
 create_dynamic_table
----------------------

(1 row)

Time: 9.646 ms
postgres=#
postgres=#
```

```
postgres=# \d customer_data
          Table "public.customer_data"
 Column |  Type   | Collation | Nullable | Default
--------+---------+-----------+----------+---------
 age    | integer |           |          |
 name   | text    |           |          |
```

As you can see, after executing this SQL query, it created a table named "customer_ data" with the specified columns and data types.

Note that this is just an example, and you can customize the table name and column definitions according to your requirements. Dynamic SQL gives you the flexibility to adapt the table structure on the fly based on the input you provide to the function.

Dynamic Query Building

Dynamic SQL can be used to build complex queries dynamically, based on user input or other runtime conditions. For example, you might need to create a query with many conditions, some of which are optional depending on the input data.

Let's look at an example. Consider a table named "records" with the following structure:

```
CREATE TABLE records (
    id integer PRIMARY KEY,
    name text,
    city text,
    state text
);

INSERT INTO records VALUES (1, 'foo', 'LA', 'California');
```

For example, consider a situation where you need to formulate a query with multiple conditions, some of which are optional and depend on the data input.

Let's create the function:

```
CREATE OR REPLACE FUNCTION search_records(id int, name text, city text,
state text)
RETURNS TABLE(v_id integer, v_name text, v_city text, v_state text)
AS $$
```

```
BEGIN
  EXECUTE 'SELECT id, name, city, state FROM records WHERE TRUE' ||
    CASE WHEN name IS NOT NULL THEN ' AND name = ' || quote_literal(name)
ELSE '' END ||
    CASE WHEN city IS NOT NULL THEN ' AND city = ' || quote_literal(city)
ELSE '' END ||
    CASE WHEN state IS NOT NULL THEN ' AND state = ' || quote_
literal(state) ELSE '' END
  INTO v_id, v_name, v_city, v_state;
  RETURN NEXT;
END;
$$ LANGUAGE plpgsql;
```

In this example, we have created a function named search_records. The function queries dynamically, where the conditions hinge on the user's inputs: name, city, and state.

Here's how it works:

- The function receives inputs: name, city, and state.

- The dynamic SQL magic starts with the EXECUTE statement, crafting a query. It uses CASE statements to add conditions only if their corresponding input isn't null.

- As the dynamic query is executed, the retrieved result is stored in the variables id, name, city, and state.

- The result is then emitted via RETURN NEXT.

Let's assume you are searching for records where the name is "foo" and the state is "California." Execute the function like this:

```
postgres=# SELECT * FROM search_records(1, 'foo', 'LA', 'California');
 v_id | v_name | v_city |   v_state
------+--------+--------+------------
    1 | foo    | LA     | California
(1 row)
```

As you can see, it returned the record from the table as expected.

Dynamic Index Creation

Dynamic SQL can be used to create indexes dynamically, based on runtime conditions. For example, you might need to create an index with a different name or structure depending on the data being processed.

Let's look at an example. Consider a table named "records" with the following structure:

```
CREATE TABLE sample_table (
    id serial PRIMARY KEY,
    column1 text,
    column2 text
);
```

In the provided example, we have a function named `create_index` that demonstrates the power of dynamic SQL for index creation:

```
CREATE OR REPLACE FUNCTION create_index(table_name text, column_name text,
index_name text)
RETURNS void AS $$
BEGIN
  EXECUTE 'CREATE INDEX ' || index_name || ' ON ' || table_name || '(' ||
column_name || ')';
END;
$$ LANGUAGE plpgsql;
```

The `create_index` function is designed to generate and execute a dynamic CREATE INDEX statement based on input parameters. The parameters include table_name (name of the table to index), column_name (name of the column to be indexed), and index_name (desired name for the index).

Here's how it works:

> `table_name`: Specify the name of the table on which you want to create the index.`column_name`: Specify the column for which you want to create the index.`index_name`: Provide a name for the index you're creating.

For instance, if you want to create an index named "sample_column1_index" on the "column1" column of the "sample_table," you would execute the function like this:

```
SELECT create_index('sample_table', 'column1', 'sample_column1_index');
```

The beauty of this function lies in its adaptability. It allows you to dynamically generate index creation statements based on various input parameters. You can customize index names and specify the columns to be indexed, enhancing query performance as needed. This feature is particularly useful when you want to create multiple indexes with varying configurations or when you need to automate index creation processes based on specific conditions.

Let's run the function:

```
postgres=# SELECT create_index('sample_table', 'column1', 'sample_column1_
index');
 create_index
--------------

(1 row)

Time: 4.745 ms
postgres=#
postgres=# \d sample_table
                          Table "public.sample_table"
 Column  |  Type   | Collation | Nullable |
    Default
---------+---------+-----------+----------+
-------------------------------------
 id      | integer |           | not null |
    nextval('sample_table_id_seq'::regclass)
 column1 | text    |           |          |
 column2 | text    |           |          |
Indexes:
    "sample_table_pkey" PRIMARY KEY, btree (id)
    "sample_column1_index" btree (column1)
```

As you can see, it created the index accordingly.

Dynamic Column Selection

Dynamic SQL can be used to select columns dynamically, based on runtime conditions. For example, you might need to select a different set of columns depending on the data being processed.

Let's look at an example. Consider a table named "employee_data" with the following structure:

```
CREATE TABLE employee_data (
    id serial PRIMARY KEY,
    first_name text,
    last_name text,
    age integer,
    department text,
    salary numeric
);
INSERT INTO employee_data VALUES (1,'foo','bar',25, 'dept',200000);
```

The provided example showcases a function named `select_columns`, which demonstrates how to dynamically select specific columns from a table based on runtime conditions:

```
CREATE OR REPLACE FUNCTION select_columns(table_name text, column_
names text[])
RETURNS record AS $$
DECLARE
rec record;
BEGIN
  EXECUTE 'SELECT ' || array_to_string(column_names, ', ') || ' FROM ' ||
  table_name  INTO rec;
  RETURN rec;
END;
$$ LANGUAGE plpgsql;
```

The `select_columns` function is designed to generate and execute a dynamic SELECT statement based on input parameters. The parameters include `table_name` (name of the table from which to select) and `column_names` (an array of column names to select).

This dynamic SQL function empowers you to select specific columns from a table based on user-defined criteria. Here's how it works:

table_name: Specify the name of the table from which you want to select columns.

column_names: Provide an array of column names you want to include in the result.

For instance, if you want to select only the "first_name" and "salary" columns from the "employee_data" table, you would execute the function like this:

```
SELECT * FROM select_columns('employee_data', ARRAY['first_name',
'salary']) as foo(fname text, sal numeric);
```

This example illustrates how dynamic SQL can enhance the flexibility of querying. The function select_columns allows you to retrieve specific column values based on your requirements, enabling more efficient data retrieval and reducing unnecessary data transfer.

By constructing the SELECT statement on the fly, you're able to tailor your queries to the exact columns you need, optimizing network bandwidth and query performance. This feature is particularly valuable when you need to retrieve different subsets of data based on varying conditions, without writing multiple static queries.

In essence, the select_columns function showcases how dynamic SQL empowers you to be more precise in your data retrieval, contributing to more efficient and effective querying in PostgreSQL.

Let's execute the function:

```
postgres=# SELECT * FROM select_columns('employee_data', ARRAY['first_
name', 'salary']) as foo(fname text, sal numeric);
 fname |   sal
-------+--------
 foo   | 200000
(1 row)
```

As you can see, it works as expected.

Best Practices and Considerations for Dynamic SQL

While dynamic SQL offers flexibility and versatility, ensuring security and maintaining performance are critical considerations. This section delves into the essential best practices to address these concerns when working with dynamic SQL in PostgreSQL.

1. Preventing SQL Injection

One of the primary concerns when dealing with dynamic SQL is the risk of SQL injection attacks. SQL injection occurs when an attacker manipulates input data to inject malicious SQL code into the query. To prevent this, follow these practices:

> **Parameterized Queries**: Use parameterized queries or prepared statements to separate data from SQL code. This approach ensures that user inputs are treated as values rather than executable code.

> **Quoting and Escaping**: When constructing dynamic SQL, use proper quoting and escaping functions to handle user inputs securely. PostgreSQL provides functions like `quote_literal` and `quote_ident` to escape and quote input values. Also, `quote_nullable` is useful when input values are null.

For example:

```
EXECUTE 'SELECT * FROM employees WHERE first_name = ' || quote_
literal(input_name);
```

2. Sanitizing and Validating Inputs

Before using user inputs in dynamic SQL, sanitize and validate them to ensure they meet expected formats and types. Perform checks to prevent unexpected behavior and reduce the likelihood of errors:

> **Data Type Validation**: Ensure that user inputs match the expected data types. Convert or validate inputs as needed before constructing the SQL query.

> **Input Length**: Check input lengths to avoid potential buffer overflows or truncation issues.

For example:

```
IF length(input_name) > 50 THEN
    RAISE EXCEPTION 'Input name is too long';
END IF;
```

3. Security Concerns

While constructing dynamic SQL, it's crucial to limit access to only authorized users and ensure that they have the appropriate permissions for executing the generated queries:

> **Grant Minimum Privileges**: Assign only the necessary permissions to the user executing the dynamic queries. Avoid granting excessive privileges.

Security definer functions in PostgreSQL allow the function to execute with the privileges of the user who defined it, rather than the privileges of the user who is executing it. While this can be useful in certain situations, such as when creating a function that accesses sensitive data, it can also be a security risk if not implemented correctly.

For example, let's say we have a security definer function called `get_sensitive_data()` that retrieves sensitive information from a table. The function is defined by a user with high privileges and is intended to be called by other users who do not have access to the sensitive data.

However, if the function is not implemented securely, a user with malicious intent could potentially exploit it to gain access to the sensitive data. For example, if the function uses dynamic SQL to construct a query based on input parameters, a user could potentially inject malicious code into the input parameters to execute unauthorized queries.

To mitigate these risks, it is important to follow best practices for writing secure functions and procedures in PostgreSQL, such as using proper input validation, limiting access to sensitive data, and testing thoroughly to ensure that the function is working as intended. Additionally, it is recommended to use security invoker functions instead of security definer functions whenever possible, to limit the potential security risks.

4. Performance Optimization

Dynamic SQL may impact performance due to query planning overhead. To maintain optimal performance, consider these strategies:

> **Plan Reuse**: Whenever possible, reuse query plans to minimize planning overhead. Prepared statements can help achieve this.

> **Use Parameterized Queries**: Parameterized queries allow PostgreSQL to cache and reuse query plans, leading to better performance over multiple executions.

For example:

```
PREPARE dynamic_query(text) AS
  SELECT * FROM employees WHERE last_name = $1;
EXECUTE dynamic_query(input_last_name);
```

By implementing best practices, sanitizing user inputs, and ensuring proper access controls, developers can harness the benefits of dynamic SQL while mitigating potential risks and maintaining efficient query execution.

Summary

In this chapter, we have provided an in-depth exploration of dynamic SQL within PostgreSQL's plpgsql environment. We have covered the essential concepts, syntax, and hands-on implementation of dynamic SQL. Real-world scenarios were examined, coupled with best practices to ensure effective utilization. Armed with this knowledge, the readers are now equipped to confidently harness the capabilities of dynamic SQL in PostgreSQL for a range of applications.

What's Next

In the next chapter, we will be covering some key features of functions and procedures of PL/pgSQL like the following:

- **Complex Function Logic**: Dive deep into advanced techniques for building complex and versatile functions and procedures.

- **Function Overloading**: Explore creating overloaded functions to provide multiple versions with varying parameter lists.

- **Function Categories**: Different types of function with use cases on how to use them effectively.

- **Modular Code Design**: Discover strategies for designing modular PL/pgSQL code using functions and procedures for reusability.

CHAPTER 12

Building Functions and Procedures

In the previous chapter, we talked about Dynamic SQL and how to create and use them in PL/pgSQL with real time use cases. In this chapter, we will discuss functions and procedures in PostgreSQL and how to build them using the PL/pgSQL programming language. We will cover the different types of available function categories and differences between them using some examples. It will help to choose the function category while developing. We will also explain the different types of procedures and how to use them with some examples.

Functions and procedures can enhance the performance of database operations by consolidating intricate logic into a single, reusable unit. It is crucial to take into account several factors when designing these functions and procedures, such as their scope of invocation, transaction handling, and parameter handling. By doing so, we can ensure that our functions and procedures are efficient, dependable, and easy to maintain. PostgreSQL functions are categorized based on their scope of invocation and their result set, which determines whether the function is executed within or outside a transaction, among other things. While implementing the business logic in PL/pgSQL functions or procedures, we should consider the factors mentioned earlier.

Functions

PL/pgSQL functions are an essential part of PostgreSQL's procedural programming capabilities, allowing developers to encapsulate custom logic and business rules directly within the database. By combining SQL statements with procedural constructs like loops and conditionals, PL/pgSQL functions enable advanced data manipulation, validation, and calculation directly within the database server. These functions can be used for

© Baji Shaik and Dinesh Kumar Chemuduru 2023
B. Shaik and D. K. Chemuduru, *Procedural Programming with PostgreSQL PL/pgSQL*,
https://doi.org/10.1007/978-1-4842-9840-4_12

tasks such as data transformation, enforcing complex constraints, and creating reusable code modules. PL/pgSQL functions can be divided into categories based on their invocation mode.

Defining Functions

To define a function in PostgreSQL, you use the CREATE FUNCTION statement. This statement specifies the name of the function, the input parameters, and the instructions that make up the function.

Here is an example of a simple function that adds two numbers together:

```
CREATE FUNCTION add_numbers(num1 INT, num2 INT)
RETURNS INT
AS $$
BEGIN
    RETURN num1 + num2;
END;
$$ LANGUAGE plpgsql;
```

This function takes two input parameters (num1 and num2) and returns the sum of those two numbers. The function is defined using the plpgsql language, which is a procedural language that supports a wide range of programming constructs.

Calling Functions

Once you have defined a function, you can call it from any program or script that has access to the database. To call a function in PostgreSQL, you use the SELECT statement and specify the name of the function and any input parameters.

Here is an example of how to call the add_numbers function from the previous example:

```
postgres=# SELECT add_numbers(5, 10);
 add_numbers
-------------
          15
(1 row)
```

This statement calls the add_numbers function with the input parameters 5 and 10 and returns the result of that function (which is 15).

Categories

When creating a PL/pgSQL function, we can specify its volatility category as IMMUTABLE, STABLE, or VOLATILE. This classification helps the optimizer to minimize the number of calls made on the result set. For instance, consider a global constant function called pi(), which always returns 3.14 as output. If we run the pi() function once or ten times, the result won't change. Thus, there is no need to execute this function multiple times if we use it in an SQL query. Consider the following example, where we run the pi() function on a table, where the table has multiple rows:

```
postgres=# CREATE TABLE test(t INT);
CREATE TABLE
postgres=# INSERT INTO test VALUES (generate_series(1, 10));
INSERT 0 10
postgres=# SELECT t/pi() FROM test;
     ?column?
-------------------
 0.318....
 0.636....
 0.954....
...
 (10 rows)
```

In the preceding example, a table named test was created, and ten rows were inserted into it. The pi() function was then called on this table, which should have been executed ten times, once for each row. However, in PostgreSQL, this function is not invoked ten times because it is globally constant. Instead, it is executed only once and the result is cached. This cached result is then utilized in subsequent executions of the function. This type of function can be classified as an IMMUTABLE function. Now, Let see what is the classification defined for this function pi() in PostgreSQL.

```
postgres=# SELECT provolatile FROM pg_proc WHERE proname = 'pi';
 provolatile
```

```
-------------
 i
(1 row)
```

Immutable Functions

To better understand the behavior of the pi() function described earlier, let's create a regular function (with the default VOLATILE classification), as well as an immutable function, and observe how many times each function is executed on the test table:

```
postgres=# CREATE OR REPLACE FUNCTION test_normal_func() RETURNS INT
AS $$
BEGIN
    RAISE NOTICE 'test_normal_func() called';
    RETURN 1;
END;
$$ LANGUAGE plpgsql;
CREATE FUNCTION

postgres=# SELECT t/test_normal_func() FROM test;
NOTICE:  test_normal_func() called
NOTICE:  test_normal_func() called
NOTICE:  test_normal_func() called
NOTICE:  test_normal_func() called
NOTICE:  test_normal_func() called
NOTICE:  test_normal_func() called
NOTICE:  test_normal_func() called
NOTICE:  test_normal_func() called
NOTICE:  test_normal_func() called
NOTICE:  test_normal_func() called
 ?column?
----------
        1
        2
        3
...
(10 rows)
```

Based on the preceding results, it is evident that the function test_normal_func() was called ten times (note: message print was called ten times), even though it always returned a static value of 1. This raises the question: Does PostgreSQL really need to execute this function ten times? Since it always returns the same value, it would be more efficient for the optimizer to execute this function once and utilize the results in subsequent function calls. To achieve this, we can declare the function as immutable. This will provide a hint to the optimizer, informing it that there is no need to execute this function multiple times and that it can be executed only once. Now, let's change the function behavior as IMMUTABLE and run the same example as follows:

```
postgres=# CREATE OR REPLACE FUNCTION test_immutable_func() RETURNS INT
AS $$
BEGIN
        RAISE NOTICE 'test_normal_func() called';
        RETURN 1;
END;
$$ LANGUAGE plpgsql IMMUTABLE;
CREATE FUNCTION

postgres=# SELECT t/test_immutable_func() FROM test;
NOTICE:  test_immutable_func() called
 ?column?
----------
        1
        2
        3
....
(10 rows)
```

The preceding output indicates that the test_immutable_func() function is only called once, regardless of the number of rows in the table. This approach helps prevent the unnecessary execution of functions that always return a global constant value. IMMUTABLE functions are recommended for mathematical expressions that always produce the same output for the same input parameters, such as log, exp, sin, and others. Additionally, string manipulation functions like lower and upper are also good examples.

STABLE Functions

Unlike IMMUTABLE functions, which always produce the same result each time they are run, STABLE functions maintain a unique result per SQL statement level. That is, the STABLE function will only execute once per entire SQL result set if the result is always the same for the given parameter. If the function produces a different result set for the given input parameters, then the SQL would execute multiple times. Consider the following example:

```
postgres=# CREATE OR REPLACE FUNCTION test_stable_func(i INT) RETURNS INT
AS $$
BEGIN
    RAISE NOTICE 'test_stable_func() called';
    RETURN 1;
END;
$$ LANGUAGE PLPGSQL STABLE;
CREATE FUNCTION

postgres=# SELECT * FROM test WHERE test_stable_func(1)=1;
NOTICE:  test_stable_func() called
 t
----
  1
  2
  3
...
...
...
(10 rows)
```

In the preceding example, the function test_stable_func is executed only once for the entire result set. This is because the function always produces the same output for the same input value of 1. Therefore, it is unnecessary for the optimizer to run this function multiple times, which ultimately improves query performance. Now, let's pass different values as input parameters to the same function and observe how many times the print message is displayed:

```
postgres=# SELECT * FROM test WHERE test_stable_func(t)=1;
```

```
NOTICE:  test_stable_func() called
NOTICE:  test_stable_func() called
NOTICE:  test_stable_func() called
NOTICE:  test_stable_func() called
NOTICE:  test_stable_func() called
NOTICE:  test_stable_func() called
NOTICE:  test_stable_func() called
NOTICE:  test_stable_func() called
NOTICE:  test_stable_func() called
NOTICE:  test_stable_func() called
 t
----
  1
  2
  3
...
...
...
(10 rows)
```

The function test_stable_func is called with the table's column name t, which contains different values. However, the function always returns the value 1 regardless of the input value. Therefore, the optimizer needs to execute the STABLE function multiple times, as the input parameter and the result differ each time. In addition, the input parameter for the function test_stable_func is of type column, with dynamic values. The optimizer does not receive any indication of whether to execute this function only once or repeatedly. Therefore, this function will be executed for each row in the table.

Let's take another built-in STABLE function, statement_timestamp, as an example and observe its behavior when invoked for each row:

```
postgres=# SELECT statement_timestamp() FROM test;
      statement_timestamp
---------------------------------
 2023-08-15 12:11:03.55166+05:30
 2023-08-15 12:11:03.55166+05:30
 2023-08-15 12:11:03.55166+05:30
```

```
...
...
...
 2023-08-15 12:11:03.55166+05:30
(10 rows)
```

Since this function is marked as STABLE, PostgreSQL will execute it only once and cache the result. The cached result will then be used for all other tuples instead of invoking the function repeatedly. For example, if we have a table with a million rows and we invoke statement_timestamp on each row, it will not make a million system time calls. Instead, it will only make one system time call and reuse the value for the other tuples.

STABLE functions will produce unique results for each SQL statement, but their behavior will change across multiple SQL statements. For example, suppose we have a transaction where we execute multiple SQL statements. In that case, each SQL statement will produce different results. Consider the following example, where multiple SQL statements produce different results inside a transaction:

```
postgres=# BEGIN WORK;
BEGIN
postgres=*# SELECT statement_timestamp() FROM test;
       statement_timestamp
----------------------------------
 2023-08-15 12:23:41.816464+05:30
 2023-08-15 12:23:41.816464+05:30
...
...
...
 2023-08-15 12:23:41.816464+05:30
(10 rows)

postgres=*# SELECT statement_timestamp() FROM test;
       statement_timestamp
----------------------------------
 2023-08-15 12:23:44.237813+05:30
 2023-08-15 12:23:44.237813+05:30
...
```

```
...
...
 2023-08-15 12:23:44.237813+05:30
(10 rows)

postgres=*# END;
COMMIT
```

From the preceding output, it is apparent that each SQL statement has a unique timestamp, while different SQL statements have different timestamps.

VOLATILE Functions

Unlike STABLE or IMMUTABLE functions, VOLATILE functions are executed for each tuple of the SQL result set. This means that they may produce different outputs for the same input value. By default, each function created in PostgreSQL is a VOLATILE function. Generally, these functions update tables in the database or process each tuple and return a different value. VOLATILE functions are not the best candidates for creating functional indexes. Consider the following example, which demonstrates the behavior of functional indexes:

```
postgres=# CREATE OR REPLACE FUNCTION public.test_volatile_func(i integer)
 RETURNS integer
 LANGUAGE plpgsql
 AS $function$
 BEGIN
 RAISE NOTICE 'test_volatile_func() called';
 RETURN 1;
 END;
$function$;
CREATE FUNCTION

postgres=# SELECT * FROM test WHERE test_volatile_func(1)=1;
NOTICE:  test_volatile_func() called
NOTICE:  test_volatile_func() called
NOTICE:  test_volatile_func() called
NOTICE:  test_volatile_func() called
```

```
NOTICE:   test_volatile_func() called
NOTICE:   test_volatile_func() called
NOTICE:   test_volatile_func() called
NOTICE:   test_volatile_func() called
NOTICE:   test_volatile_func() called
NOTICE:   test_volatile_func() called
 t
----
  1
  2
  3
...
...
...
(10 rows)
```

The function test_volatile_func(1), which accepts an input parameter value of 1 and returns a value of 1, was executed for each row in the preceding output. These types of functions should not be declared as VOLATILE because there is no need to execute them for each tuple. As we mentioned, the best candidates for VOLATILE functions are those that return a different value for each tuple when executed on the table rows. Consider the following example, which is a better illustration for this type of function:

```
postgres=# CREATE OR REPLACE FUNCTION public.process_each_row(t int)
 RETURNS integer
 LANGUAGE plpgsql
 AS $function$
 BEGIN
    RAISE NOTICE 'process_each_row() called';
    RETURN t+1;
END;
$function$;
CREATE FUNCTION
postgres=# SELECT process_each_row(t) FROM test;
NOTICE:   process_each_row() called
NOTICE:   process_each_row() called
```

```
NOTICE:   process_each_row() called
NOTICE:   process_each_row() called
NOTICE:   process_each_row() called
NOTICE:   process_each_row() called
NOTICE:   process_each_row() called
NOTICE:   process_each_row() called
NOTICE:   process_each_row() called
NOTICE:   process_each_row() called
 process_each_row
-------------------
                 2
                 3
                 4
...
...
...
(10 rows)
```

In the preceding example, the function traversed each tuple and added the value 1 to each row before returning the value. This is a case where volatile functions are recommended to be used, as the business logic needs to be invoked for each tuple. Let's take another built-in VOLATILE function, clock_timestamp, as an example and observe its behavior when invoked for each row:

```
postgres=# SELECT clock_timestamp() FROM test;
          clock_timestamp
-----------------------------------
 2023-08-15 12:05:31.426333+05:30
 2023-08-15 12:05:31.426727+05:30
 2023-08-15 12:05:31.426728+05:30
...
...
...
 2023-08-15 12:05:31.426731+05:30
(10 rows)
```

The preceding output suggests that the clock_timestamp function was executed for each row in the table, resulting in a different timestamp value for each tuple. Unlike STABLE and IMMUTABLE functions, VOLATILE functions always produce different timestamp values inside a transaction.

Procedures

Starting from PostgreSQL 11, PL/pgSQL allows the creation of procedures. Procedures, like functions, consist of a series of business logic steps that may include the use of LOOP and control statements. However, unlike functions, procedures do not return any values to the calling environment. To obtain values from procedures, we can use OUT parameters.

Procedures cannot be invoked as part of SQL statements. Instead, we must use an explicit "CALL procedure_name()" statement to execute them. Consider the following simple example:

```
postgres=# CREATE OR REPLACE PROCEDURE reset_test_data() AS $$
BEGIN
    -- Delete all the data from the table
    DELETE FROM test;
    -- Reset the sequence
    INSERT INTO test VALUES (generate_series(1, 100));
    -- Commit changes
    COMMIT;
END;
$$ LANGUAGE plpgsql;
CREATE PROCEDURE

postgres=# CALL reset_test_data();
CALL
```

In the preceding example, we have created a procedure to reset the test data. When the procedure is invoked, it deletes all data from the test table, inserts some dummy rows, and then commits the changes. We cannot achieve the same behavior with functions because the execution of a function is always an integral part of the same transaction. Procedure execution is not an integral part of the transaction, as procedures prefer to execute in their own transactional context. Therefore, COMMIT/ROLLBACK operations are supported in procedures, while functions will raise an exception if they encounter any COMMIT/ROLLBACK operation. Consider writing the preceding example as a function and see the execution result as follows:

```
postgres=# CREATE OR REPLACE FUNCTION reset_test_data_func() RETURNS
VOID AS $$
 BEGIN
     -- Delete all the data from the table
     DELETE FROM test;
     -- Reset the sequence
     INSERT INTO test VALUES (generate_series(1, 100));
     -- Commit changes
     COMMIT;
 END;
 $$ LANGUAGE plpgsql;
CREATE FUNCTION
postgres=# SELECT reset_test_data_func();
ERROR:  invalid transaction termination
CONTEXT:  PL/pgSQL function reset_test_data_func() line 8 at COMMIT
```

As you can see, we received an error message because the function execution occurs within an implicit transaction, and a nested COMMIT operation was invoked before completing the implicit transaction. We will discuss this further in the upcoming chapter on transaction management.

Temporary Functions/Procedures

In PostgreSQL, temporary functions/procedures can be created that are automatically dropped when the session is closed. These objects are scoped to the session and are more advantageous than anonymous functions because they allow for input parameters and return values to be passed to the calling environment. Temporary objects in PostgreSQL are created in the pg_temp schema, a special schema that is only visible and accessible to the session that created them. At the end of the session, these objects are automatically dropped. This is useful for creating temporary tables, indexes, or other database objects that are only needed for the duration of a session. Consider the following example:

```
postgres=# CREATE OR REPLACE FUNCTION pg_temp.temp_test_func() RETURNS
void AS $$
postgres$# BEGIN
postgres$#     RAISE NOTICE 'temporary function called';
postgres$#     END;
postgres$# $$ LANGUAGE plpgsql;
CREATE FUNCTION

postgres=# SELECT pg_temp.temp_test_func();
NOTICE:  temporary function called
 temp_test_func
----------------

(1 row)

postgres=# \q
Press any key to continue . . .
```

From the preceding output, we created a temporary function called temp_test_func() and closed the session. To test if the function was dropped automatically, open a new session and attempt to execute the function:

```
postgres=# SELECT pg_temp.temp_test_func();
ERROR:  schema "pg_temp" does not exist
LINE 1: SELECT pg_temp.temp_test_func();
```

The preceding output indicates that an error occurred while executing the temporary function (which was deleted as the previous session closed) that was created in the previous session.

VARIADIC Functions/Procedures

In some of the cases, functions or procedures may need to accept an unknown number of inputs as arguments, and declaring a function with a fixed amount of parameters would not be ideal. For example, consider the following logging method, which accepts the log level as the first parameter, and a variable number of parameters to log the actual message:

```
log_message('INFO', 'This is notification message to user');
log_message('ERROR', 'Error message', 'Why this happened', 'Hint message to user', 'Stack trace');
```

In the log_message() method shown earlier, the app sends only two parameters if the log level is 'INFO', but sends more than two parameters if the log level is 'ERROR'. To support this dynamic number of parameters in procedures/functions, PL/pgSQL offers VARIADIC parameter types that can accept a dynamic number of input parameters in functions/procedures. Consider the following example, which demonstrates the behavior described earlier:

```
postgres=# CREATE OR REPLACE PROCEDURE log_message(level text, VARIADIC
messages text[])
LANGUAGE plpgsql AS $$
DECLARE
    log_time timestamp := now();
    log_entry text;
BEGIN
    -- Construct the log entry
    log_entry := log_time || ' [' || level || '] ';
    FOR i IN 1 .. array_length(messages, 1) LOOP
        log_entry := log_entry || messages[i] || ' - ';
    END LOOP;
    RAISE NOTICE 'Log entry %', log_entry;
END;
$$;
CREATE PROCEDURE
```

As shown earlier, we have created a procedure named log_message with two input parameters. The first parameter, log_level, only accepts text values. The second parameter is of type VARIADIC, which can accept multiple parameters and consolidate them into the array parameter named "messages". To retrieve all the input parameters provided, we should iterate over the "messages" parameter.

Now, let's test this procedure with the log level "INFO," which only sends a text message along with it:

```
postgres=# CALL log_message('INFO', 'This is notification message to user');
NOTICE: Log entry 2023-08-15 16:37:33.987388 [INFO] This is notification
message to user -
CALL
```

Now, try setting the log level to 'ERROR' and providing a greater number of input parameters, as follows:

```
postgres=# CALL log_message('ERROR', 'Error message', 'Why this happened',
'Hint message to user', 'Stack trace');
NOTICE: Log entry 2023-08-15 16:35:00.537965 [ERROR] Error message - Why
this happened - Hint message to user - Stack trace -
CALL
```

The preceding demonstration shows that VARIADIC functions/procedures provide flexibility in accepting any number of parameters of the same type and processing them as required.

Best Practices

When designing and implementing functions and procedures in PostgreSQL, it is important to follow best practices to ensure that your code is efficient, maintainable, and secure.

Here are some best practices to consider:

- Use descriptive function and procedure names that accurately describe the operation being performed.

- Use input parameters to make your functions and procedures more flexible and reusable.

- Use comments to document your functions and procedures and make them more understandable.

- Follow PostgreSQL security best practices to ensure that your code is secure and protected from attacks.

- Test your functions and procedures thoroughly to ensure that they are working correctly and efficiently.

By following these best practices, you can create functions and procedures that are efficient, maintainable, and secure and can help you manage and manipulate your data more effectively in PostgreSQL.

Summary

In this chapter, we have covered functions and procedures which can improve database performance by consolidating complex logic into a single, reusable unit. When designing these functions and procedures, it is important to consider factors such as their scope of invocation, transaction handling, and parameter handling. PostgreSQL functions are categorized based on their volatility. IMMUTABLE functions always produce the same output for the same input. These functions are used in query optimization and can be cached by the server. STABLE functions produce the same output for the same input and different results for different inputs. VOLATILE functions always produce different outputs for the same input. Choosing the appropriate volatility category is crucial for optimizing query performance.

What's Next

In the next chapter, we will be covering some key features of return values and parameters in PL/pgSQL like the following:

- **Advanced Return Values**: Learn about returning complex data types, arrays, and record types from PL/pgSQL functions and procedures.

- **Output Parameters**: Explore using output parameters for returning multiple values or complex data structures from functions.

- **Dynamic Result Sets**: Discover how to return dynamic result sets using refcursor parameters for versatile data retrieval.

- **Parameter Modes**: Dive into the intricacies of different parameter modes (IN, OUT, INOUT) and their use cases.

CHAPTER 13

Return Values and Parameters

In the previous chapter, we talked about building functions and procedures. We covered examples of using IMMUTABLE, STABLE and VOLATILE functions besides to temporary functions and variadic functions. In this chapter, we will cover the importance of returning a value in a function and the different types of options available to return the values in PL/pgSQL. We will walk through some real-world examples of where and when to use each type of return value based on the requirements.

Return Values

In PL/pgSQL, returning a value means that the function will produce a result that can be used by other parts of the program. The RETURNS keyword is used to specify the data type of the value that the function will return. This can be any valid PostgreSQL data type, such as INTEGER, VARCHAR, or even custom composite types.

When the function is executed, it can use the RETURN statement to provide a value as output. This value can be derived from any operation or calculation performed within the function and can be based on input parameters, the state of the database, or any other relevant factors.

By returning a value, PL/pgSQL functions enable developers to create reusable code that can perform specific tasks and return results that can be used by other parts of the application. This can help to streamline programming and reduce redundancy by allowing common operations to be encapsulated in a single function.

© Baji Shaik and Dinesh Kumar Chemuduru 2023
B. Shaik and D. K. Chemuduru, *Procedural Programming with PostgreSQL PL/pgSQL*,
https://doi.org/10.1007/978-1-4842-9840-4_13

In addition to returning simple data types, PL/pgSQL functions can also return complex data structures, such as arrays, tables, or custom composite types. This allows developers to create flexible and powerful functions that can generate custom output based on complex input parameters.

Simple Example

Let's look at a simple example of a PL/pgSQL function that returns a value:

```
CREATE OR REPLACE FUNCTION calc_area(length INTEGER, width INTEGER)
RETURNS INTEGER AS $$
DECLARE
    area INTEGER;
BEGIN
    area := length * width;
    RETURN area;
END;
$$ LANGUAGE plpgsql;
```

In this example, the calc_area function takes two integer parameters: length and width. The function multiplies these parameters to calculate the area of a rectangle, which is assigned to a local variable called area. Finally, the RETURN statement is used to return the value of area as the function's output. When calling this function, the returned value can be stored in a variable or used directly in an expression.

Let's run the function:

```
book=# SELECT calc_area(20,10);
 calc_area
-----------
       200
(1 row)
```

As you can see, the area of a rectangle with length 20 and width 10 is returned as 200 by the function. By returning a value, PL/pgSQL functions can be used to perform calculations, manipulate data, or generate custom output based on input parameters.

Different Ways to Return Values

There are several ways to return values in PL/pgSQL. In addition to using the RETURN statement to return a value from a function as described in the previous section, PL/pgSQL also provides other ways for returning values.

RETURNS

This keyword is used to specify the data type of the value that the function will return. This can be any valid PostgreSQL data type, and the function can use the RETURN statement to provide a value as output. The following is the syntax:

```
CREATE OR REPLACE FUNCTION <function_name>
RETURNS VARCHAR AS $$
DECLARE
    --variables
BEGIN
    -  your code
    RETURN <var>;
END;
$$ LANGUAGE plpgsql;
```

Advantages of using RETURNS

- Can return a single row with a custom structure, which can be useful in situations where the data needs to be manipulated or processed further by other parts of the application

- Allows for a more concise and readable function definition

Disadvantages of using RETURNS

- Cannot return a set of rows, which limits the flexibility of the function

RETURNS SETOF

This syntax allows a PL/pgSQL function to define a custom record type as the output and then return a set of rows, each of which is a record with that specific structure. The following is the syntax:

```
CREATE OR REPLACE FUNCTION <function_name>
RETURNS SETOF <table> AS $$
BEGIN
    RETURN QUERY <your select query>;
END;
$$ LANGUAGE plpgsql;
```

Advantages of using RETURNS SETOF

- Can return a set of rows, each of which is a record with a specific structure, which provides more flexibility in the function's output

- Can be used to return the results of complex queries that involve multiple tables

Disadvantages of using RETURNS SETOF

- Can be more difficult to define and work with compared to other return types

RETURNS TABLE

This syntax is similar to RETURNS SETOF, but allows the function to define a custom table type that contains one or more columns with specific data types. The following is the syntax:

```
CREATE OR REPLACE FUNCTION <function_name>
RETURNS TABLE (col1 type, col2...) AS $$
BEGIN
    RETURN QUERY <your select query>;
END;
$$ LANGUAGE plpgsql;
```

Advantages of using RETURNS TABLE

- Provides a clear and easy-to-understand definition of the function's output

- Can be used to return a set of rows with columns that are predefined by the table type

Disadvantages of using RETURNS TABLE

- Can be more verbose compared to other return types, which can make the function definition less readable

- Can be more difficult to define and work with compared to other return types

- Is not allowed to use explicit OUT or INOUT parameters with the RETURNS TABLE notation

OUT

This keyword is used to define output parameters that can be set within the function using the SELECT INTO statement. These parameters can be used to return values in a variety of ways, such as returning a single value, a set of values, or a record type. The following is the syntax:

```
CREATE OR REPLACE FUNCTION <function_name>(OUT <parameter> INTEGER)
AS $$
BEGIN
    SELECT <col> INTO <parameter> FROM <table>;
END;
$$ LANGUAGE plpgsql;
```

Advantages of using OUT parameters

- Can be used to return a single row with a custom structure, which provides more flexibility in the function's output

- Allows for the use of existing variable names in the function definition

Disadvantages of using OUT parameters

- Can be more verbose compared to other return types, which can make the function definition less readable

- Cannot return a set of rows, which limits the flexibility of the function

Simple Difference Matrix

The following is a difference matrix for the different return types in PL/pgSQL:

Return Type	Structure	Usage
RETURNS	Custom record type	Returns a single row with a custom structure
RETURNS SETOF	Custom record type	Returns a set of rows, each of which is a record with a specific structure
RETURNS TABLE	Custom table type	Returns a set of rows, each of which has columns defined by the table type
OUT parameters	Custom record type	Returns a single row with a custom structure

The choice of return type depends on the specific requirements of the function and the application as a whole. RETURNS SETOF may be the most flexible, but it may also be more difficult to define and work with. RETURNS and OUT parameters may be simpler to use, but they have their own limitations. RETURNS TABLE provides a clear definition of the function's output, but it may be more verbose compared to other return types.

Different Examples for Each RETURN Type

The following are the different methods to use RETURN values:

- Using SELECT statements

- Using RETURNS TABLE

- Using RETURN NEXT

- Using RETURNS SETOF TABLE

- Using RETURNS SETOF data type

- Using RETURNS RECORD

- Using RETURNS SETOF RECORD

- Using OUT parameters

- Using INOUT parameters

Using SELECT Statements

A simple way to return values from a PL/pgSQL function is to use a SELECT statement to return the desired value.

Let's look at an example:

```
CREATE TABLE users (user_id int, name varchar, email varchar);

INSERT INTO users VALUES (1, 'foo', 'foo@example.com'),
(2, 'bar', 'bar@example.com');

CREATE OR REPLACE FUNCTION get_name_using_SELECT(id INTEGER)
RETURNS VARCHAR AS $$
DECLARE
    result VARCHAR;
BEGIN
    SELECT name INTO result FROM users WHERE user_id = id;
    RETURN result;
END;
$$ LANGUAGE plpgsql;
```

In this example, the get_name_using_SELECT function takes an integer parameter called id. The function uses a SELECT statement to retrieve the name column from the users table where user_id matches the id parameter. The retrieved name value is stored in the result variable, which is then returned as the output of the function.

Let's run the function:

```
book=# SELECT get_name_using_SELECT(1);
 get_name_using_select
-----------------------
 foo
(1 row)
```

As you can see, it returned the value from the variable as expected.

Using RETURNS TABLE

PL/pgSQL also allows functions to return a table as output, using the RETURNS TABLE syntax.

Let's look at the example with the same table:

```
CREATE OR REPLACE FUNCTION get_users_return_TABLE()
RETURNS TABLE (id INTEGER, username VARCHAR) AS $$
BEGIN
    RETURN QUERY SELECT user_id, name FROM users;
END;
$$ LANGUAGE plpgsql;
```

In this example, the get_users_return_TABLE function returns a table with two columns: user_id and name. Inside the function, the RETURN QUERY statement is used to return the result of a SELECT statement that retrieves these two columns from the users table. When the function is called, the resulting table is returned as output.

Let's run the function:

```
book=# SELECT * FROM get_users_return_TABLE();
id | username
----+----------
1 | foo
2 | bar
(2 rows)
```

As you can see, it returned the output of the table.

Using RETURN NEXT

In PL/pgSQL, RETURN NEXT is a statement used to return the next row of a result set from a function. This statement is often used in conjunction with a FOR loop to iterate through a set of rows and return them one at a time.

Here's an example of a PL/pgSQL function that uses RETURN NEXT to return each row of a table:

```
CREATE OR REPLACE FUNCTION get_users_return_NEXT()
RETURNS TABLE (id INTEGER, username VARCHAR) AS $$
BEGIN
    FOR id, username IN SELECT * FROM users LOOP
        RETURN NEXT;
    END LOOP;
    RETURN;
END;
$$ LANGUAGE plpgsql;
```

In this example, the get_users_return_NEXT function returns a table with two columns: id and username. Inside the function, a FOR loop is used to iterate through each row of the users table. The RETURN NEXT statement is used to return each row of the table one at a time.

The RETURN statement is used to indicate that the end of the set has been reached.

Let's run the function:

```
postgres=# SELECT get_users_return_NEXT();
 get_users_return_next
-----------------------
 (1,foo)
 (2,bar)
(2 rows)
```

This SQL statement returned a table with all user_id and name values from the users table.

By providing RETURN NEXT, PL/pgSQL allows developers to return result sets one row at a time, which can be useful in situations where it is not practical to return the entire set at once.

Using RETURNS SETOF TABLE

Another way to return a record type in PL/pgSQL is to use the RETURNS SETOF syntax. This allows the function to return a set of rows, each of which is a record with a specific structure.

Here's an example:

```
CREATE OR REPLACE FUNCTION get_users_return_SETOF_table(id INTEGER)
RETURNS SETOF users AS $$
BEGIN
    RETURN QUERY SELECT * FROM users WHERE user_id = id;
END;
$$ LANGUAGE plpgsql;
```

In this example, the get_users_return_SETOF_table function returns a set of rows, each of which is a record of type users. The function uses a SELECT statement to retrieve the row from the users table where user_id matches the id parameter. The RETURN QUERY statement is used to return the result of the SELECT statement as a set of rows.

Let's run the function:

```
postgres=# SELECT get_users_return_SETOF_table(1);
 get_users_return_setof_table
-------------------------------
 (1,foo,foo@example.com)
(1 row)
```

This SQL statement returned a set of rows, each of which is a record of type users.

Using RETURNS SETOF Data Type

To return a set of integers in PL/pgSQL, you can use the RETURNS SETOF syntax. This allows the function to return a set of rows, each of which is an integer value. Here's an example:

```
CREATE OR REPLACE FUNCTION get_users_return_SETOF_integers()
RETURNS SETOF INTEGER AS $$
BEGIN
    RETURN QUERY SELECT user_id FROM users;
```

```
END;
$$ LANGUAGE plpgsql;
```

In this example, the get_users_return_SETOF_integers function returns a set of integers. The function uses a SELECT statement to retrieve the user_id from the users table. The RETURN QUERY statement is used to return the result of the SELECT statement as a set of rows.

Let's run the function:

```
postgres=# SELECT * FROM get_users_return_SETOF_integers();
 get_users_return_setof_integers
---------------------------------
                               1
                               2
(2 rows)
```

This SQL statement returned a set of rows, each of which is an integer value.

Using RETURNS RECORD

Another way to return a record data type in PL/pgSQL is to use the RETURNS with RECORD type. This allows the function to define a custom record type as the output. Here's an example:

```
CREATE OR REPLACE FUNCTION get_users_return_RECORD(id INTEGER)
RETURNS RECORD AS $$
DECLARE
    user_row RECORD;
BEGIN
    SELECT * INTO user_row FROM users WHERE user_id = id;
    RETURN user_row;
END;
$$ LANGUAGE plpgsql;
```

In this cxample, the get_users_return_RECORD function takes an integer parameter called id and returns a record type as output. Inside the function, the SELECT statement retrieves all the columns from the users table where user_id matches the id parameter. The INTO statement is used to set the value of the user_row variable to the corresponding record.

To return the result, we use the RETURN statement to return the user_row variable as the output of the function.

Let's run the function:

```
book=# SELECT get_users_return_RECORD(1);
 get_users_return_record
--------------------------
 (1,foo,foo@example.com)
(1 row)
```

This SQL statement returned a single row with three columns: name, department, and salary. By using RETURNS RECORD, PL/pgSQL functions can return a single row with a custom structure, which can be useful in situations where the data needs to be manipulated or processed further by other parts of the application.

Using RETURNS SETOF RECORD

In PL/pgSQL, it is possible to return a set of record data types using the RETURNS SETOF or RETURNS TABLE syntax. Using the RETURNS SETOF syntax, a PL/pgSQL function can define a custom record type as the output and then return a set of rows, each of which is a record with that specific structure. For example:

```
CREATE OR REPLACE FUNCTION get_users_return_SETOF_RECORD()
RETURNS SETOF RECORD AS $$
BEGIN
    RETURN QUERY SELECT * FROM users;
END;
$$ LANGUAGE plpgsql;
```

In this example, the get_users_return_SETOF_RECORD function returns a set of rows, each of which is a record type. Inside the function, the SELECT statement retrieves all columns from the users table. The RETURN QUERY statement is used to return the result of the SELECT statement as a set of rows.

While running the function, you will need a structure defined at runtime as it's a generic record type. Let's run the function:

```
postgres=# SELECT * FROM get_users_return_SETOF_RECORD() AS (user_id int,
name varchar, email varchar);
 user_id | name |        email
---------+------+------------------
       1 | foo  | foo@example.com
       2 | bar  | bar@example.com
(2 rows)
```

This SQL statement returned a set of rows, each of which is a record type.

It is also possible that we can return multiple SQL statement results from a single function as follows:

```
postgres=# CREATE OR REPLACE FUNCTION public.test_multiple()
RETURNS SETOF integer
LANGUAGE plpgsql
AS $function$
BEGIN
        RETURN QUERY SELECT generate_series(1,5);
        RETURN QUERY SELECT 2;
        RETURN;
END;
$function$;
CREATE FUNCTION

postgres=# SELECT public.test_multiple();
 test_multiple
---------------
             1
             2
             3
             4
             5
             2
(6 rows)
```

As seen in the preceding results, we utilized two RETURN QUERY statements to combine the results of two queries into a single result set and return a unified result from the function execution.

By providing these different ways to return sets of record data types, PL/pgSQL allows developers to choose the most appropriate method for their specific use case.

Using OUT Parameters

It is also possible to return a set of integers in PL/pgSQL using OUT parameters. This method requires defining a new record variable with the desired structure and then setting its values before returning it as output. Here's an example:

```
CREATE OR REPLACE FUNCTION get_users_return_OUT_params(OUT integer_column
INTEGER)
AS $$
BEGIN
    SELECT user_id INTO integer_column FROM users LIMIT 1;
END;
$$ LANGUAGE plpgsql;
```

In this example, the get_users_return_OUT_params function defines a single OUT parameter called integer_column. Inside the function, the SELECT statement retrieves the user_id value from the users table and sets it to the integer_column parameter.

Let's run the function:

```
postgres=# SELECT * FROM get_users_return_OUT_params();
 integer_column
----------------
             1
(1 row)
```

This SQL statement returned a single row with one integer value.

Here is another example where we return multiple rows via multiple OUT parameters:

```
postgres=# CREATE OR REPLACE FUNCTION public.testout(OUT p_output1 integer,
OUT p_output2 text)
 RETURNS SETOF record
```

```
  LANGUAGE plpgsql
AS $function$
DECLARE
        v_rec RECORD;
BEGIN
        FOR v_rec IN (SELECT generate_series(1, 10) i, 'abcd' a ) LOOP
                p_output1 := v_rec.i;
                p_output2 := v_rec.a;
                RETURN NEXT;
        END LOOP;
        RETURN;
END;
$function$;
CREATE FUNCTION

postgres=# SELECT * FROM testout();
p_output1 | p_output2
-----------+-----------
1 | abcd
2 | abcd
...
...
9 | abcd
10 | abcd
(10 rows)
```

In the preceding example, we declared two OUT variables named p_output1 and p_output2. Then, we assigned the column value of the record to each OUT variable type. After that, we called RETURN NEXT, which keeps the result queue in the heap. Finally, the RETURN statement returns the result heap to the calling environment.

Using INOUT Parameter

Using an INOUT parameter type allows a single parameter to act as both an input and output parameter, enabling the return of data to the calling environment. Consider the following example:

```
CREATE OR REPLACE FUNCTION testinout(p_output1 INOUT INT, p_output2 OUT
TEXT) RETURNS RECORD
AS
$$
BEGIN

        RAISE NOTICE 'Got value for 1st parameter as %', p_output1;
        p_output1 := 10;
        p_output2 := 'Testing';
END;
$$ LANGUAGE PLPGSQL;

postgres=# SELECT * FROM testinout(5);
NOTICE:  Got value for 1st parameter as 5
 p_output1 | p_output2
-----------+-----------
        10 | Testing
(1 row)
```

The preceding code declares two variables. The p_output1 parameter is declared as INOUT, while the p_output2 parameter is declared as an OUT parameter. An input value of 5 is passed to the INOUT parameter, p_output1, which is then updated to a different output value of 10. This demonstrates the behavior of returning values to the calling environment via an INOUT parameter.

Summary

In this chapter, we talked about various ways to return values in PL/pgSQL functions, including using the RETURN statement to return a single value of any valid PostgreSQL data type, using RETURNS TABLE or RETURNS SETOF to return a set of rows with a specific structure, and using OUT parameters to set the value of variables that are returned as output. We also included examples of functions that return different types of data, such as integers, record types, and tables.

What's Next

In the next chapter, we will be covering some key features of exception handling in PL/pgSQL like the following:

- **Advanced Exception Handling**: Explore handling multiple exceptions, nesting exception blocks, and gracefully recovering from errors.

- **Custom Exception Types**: Learn how to create and raise custom exceptions to provide meaningful error messages and context.

- **Logging and Debugging**: Discover techniques for logging exception details and debugging your PL/pgSQL code.

- **Exception Propagation**: Explore strategies for propagating exceptions to higher levels for centralized error handling.

- **Error Recovery**: Dive into techniques for recovering from exceptions and ensuring that your application remains operational.

CHAPTER 14

Handling Exceptions

In the previous chapter, we talked about returning complex data types, arrays, and record types from PL/PGSQL functions and procedures and explored output parameters for returning multiple values. In this chapter, we will cover different types of exceptions in PostgreSQL. It will start with the introduction of exceptions and how to use them within PL/pgSQL code with a simple example. We will walk through some real-world examples of where and when to use these exceptions using PL/pgSQL functions or procedures. We will also cover the advantages and disadvantages of exceptions.

Exceptions

Let's start with exploring how to determine the effect of a command in PL/pgSQL which helps to return meta-information. This will help with the exceptions in PL/pgSQL to return necessary information. In PL/pgSQL, there are several ways to retrieve meta-information about the last command run inside a function or procedure. Some of the most commonly used methods are GET DIAGNOSTICS and FOUND.

GET DIAGNOSTICS

This command is used to retrieve information about the last executed statement. It can be used to retrieve the row count, the number of affected rows, and the SQLSTATE of the last executed statement.

The syntax for GET DIAGNOSTICS is as follows:

```
GET DIAGNOSTICS <variable> = <item>;
```

© Baji Shaik and Dinesh Kumar Chemuduru 2023
B. Shaik and D. K. Chemuduru, *Procedural Programming with PostgreSQL PL/pgSQL*,
https://doi.org/10.1007/978-1-4842-9840-4_14

Here, <variable> is the name of a variable that will hold the value of the item being retrieved, and <item> is the item to be retrieved. The item can be one of the following:

- ROW_COUNT: The count of rows impacted by the most recently executed statement

- PG_CONTEXT: The context in which the last executed statement occurred

Let's look at an example where we can get how many rows were updated through an UPDATE within a function.

Create a table named test_table:

```
CREATE TABLE test_table (
id INT NOT NULL,
name VARCHAR NOT NULL
);
```

Insert a few values:

```
INSERT INTO test_table VALUES (generate_series(1,10), 'first'||generate_
series(1,10));
INSERT INTO test_table VALUES (generate_series(1,10), 'second'||generate_
series(1,10));
```

Here is the function with the use of GET DIAGNOSTICS to retrieve the row count of the last executed statement:

```
CREATE OR REPLACE FUNCTION test_func () RETURNS integer AS $$
DECLARE
  rowcount integer;
BEGIN
  UPDATE test_table SET name = 'updated' where name like 'first%';
  GET DIAGNOSTICS rowcount = ROW_COUNT;
  RETURN rowcount;
END;
$$ LANGUAGE plpgsql;
```

In this example, we are creating a function called test_func. Within the function, we are updating a table and using GET DIAGNOSTICS to retrieve the row count of the update statement. We are then returning the row count as the output of the function.

Let's run this function:

```
book=# SELECT test_func ();
 my_function
-------------
          10
(1 row)
```

As you can see, it returned 10, which means 10 rows in the table were updated through this function.

However, if you go into the details, how can we use the row count? Let's consider an example of a function which is used to update employee salaries.

Let's create the employees table with some data:

```
CREATE TABLE employees (
  id SERIAL PRIMARY KEY,
  name VARCHAR(50) NOT NULL,
  email VARCHAR(50) NOT NULL,
  salary NUMERIC(8,2) NOT NULL
);

INSERT INTO employees (name, email, salary)
VALUES
  ('f1', 'f1@example.com', 50000.00),
  ('f2', 'f2@example.com', 60000.00),
  ('f3', 'f3@example.com', 70000.00),
  ('f4', 'f4@example.com', 80000.00);
```

Let's create the function which updates the employee salary:

```
CREATE OR REPLACE FUNCTION update_employee_salary(
    IN employee_id INTEGER,
    IN new_salary NUMERIC
) RETURNS BOOLEAN AS $$
DECLARE
```

```
    row_count INTEGER;
BEGIN
    UPDATE employees
    SET salary = new_salary
    WHERE id = employee_id;

    GET DIAGNOSTICS row_count = ROW_COUNT;

    IF row_count = 1 THEN
        RETURN TRUE;
    ELSE
        RETURN FALSE;
    END IF;
END;
$$ LANGUAGE plpgsql;
```

In this example, we are using GET DIAGNOSTICS to retrieve the number of rows affected by an update statement. We first update the salary of an employee with a given ID and then use GET DIAGNOSTICS to retrieve the number of rows affected by the update.

We then use the IF statement to check if the update affected exactly one row. If it did, we return TRUE, indicating that the update was successful. If it affected zero or more than one row, we return FALSE, indicating that the update was not successful.

Let's run this function:

```
postgres=# select * from employees;
 id |      name       |         email         |  salary
----+-----------------+-----------------------+----------
  1 | f1              | f1@example.com        | 50000.00
  2 | f2              | f2@example.com        | 60000.00
  3 | f3              | f3@example.com        | 70000.00
  4 | f4              | f4@example.com        | 80000.00
(4 rows)

postgres=# SELECT update_employee_salary(1,100000.00);
 update_employee_salary
------------------------
 t
```

```
(1 row)

postgres=# select * from employees;
 id |     name      |        email        |  salary
----+---------------+---------------------+-----------
  2 | f2            | f2@example.com      |  60000.00
  3 | f3            | f3@example.com      |  70000.00
  4 | f4            | f4@example.com      |  80000.00
  1 | f1            | f1@example.com      | 100000.00
(4 rows)
```

As you can see, the function returned TRUE as it was able to UPDATE one row as per the employee ID. Let's see what happens if we run this function with an employee ID which does not exist in the table, for example, 5:

```
book=# SELECT update_employee_salary(5,100000.00);
 update_employee_salary
------------------------
 f
(1 row)
```

As you can see, it returned FALSE as there were no rows to UPDATE.

FOUND

This command is used to determine if the last executed statement returned any rows. It can be used in conjunction with other commands, such as SELECT, to determine if the query returned any rows.

Let's look at an example of how to use FOUND to determine if a SELECT statement returned any rows:

```
CREATE OR REPLACE FUNCTION test_func(nm varchar) RETURNS boolean AS $$
DECLARE
result varchar;
BEGIN
  SELECT name INTO result FROM test_table WHERE name = nm;
  IF FOUND THEN
  RETURN TRUE;
```

```
  ELSE
  RETURN FALSE;
  END IF;
END;
$$ LANGUAGE plpgsql;
```

In this example, we are creating a function called test_func. Within the function, we are using a SELECT statement to retrieve data from a table. We are then using FOUND to determine if the SELECT statement returned any rows and returning a boolean value based on the result.

Let's run the SELECT statement and see if the row exists:

```
postgres=# SELECT name FROM test_table WHERE name = 'second1';
  name
--------
 second1
(1 row)
```

This row exists. So, the function with input second1 should return TRUE:

```
postgres=# SELECT  test_func('second1');
 test_func
-----------
 t
(1 row)
```

If we consider another row which does not exist, it will return FALSE:

```
postgres=# SELECT name FROM test_table WHERE name = 'second100';
 name
------
(0 rows)

postgres=# SELECT  test_func('second100');
 test_func
-----------
 f
(1 row)
```

Exceptions in PL/pgSQL

An exception in PL/pgSQL is an error condition that occurs during the execution of a program. In PostgreSQL, exceptions are used to handle errors that can occur during database operations, such as syntax errors, constraint violations, data type mismatches, and object not found errors.

- **Syntax Errors**: These are errors that occur when the SQL code is malformed or incorrect. Examples include missing or extra parentheses, incorrect syntax for a function or keyword, and misspelled table and column names.

- **Constraint Violations**: These are errors that occur when a constraint is violated, such as a primary key or unique constraint. Examples include trying to insert a duplicate value into a column with a unique constraint or trying to delete a row that is referenced by a foreign key constraint.

- **Foreign Key Violations**: These are errors that occur when a foreign key constraint is violated. Examples include trying to insert a value into a column that does not exist in the referenced table or trying to delete a row that is still referenced by another table.

- **Data Type Mismatch Errors**: These are errors that occur when the data type of a column does not match the data being inserted or updated. Examples include trying to insert a string into a numeric column or trying to insert a value that is too large for the column.

- **Object Not Found Errors**: These are errors that occur when an object referenced in the SQL code does not exist. Examples include trying to select data from a table that does not exist or trying to create a trigger on a nonexistent table.

These are some examples of what kind of errors we can see. However, there would be a lot more.

Different Ways to Handle Exceptions in PL/pgSQL

In this section, we will go through different ways to handle exceptions such as the following:

- Using the BEGIN and END statements

- Using the RAISE statement

- Using the GET STACKED DIAGNOSTICS statement

Using the BEGIN and END Statements

One way to handle exceptions in PL/pgSQL is by using the BEGIN and END statements. These statements define a block of code that can be executed as a single unit. Within a BEGIN block, users can define exception handlers that catch specific errors and perform appropriate actions.

The following is the syntax:

```
BEGIN
    -- code block
EXCEPTION
    WHEN SQLSTATE '<error_number>' THEN
        -- handle the unique constraint violation error
    WHEN OTHERS THEN
        -- handle all other errors
END;
```

In the syntax, SQLSTATE '<error_number>' is used to catch the specific error based on the error code. If that specific error occurs, the code block defined in the WHEN SQLSTATE '<error_number>' THEN section will be executed. If any other error occurs, the code block defined in the WHEN OTHERS THEN section will be executed. There are some predefined error codes available in PostgreSQL. You can find the list of error codes in the PostgreSQL Error Codes (https://www.postgresql.org/docs/current/errcodes-appendix.html) documentation.

To begin understanding exceptions, consider the following simple example:

```
postgres=# DO $$
DECLARE
    v_result INT;
```

```
BEGIN
    v_result = 1/0;
EXCEPTION
    WHEN OTHERS THEN
    RAISE NOTICE 'Got error';
END;
$$;
NOTICE:  Got error
DO
```

In the preceding example, we explicitly raised a generic mathematical exception by dividing 1 by 0. In the exception block, we printed the message "Got error". PL/pgSQL is so flexible that we can put another block of PL/pgSQL within an exception block, which can be useful in some cases where you want to write some work to print the error. Consider the following extended example:

```
postgres=# DO $inline$
DECLARE
        v_result INT;
BEGIN
        v_result = 1/0;
        RAISE NOTICE 'Hello World!';
EXCEPTION
        WHEN OTHERS THEN
        DO $$
        BEGIN
                RAISE NOTICE 'Got error';
        END;
        $$;
END;
$inline$;
NOTICE:  Got error
DO
```

In the preceding example, an anonymous block of code is added within an exception block to execute whenever an exception occurs. This kind of code flexibility is offered by PL/pgSQL, helpful in handling exceptions.

Now, consider an example with the GET DIAGNOSTICS. Create a test table and insert some rows as follows:

```
CREATE TABLE employees (
  id SERIAL PRIMARY KEY,
  name VARCHAR(50) NOT NULL,
  email VARCHAR(50) NOT NULL,
  salary NUMERIC(8,2) NOT NULL
);

INSERT INTO employees (name, email, salary)
VALUES
  ('f1', 'f1@example.com', 50000.00),
  ('f2', 'f2@example.com', 60000.00),
  ('f3', 'f3@example.com', 70000.00),
  ('f4', 'f4@example.com', 80000.00);
```

As the salary column is not null, you will see a not-null violation error when you try to update the salary as null:

```
postgres=# UPDATE employees SET salary = null WHERE id=1;
ERROR:  null value in column "salary" of relation "employees" violates not-
null constraint
DETAIL:  Failing row contains (1, f1, f1@example.com, null).
```

Let's create a function to handle not-null violation errors. From PostgreSQL error codes, 23502 is the error code for not-null violation:

```
CREATE OR REPLACE FUNCTION update_employee_salary(
    IN employee_id INTEGER,
    IN new_salary text
) RETURNS BOOLEAN AS $$
DECLARE
    rowcount INTEGER;
BEGIN
        UPDATE employees
    SET salary = new_salary::numeric
    WHERE id = employee_id;
```

```
    GET DIAGNOSTICS rowcount = ROW_COUNT;
    RETURN rowcount;
EXCEPTION
    WHEN SQLSTATE '23502' THEN
        RAISE NOTICE 'customer error: not-null violation error';
        RETURN FALSE;
    WHEN OTHERS THEN
        RAISE NOTICE 'other error';
        RETURN FALSE;
END;

$$ LANGUAGE plpgsql;
```

From the function, if it is a not-null violation error, it throws the message that we are passing 'customer error: not-null violation error'. If it's another error, it will go to the WHEN OTHERS block and throw the 'other error' message.

Let's test with updating a null value:

```
postgres=# select update_employee_salary(1,null);
NOTICE:  customer error: not-null violation error
 update_employee_salary
------------------------
 f
(1 row)
```

As you can see, it has thrown the custom message from the function for not-null violation. But let's try updating a text value to a numeric field:

```
postgres=# select update_employee_salary(1,'abc');
NOTICE:  other error
 update_employee_salary
------------------------
 f
(1 row)
```

As you can see, it went to the WHEN OTHERS block and threw the other error message. However, if you want to know the exact error instead of the custom message when it went to WHEN OTHERS, you can trap the error using SQLSTATE and SQLERRM.

Let's modify the function as follows to trap the error:

```
CREATE OR REPLACE FUNCTION update_employee_salary(
    IN employee_id INTEGER,
    IN new_salary text
) RETURNS BOOLEAN AS $$
DECLARE
    rowcount INTEGER;
    err_num int;
    err_msg varchar;
BEGIN
        UPDATE employees
    SET salary = new_salary::numeric
    WHERE id = employee_id;

    GET DIAGNOSTICS rowcount = ROW_COUNT;
    RETURN rowcount;

EXCEPTION
    WHEN SQLSTATE '23502' THEN
        RAISE NOTICE 'customer error: not-null violation error';
        RETURN FALSE;
    WHEN OTHERS THEN
        err_num := SQLSTATE;
        err_msg := SUBSTR(SQLERRM, 100);
        RAISE NOTICE 'other error is: %:%', err_num, err_msg;
        RETURN FALSE;
END;

$$ LANGUAGE plpgsql;
```

Let's run and see the exact error:

```
postgres=# select update_employee_salary(1,'abc');
ERROR:  invalid input syntax for type integer: "22P02"
CONTEXT:  PL/pgSQL function update_employee_salary(integer,text) line 20 at
assignment
```

As you can see, it has thrown the exact error.

Using the RAISE Statement

Another way to handle exceptions in PL/pgSQL is by using the RAISE statement. This statement is used to raise an exception explicitly, allowing users to define their own custom exceptions and error messages.

Let's use the same example again with RAISE EXCEPTION implementation:

```
CREATE OR REPLACE FUNCTION update_employee_salary(
    IN employee_id INTEGER,
    IN new_salary numeric
) RETURNS BOOLEAN AS $$
DECLARE
    rowcount INTEGER;
BEGIN
        UPDATE employees
    SET salary = new_salary::numeric
    WHERE id = employee_id;

    IF new_salary < 50000 OR new_salary > 80000 THEN
    RAISE EXCEPTION 'Salary must be between $50,000 and $80,000';
    RETURN FALSE;
    END IF;

    RETURN TRUE;
END;

$$ LANGUAGE plpgsql;
```

In this example, if the new salary is outside of the range of $50,000 to $80,000, a custom exception with the error message "Salary must be between $50,000 and $80,000" will be raised.

Let's test this function with a salary which is higher than $80,000 and between $50,000 and $80,000:

```
postgres=# select update_employee_salary(1,100000);
ERROR:  Salary must be between $50,000 and $80,000
CONTEXT:  PL/pgSQL function update_employee_salary(integer,numeric) line 10
at RAISE
Time: 4.083 ms
```

```
postgres=# select update_employee_salary(1,70000);
 update_employee_salary
------------------------
 t
(1 row)

Time: 0.790 ms
postgres=# SELECT * FROM employees WHERE id=1;
 id | name |     email      |  salary
----+------+----------------+----------
  1 | f1   | f1@example.com | 70000.00
(1 row)
```

As you can see, it has raised an exception with $100,000 as it is higher than $80,000 and updated the value as expected when the salary is $70,000.

Custom Exceptions

Sometimes, an application needs to raise custom exceptions with its own error messages, codes, and even custom hint messages. PL/pgSQL's RAISE EXCEPTION clause allows you to do this by setting exception attributes like MESSAGE, DETAIL, HINT, and ERRCODE. Consider the following example:

```
postgres=# DO
$$
BEGIN
    RAISE EXCEPTION USING MESSAGE='This is error message', DETAIL='These
are the details about this error', HINT='Hint message which may fix this
error',ERRCODE='P1234';
END;
$$;
ERROR:  This is error message
DETAIL:  These are the details about this error
HINT:  Hint message which may fix this error
CONTEXT:  PL/pgSQL function inline_code_block line 3 at RAISE
```

The preceding output shows that we raised a custom exception with custom messages and error codes. Since we are raising the plpgsql custom error, the error code should start with "P". To specify the error codes, we should follow the PostgreSQL error code formats, which are mentioned in the documentation.

You can refer to PostgreSQL error codes here: `www.postgresql.org/docs/current/errcodes-appendix.html`.

We can use both custom exceptions and predefined PL/pgSQL exceptions to raise exceptions. The following example raises a predefined exception:

```
postgres=# DO
$$
BEGIN
    RAISE division_by_zero USING MESSAGE='Number zero can not be divisor';
END;
$$;
ERROR:  Number zero can not be divisor
CONTEXT:  PL/pgSQL function inline_code_block line 3 at RAISE
```

Rethrow Exceptions

In the preceding example, an anonymous block of code is added within an exception block to execute whenever an exception occurs. This kind of code flexibility is offered by PL/pgSQL, helpful in handling exceptions. In the previous example, we learned how to raise an exception. Now, let's discuss how to catch an exception and then throw it. Consider the following simple example, which raises a custom exception and then throws it from the place where it caught the exception:

```
postgres=# DO $$
DECLARE
            v_test INT:=0;
BEGIN
      BEGIN
            v_test:= 1/0;
            RAISE NOTICE 'value is %', v_test;
```

```
            EXCEPTION
                WHEN OTHERS THEN
                    RAISE EXCEPTION 'got some error %', SQLERRM;
        END;
EXCEPTION
        WHEN OTHERS THEN
        RAISE NOTICE 'exception from outer block %', SQLERRM;
END;
$$;
NOTICE:  exception from outer block got some error division by zero
DO
```

As you can see in the preceding example, we have nested blocks in which a custom exception is raised from inside the inner block and caught by the outer block.

ASSERT

Assertions are used in PL/pgSQL to enforce business rules or check assumptions about data. They are used to ensure that the data in the database conforms to certain requirements. Assertions can be used to check the validity of input values, the correctness of business logic, or the consistency of data in the database. If an assertion fails, it will raise an exception, which can be caught and handled by the application. If an assertion passes, then it won't raise any exception. Consider the following simple example, which demonstrates the assertion behavior:

```
postgres=# DO
$$
BEGIN
    ASSERT 1=1, 'this assertion should not raise';
    ASSERT 1=0, 'assertion failed, as 1 is not equal to 0';
END;
$$;
ERROR:  assertion failed, as 1 is not equal to 0
CONTEXT:  PL/pgSQL function inline_code_block line 4 at ASSERT
```

In the preceding output, we have specified two assert statements. One assert statement's condition is true, while the other's condition is false. An exception only occurs when the condition is false.

Get Call Stack

In PL/pgSQL, if you want to get a call stack or stack trace regardless of the exception, you can use the GET DIAGNOSTIC command to retrieve the call stack information. Unlike other programming languages where only the call stack dump is available when an exception occurs, PL/pgSQL offers to fetch the call stack whenever it is required.

```
postgres=# DO $$
DECLARE
v_text TEXT:='';
BEGIN
    BEGIN
        GET DIAGNOSTICS v_text = PG_CONTEXT;
        RAISE NOTICE '%', v_text;
    END;
END;
$$;
NOTICE:  PL/pgSQL function inline_code_block line 6 at GET DIAGNOSTICS
DO
```

As shown in the preceding example, we can print the CALL stack using PG_CONTEXT to determine where the GET DIAGNOSTIC was executed from. Now, extend the same behavior with the following function calls, and see the function call stack:

```
postgres=# CREATE OR REPLACE FUNCTION function_one()
RETURNS void AS $$
BEGIN
  RAISE NOTICE 'Function One called';
  -- Call Function Two
  PERFORM function_two();
END;
$$ LANGUAGE plpgsql;
CREATE FUNCTION
```

```
postgres=# CREATE OR REPLACE FUNCTION function_two()
RETURNS void AS $$
BEGIN
  RAISE NOTICE 'Function Two called';
  -- Call Function Three
  PERFORM function_three();
END;
$$ LANGUAGE plpgsql;
CREATE FUNCTION

postgres=# CREATE OR REPLACE FUNCTION function_three()
RETURNS void AS $$
DECLARE
    v_text TEXT:='';
BEGIN
  RAISE NOTICE 'Function Three called';
  GET DIAGNOSTICS v_text=PG_CONTEXT;
  RAISE NOTICE 'Call stack %', v_text;
END;
$$ LANGUAGE plpgsql;
CREATE FUNCTION

postgres=# SELECT function_one();
NOTICE:   Function One called
NOTICE:   Function Two called
NOTICE:   Function Three called
NOTICE:   Call stack PL/pgSQL function function_three() line 6 at GET
DIAGNOSTICS
SQL statement "SELECT function_three()"
PL/pgSQL function function_two() line 5 at PERFORM
SQL statement "SELECT function_two()"
PL/pgSQL function function_one() line 5 at PERFORM
 function_one
--------------

(1 row)
```

Using the GET STACKED DIAGNOSTICS Statement

The GET STACKED DIAGNOSTICS statement is used to retrieve information about an exception that has been raised. This statement can be used to retrieve the error message, the SQLSTATE, and other information about the exception.

Again, the same example:

```
CREATE OR REPLACE FUNCTION update_employee_salary(
    IN employee_id INTEGER,
    IN new_salary text
) RETURNS BOOLEAN AS $$
DECLARE
    rowcount INTEGER;
    err_msg varchar;
BEGIN
        UPDATE employees
    SET salary = new_salary::numeric
    WHERE id = employee_id;

    GET DIAGNOSTICS rowcount = ROW_COUNT;
    RETURN rowcount;

EXCEPTION
    WHEN SQLSTATE '23502' THEN
        RAISE NOTICE 'customer error: not-null violation error';
        RETURN FALSE;
    WHEN OTHERS THEN
        GET STACKED DIAGNOSTICS err_msg = MESSAGE_TEXT;
        RAISE NOTICE 'Error: %', err_msg;
        RETURN FALSE;
END;                     .

$$ LANGUAGE plpgsql;
```

In this example, the GET STACKED DIAGNOSTICS statement is used to retrieve the error message associated with an exception that has been raised. The error message is stored in the variable err_msg and is printed to the console using the RAISE NOTICE statement.

Let's run the function:

```
postgres=# select update_employee_salary(1,'abc');
NOTICE:  Error: invalid input syntax for type numeric: "abc"
 update_employee_salary
------------------------
 f
(1 row)
```

As you can see, the exact error has been caught with GET STACKED DIAGNOSTICS using the MESSAGE_TEXT item. For all available items, you can go through the Trapping Errors (https://www.postgresql.org/docs/current/plpgsql-control-structures. html#PLPGSQL-ERRORTRAPPING) documentation.

The difference between GET DIAGNOSTICS and GET STACKED DIAGNOSTICS is that the latter retrieves information about the latest exception, while the former fetches information about the previous statement's execution status.

By using exception handling, users can define exception handlers that catch specific errors and perform appropriate actions. However, there are both advantages and disadvantages to using exceptions inside PL/pgSQL.

Advantages of Using Exceptions

1. **Improved Error Handling**: Exceptions provide a way to handle errors that occur during database operations, such as syntax errors, constraint violations, data type mismatches, and object not found errors. By handling these errors, users can write more robust and error-resistant database applications.

2. **Better Control Flow**: Exceptions provide a way to control the flow of execution in PL/pgSQL programs. By using exception handlers, users can define what actions to take when specific errors occur. This can lead to more efficient and effective error handling.

3. **Custom Error Messages**: By using the RAISE command, users can define their own custom exceptions and error messages. This can be useful when creating complex PL/pgSQL programs that require specific error messages.

4. **Simplified Code**: Exception handling can simplify code by allowing users to handle errors in a centralized location. This can make code easier to read and maintain.

Disadvantages of Using Exceptions

1. **Increased Complexity**: Exception handling can add complexity to PL/pgSQL programs. Users must define exception handlers for each potential error, which can make code more difficult to read and maintain.

2. **Performance Overhead**: Exception handling can have a performance overhead due to the additional processing required. Users must define exception handlers for each potential error, which can slow down the execution of PL/pgSQL programs.

3. **Potential for Overuse**: If users define too many exception handlers, it can lead to overuse of exceptions. This can make code more difficult to read and maintain and can also impact performance.

4. **Debugging Complexity**: Exception handling can make debugging more complex. When an exception is raised, it can be difficult to determine the root cause of the error.

Summary

In this chapter, we have discussed the types of exceptions in PostgreSQL, their syntax, and usage. We also covered some real-world examples where these exceptions are useful. We talked about the advantages and disadvantages of exceptions, which will help to use them carefully based on the requirements.

What's Next

In the next chapter, we will be covering some key features of triggers in PL/pgSQL like the following:

- **Trigger Types**: Explore advanced trigger scenarios, including BEFORE and AFTER triggers, row-level and statement-level triggers, and nested triggers.

- **Combining Triggers**: Learn techniques for combining multiple triggers on the same table to implement complex behaviors.

- **Trigger Performance**: Dive into trigger performance considerations and optimization techniques for efficient data manipulation.

- **Real-Time Data Manipulation**: Explore how to use triggers to maintain real-time data integrity and enforce complex business rules.

CHAPTER 15

Triggers

In the previous chapter, we talked about the different types of exceptions available in PL/pgSQL and how to handle them with some examples. In this chapter, we will cover triggers in PostgreSQL. It will start with the introduction of triggers and how to create them using PL/pgSQL code with a simple example. We will then talk about the types of triggers with some use cases and real-world examples of where and when to use these triggers using PL/pgSQL functions. We will also cover the advantages and disadvantages of triggers.

What Are Triggers?

In PostgreSQL, a trigger is a function that is automatically executed in response to a certain event or action performed on a table. It can be used to enforce business rules, modify data before it is inserted or updated, replicate data across different tables or databases, or even notify external systems of changes. In this chapter, we will discuss the types of triggers in PostgreSQL, their syntax and usage, as well as their advantages and disadvantages with real-world use cases.

Unlike most of the RDBMS databases, the PostgreSQL trigger itself cannot have the code (that should be performed on the trigger event) inside it. There will be a trigger function with the trigger. The trigger function is a PL/pgSQL function that is executed automatically when the trigger event occurs. The function can contain any valid SQL statements or PL/pgSQL code and can perform any necessary actions based on the data that caused the trigger event.

Syntax

You can use the CREATE TRIGGER command to create the trigger:

```
CREATE TRIGGER <name_of_the_trigger> { BEFORE/AFTER/INSTEAD OF } {event}
    ON <name_of_the_table>
    ( FOREACH { ROW/STATEMENT })
    [ WHEN ( with_condition ) ]
    EXECUTE ( FUNCTION/PROCEDURE } func_name ( arguments )
```

This is a basic syntax. For a detailed version of the syntax, you can go through the CREATE TRIGGER (https://www.postgresql.org/docs/current/sql-createtrigger.html) documentation.

The trigger's execution timing is determined by the BEFORE and AFTER keywords, indicating whether it should execute prior to or following the triggering event.

This event can be an INSERT, UPDATE, and DELETE on the table so that it will execute the trigger operation.

Using the ON keyword, you define the table on which the trigger will be executed. The FOREACH ROW clause specifies that the trigger will be executed for each individual row impacted by the triggering event.

The WHEN clause specifies a condition that must be met for the trigger to be executed. The EXECUTE FUNCTION clause specifies the name of the function that will be executed when the trigger is triggered.

Make sure that you're creating a trigger and trigger function that will meet your needs and serve your intended purpose. It can also help you to avoid mistakes or errors that might occur if you're not clear about what you're trying to accomplish.

When creating a trigger and trigger function, it can be helpful to consider the following questions:

- What is the purpose of the trigger and trigger function?

- What table or tables will the trigger and trigger function be associated with?

- What event or events should trigger the execution of the trigger function?

- What actions should the trigger function perform in response to the triggering event?

By answering these questions, you can create a trigger and the associated trigger function that will be effective and efficient in meeting your needs.

Simple Example

The best examples of triggers in PostgreSQL, or any database system, are referential integrity triggers. These triggers are implicit in the database system and take care of handling the relationship between child and parent tables created using primary and foreign keys. Consider the following example.

Create a table test and its child table test_child with PRIMARY KEY and FOREIGN KEY:

```
CREATE TABLE test(t INT PRIMARY KEY);

CREATE TABLE test_child(t INT REFERENCES test(t));
```

To view the internal referential integrity constraints, query the pg_trigger catalog table. These triggers are created and maintained by PostgreSQL internally:

```
postgres=# SELECT tgname FROM pg_trigger WHERE tgisinternal is TRUE AND
tgrelid::regclass = 'test_child'::regclass;
             tgname
---------------------------------
 RI_ConstraintTrigger_c_830125
 RI_ConstraintTrigger_c_830126
(2 rows)
```

In general, PostgreSQL creates two referential integrity triggers on the "referencing" table: one to perform validations before update/insert/delete and another trigger after performing the cascading actions.

Let's go through an example to understand the triggers better. Consider an example of creating a trigger function and a trigger on an employees table:

```
CREATE TABLE employees (
    eid SERIAL PRIMARY KEY,
    name VARCHAR(50) NOT NULL,
    salary NUMERIC(10, 2) NOT NULL,
    last_modified TIMESTAMP
);
```

The eid column is an auto-incrementing integer and serves as the primary key. The name column is a string that cannot be null, and the salary column is a numeric value with two decimal places that cannot be null. The last_modified column is a timestamp that will be updated automatically by the trigger.

Let's create a trigger function and a trigger on the table:

```
CREATE OR REPLACE FUNCTION func_update_last_modified()
RETURNS TRIGGER AS $$
BEGIN
    NEW.last_modified = current_timestamp;
    RETURN NEW;
END;
$$ LANGUAGE plpgsql;
```

The trigger function will automatically update the last_modified column of the table to the current timestamp whenever a row is updated. The trigger will execute the trigger function before an update operation on the table.

This will allow us to track changes to the employees table and ensure that the last_modified column is always up to date without having to manually update it every time a row is updated.

The terms NEW and OLD refer to the new and old values of a row impacted by an INSERT, UPDATE, or DELETE operation that triggered a trigger function.

When a trigger function is executed, the NEW variable contains the new values of the row that was impacted by the triggering operation, while the OLD variable contains the old values of the row, before the triggering operation was executed.

```
CREATE TRIGGER trig_update_last_modified
    BEFORE UPDATE
    ON employees
    FOREACH ROW
    EXECUTE FUNCTION func_update_last_modified();
```

The trigger trig_update_last_modified is created that is executed before an update operation on the employees table. The trigger is defined as a row-level trigger that executes the func_update_last_modified function for each row affected by the update operation.

Let's INSERT some data into the employees table:

```
INSERT INTO employees (name, salary) VALUES ('foo bar', 50000.00),
('bar foo', 75000.00);
```

Since we did not specify a value for the last_modified column, it will be null for each row.

You can test the trigger by updating a row and checking that the last_modified column has been automatically updated:

```
UPDATE employees SET salary = 60000.00 WHERE name = 'foo bar';
```

You should see that the last_modified column has been automatically updated with the current timestamp:

```
postgres=# SELECT * FROM employees where name='foo bar';
 id |  name   | salary  |       last_modified
----+---------+---------+---------------------------
  1 | foo bar | 60000.00 | 2023-07-14 22:19:27.135842
(1 row)
```

In this example, the purpose of the trigger is clear that will automatically update the last_modified column of a table whenever a row is updated. This will allow us to track changes to the table and ensure that the last_modified column is always up to date.

Types of Triggers in PostgreSQL

PostgreSQL supports three types of triggers:

- Row-level triggers
- Statement-level triggers
- Event triggers

In this section, we'll explain each type in detail, along with code examples.

Row-Level Triggers

For each row impacted by the triggering event, like an insert, update, or delete operation, a row-level trigger is executed. Row-level triggers can be used to enforce data constraints or replicate data across tables.

Creating Row-Level Triggers

The syntax for creating a row-level trigger in PostgreSQL is as follows:

```
CREATE TRIGGER <name_of_the_trigger>
    {BEFORE/AFTER}
    {INSERT/UPDATE/DELETE}
    ON <name_of_the_table>
    [FOREACH ROW]
    [WHEN (required_condition)]
    EXECUTE FUNCTION function_name();
```

Example 1: Enforce Data Constraint

Let's look at an example where we apply a discount to order value before it gets inserted into the table with all the orders. Consider a table called orders as follows:

```
CREATE TABLE orders (
    order_id SERIAL PRIMARY KEY,
    order_date DATE NOT NULL,
    order_value NUMERIC(10,2) NOT NULL,
    discount NUMERIC(10,2) NOT NULL DEFAULT 0
);
```

Next, let's insert some sample data into the orders table:

```
INSERT INTO orders (order_date, order_value, discount) VALUES
    ('2023-07-01', 100.00, 10.00),
    ('2023-07-02', 200.00, 20.00),
    ('2023-07-03', 300.00, 30.00);
```

Now, let's create a trigger function called update_order_value that will update the order_value column to reflect the discount whenever a row is inserted:

```
CREATE OR REPLACE FUNCTION update_order_value()
    RETURNS TRIGGER AS $$
BEGIN
    NEW.order_value = NEW.order_value - NEW.discount;
    RETURN NEW;
END;
$$ LANGUAGE plpgsql;
```

Finally, let's create a trigger called update_order_value_trigger that will execute the update_order_value function whenever the customers table gets inserted with a new row:

```
CREATE TRIGGER update_order_value_trigger
    BEFORE INSERT
    ON orders
    FOREACH ROW
    EXECUTE FUNCTION update_order_value();
```

Now, whenever the customers table gets inserted with a new row, the update_order_value function will automatically update the order_value column to reflect the discount.

For example, if we insert a new row with an order value of 150.00 and a discount of 15.00, the order_value column will be automatically updated to 135.00:

```
INSERT INTO orders (order_date, order_value, discount) VALUES
    ('2023-07-04', 150.00, 15.00);

SELECT * FROM orders ORDER BY order_date DESC limit 1;
 order_id | order_date | order_value | discount
----------+------------+-------------+----------
        7 | 2023-07-04 |      135.00 |    15.00
(1 row)
```

As you can see, order_value has been updated as 135.00 after the discount of 15.00.

Example 2: Creating Multiple Triggers on the Same Table

In PostgreSQL, we can create multiple triggers on a table. We are not limited to creating just one table and one trigger; we can create any number of triggers for events like BEFORE/AFTER. Consider the following example:

```
CREATE TABLE test(t INT);
```

```
CREATE OR REPLACE FUNCTION trig_func_a()
RETURNS TRIGGER AS $$
DECLARE
var varchar;
BEGIN
var:= 'executing trigger A';
RAISE NOTICE '%', var;
RETURN NEW;
END;
$$ LANGUAGE plpgsql;
```

```
CREATE OR REPLACE FUNCTION trig_func_b()
RETURNS TRIGGER AS $$
DECLARE
var varchar;
BEGIN
var:= 'executing trigger B';
RAISE NOTICE '%', var;
RETURN NEW;
END;
$$ LANGUAGE plpgsql;
```

```
CREATE TRIGGER a_trig
AFTER INSERT ON test
FOREACH ROW
EXECUTE FUNCTION trig_func_a();
```

```
CREATE TRIGGER b_trig
AFTER INSERT ON test
FOREACH ROW
EXECUTE FUNCTION trig_func_b();
```

```
postgres=# INSERT INTO test VALUES (0);
NOTICE: Trigger A
NOTICE: Trigger B
INSERT 0 1
```

In the preceding example, we created two triggers (a_trigger, b_trigger) on the test table for the same AFTER INSERT event. When we inserted data into the test table, the Trigger A function was invoked first, followed by Trigger B. If more than one trigger is defined for the same event on the same relation, the triggers will be fired in alphabetical order by trigger name. As PostgreSQL supports multiple pluggable languages like PL/V8, PL/TCL, and PL/Python, we can attach any of these functions as trigger invocation methods.

Example 3: Prevent Nested Invocations

Triggers are specific events that are fired whenever a certain event occurs. However, in some cases, these events can trigger recursive behavior, leading to unwanted consequences. To control the nested invocations of triggers in PostgreSQL, you can use the function pg_trigger_depth(), which returns the current trigger invocation depth. For instance, a trigger on a table called "test" may repeatedly retrigger itself, causing recursive behavior that can eventually lead to a procedural call stack overflow and transaction failure. Sometimes, we may want to limit the number of times a retrigger is executed to only three or four times. In such cases, we can control this behavior using the pg_trigger_depth() function to ensure that the limit is not exceeded. Consider the following example:

```
postgres=# CREATE TABLE test (
    id SERIAL PRIMARY KEY,
    name VARCHAR(50)
);

postgres=# CREATE OR REPLACE FUNCTION trigger_function()
RETURNS TRIGGER AS $$
 DECLARE
   nested_trigger_depth INTEGER;
 BEGIN
   nested_trigger_depth := pg_trigger_depth();
```

```
    -- Perform different actions based on the trigger depth
    CASE nested_trigger_depth
      WHEN 1 THEN
        RAISE NOTICE 'This is the outermost trigger';

      WHEN 2 THEN
        RAISE NOTICE 'This is the first nested trigger, and stop further
        nested calls';
        RETURN NEW;
      ELSE
        RAISE NOTICE 'This is a nested trigger at depth %',
        nested_trigger_depth;
    END CASE;

    INSERT INTO test(name) VALUES ('Test2');
    RETURN NEW;
  END;
$$ LANGUAGE plpgsql;

postgres=# CREATE TRIGGER test_trg
postgres-# AFTER INSERT ON test
postgres-# FOREACH ROW
postgres-# EXECUTE FUNCTION trigger_function();
CREATE TRIGGER

postgres=# INSERT INTO test (name) VALUES ('Test');
NOTICE:  This is the outermost trigger
NOTICE:  This is the first nested trigger, and stop further nested calls
INSERT 0 1
```

As you can see in the preceding example, we fixed the issue of nested trigger invocation exceeding the allowed level by using the pg_trigger_depth() function.

Example 4: Replicating Data Across Tables

Let's take another example where row-level triggers can be used to replicate the data of a table. Let's start by creating a simple example table and then create a trigger function and a row-level trigger to replicate data from the example table to a separate reporting table.

Consider a table called customers as follows:

```
CREATE TABLE customers (
    customer_id serial PRIMARY KEY,
    customer_name text,
    customer_email text,
    customer_phone text
);
```

Next, we will create a separate reporting table called customer_reports that we will use to replicate data from the customers table. The customer_reports table will have the same columns as the customers table, but with an additional "report_date" column to track when the data was replicated.

Create the customer_reports table:

```
CREATE TABLE customer_reports (
    report_id serial PRIMARY KEY,
    cust_id integer,
    cust_name text,
    cust_email text,
    cust_phone text,
    report_date timestamp DEFAULT now()
);
```

Now that we have our two tables, we can create a trigger function that will replicate data from the customers table to the customer_reports table. The trigger function will be called replicate_customer_data and will take one argument: the "NEW" row that triggered the trigger.

Create the replicate_customer_data trigger function:

```
CREATE FUNCTION replicate_customer_data()
    RETURNS TRIGGER AS $$
BEGIN
    INSERT INTO customer_reports (cust_id, cust_name, cust_email, cust_phone)
    VALUES (NEW.customer_id, NEW.customer_name, NEW.customer_email,
    NEW.customer_phone);
    RETURN NEW;
END;
$$ LANGUAGE plpgsql;
```

As you can see, the trigger function simply inserts the new row from the customers table into the customer_reports table, using the "NEW" keyword to reference the row that triggered the trigger.

Now, we can create the row-level trigger that will call the replicate_customer_data function whenever the customers table gets inserted with a new row. The row-level trigger will be called insert_customer_report and will be executed "AFTER INSERT" on the customers table.

Create the insert_customer_report row-level trigger:

```
CREATE TRIGGER insert_customer_report
    AFTER INSERT
    ON customers
    FOREACH ROW
    EXECUTE FUNCTION replicate_customer_data();
```

Now, whenever the customers table gets inserted with a new row, the insert_customer_report row-level trigger will be called, which in turn will call the replicate_customer_data trigger function to insert the new row into the customer_reports table.

```
INSERT INTO customers VALUES (1, 'foo', 'foo.bar@example.com',
'111-111-1111');

postgres=# SELECT * FROM customer_reports;
-[ RECORD 1 ]--+---------------------------
report_id      | 1
cust_id        | 1
cust_name      | foo
cust_email     | foo.bar@example.com
cust_phone     | 111-111-1111
report_date    | 2023-07-14 23:12:52.700729
```

As you can see, the data inserted in the customers table is replicated to the customer_reports table.

INSTEAD OF Triggers

An INSTEAD OF trigger in PostgreSQL allows for the execution of a different action than the default action when a specific event occurs. This type of trigger is commonly used for views, which cannot be updated in the same way as tables. Instead, the trigger can execute a stored procedure that performs the update in a different way. INSTEAD OF triggers are useful when dealing with complex views that require more than one table to be updated. The trigger can execute a stored procedure that updates the necessary tables in the correct order. Additionally, this type of trigger can be used to enforce business rules and data constraints when inserting or updating data in a view. Consider the following example:

```
postgres=# CREATE TABLE employee (
  id SERIAL PRIMARY KEY,
  name VARCHAR(50),
  age INTEGER,
  department VARCHAR(100)
);
CREATE TABLE

postgres=# INSERT INTO employee (name, age, department) VALUES
('John', 30, 'HR');
INSERT 0 1

postgres=# INSERT INTO employee (name, age, department) VALUES
('Jane', 28, 'IT');
INSERT 0 1
```

Create a view on the preceding table as follows:

```
CREATE VIEW employee_viewAS
SELECT *
FROM employee
WHERE age >= 30;
CREATE VIEW
```

Create a trigger function, which gets executed on the VIEW:

```
CREATE OR REPLACE FUNCTION instead_of_insert_trigger()
RETURNS TRIGGER AS $$
BEGIN
    -- Perform custom logic instead of the default INSERT operation
RAISE NOTICE 'Custom INSERT logic executed';
RETURN NULL; -- Do not perform the default INSERT operation
END;
$$ LANGUAGE plpgsql;
```

Create an INSTEAD OF trigger on the preceding view, which we created:

```
CREATE TRIGGER insert_trigger
INSTEAD OF INSERT ON employee_view
FOREACH ROW
EXECUTE FUNCTION instead_of_insert_trigger();
```

Try to insert data into the view.

```
postgres=# INSERT INTO employee_view (name, age, department) VALUES
('Alice', 32, 'Sales');
NOTICE:  Custom INSERT logic executed
INSERT 0 0
```

As you can see, we were able to perform DML operations on views with the help of INSTEAD OF triggers.

Statement-Level Triggers

Regardless of the number of rows affected, a statement-level trigger executes only once for each triggering event. Statement-level triggers can be used to log changes to a table or database.

Creating Statement-Level Triggers

The syntax is similar to that of a row-level trigger, except that the FOREACH ROW clause is omitted:

```
CREATE TRIGGER <name_of_the_trigger>
    (BEFORE/AFTER)
    (INSERT/UPDATE/DELETE)
    ON <name_of_the_table>
    (WHEN <your_condition> )
    EXECUTE FUNCTION function_name();
```

Example: Logging Changes to a Table

Let's consider a table that holds customer orders, and you want to log all INSERT,
UPDATE, and DELETE statements executed on the table. You can create a statement-level
trigger to log the statements to a separate table.

Create the orders table as follows:

```
CREATE TABLE orders (
    id SERIAL PRIMARY KEY,
    order_date DATE NOT NULL,
    order_value NUMERIC(10,2) NOT NULL
);
```

Create another table order_log to store the log data:

```
CREATE TABLE order_log (
    id SERIAL PRIMARY KEY,
    operation TEXT,
    t_time TIMESTAMP,
    order_id INTEGER
);
```

The id column is for the log entry, the operation is the operation that triggered the
log entry (insert, update, or delete), the timestamp is the log entry time, and the order_
id is the order that was affected.

Create a trigger function to log the changes:

```
CREATE OR REPLACE FUNCTION log_order_changes()
    RETURNS TRIGGER AS $$
BEGIN
    IF TG_OP = 'INSERT' THEN
        INSERT INTO order_log (operation, t_time, order_id)
```

255

```
        VALUES ('INSERT', NOW(), NEW.id);
    ELSIF TG_OP = 'UPDATE' THEN
        INSERT INTO order_log (operation, t_time, order_id)
        VALUES ('UPDATE', NOW(), NEW.id);
    ELSIF TG_OP = 'DELETE' THEN
        INSERT INTO order_log (operation, t_time, order_id)
        VALUES ('DELETE', NOW(), OLD.id);
    END IF;
    RETURN NULL;
END;
$$ LANGUAGE plpgsql;
```

This trigger function will be executed whenever an insert, update, or delete operation is performed on the table. It will check the type of operation that triggered the function (TG_OP) and then insert a new log entry into the order_log table with the appropriate operation type, timestamp, and order ID.

TG_OP is a system variable that is available in trigger functions. It contains the operation that triggered the trigger function, such as INSERT, UPDATE, or DELETE.

The TG_OP variable can be used to perform different actions based on the type of operation that triggered the trigger function.

Create the trigger to execute the trigger function:

```
CREATE TRIGGER order_log_trigger
    AFTER INSERT OR UPDATE OR DELETE
    ON orders
    FOREACH STATEMENT
    EXECUTE FUNCTION log_order_changes();
```

This trigger will execute the log_order_changes function after each DML operation on the orders table. It executes the function for each affected row individually.

Now, whenever a DML operation is performed on the orders table, a log entry will be inserted in the order_log table with the operation type, timestamp, and order ID. This can be useful for tracking changes to the table and auditing user activity.

Let's try inserting a row in the orders table and check the rows in the order_ log table:

```
INSERT INTO orders (id,order_date, order_value) VALUES (100,now(),
'150.00');
```

```
postgres=# SELECT * FROM order_log;
 id | operation |          timestamp          | order_id
----+-----------+-----------------------------+----------
  2 | INSERT    | 2023-07-14 23:31:42.729388 |      100
(1 row)
```

As you can see, the data inserted in the orders table is updated to the order_log table.

There are a few other trigger arguments like TG_OP:

- TG_OP: A string indicating the operation for which the trigger was fired. The trigger operation can be INSERT, UPDATE, DELETE, or TRUNCATE, based on how the trigger is defined. This variable helps you determine the type of action that triggered the trigger.

- TG_NAME: This refers to a variable holding the name of the trigger that was executed. It allows you to identify which specific trigger function is currently executing, useful when multiple triggers are defined on the same table.

- TG_WHEN: A string representing the timing of the trigger's execution, which can be one of BEFORE, AFTER, or INSTEAD OF. The timing specifies whether the trigger action occurs before the operation, after the operation, or instead of the operation itself.

- TG_LEVEL: A string denoting the execution level of the trigger, which can take two values: ROW or STATEMENT. When defined as a row-level trigger, it executes for each affected row individually. In contrast, as a statement-level trigger, it executes once for the entire statement.

- TG_TABLE_NAME: The table name assists in identifying the specific table where the triggering event took place.

- TG_RELNAME: Similar to TG_TABLE_NAME, it also provides the name of the table that caused the trigger invocation.

- TG_RELID: This object or table ID is useful if you need to perform dynamic queries or operations on the triggering table.

- TG_TABLE_SCHEMA: This variable provides the name of the schema for the table involved in the trigger event.

- TG_NARGS: It represents the count of arguments provided to the underlying procedure of the trigger when creating the trigger using the CREATE TRIGGER statement. This can be useful for dynamic trigger functions that require different sets of arguments.

- TG_ARGV[]: An array containing the arguments passed to the underlying procedure of the trigger during the creation of the trigger. The elements in this array can be accessed using an index, such as TG_ARGV[0], TG_ARGV[1], and so on.

Event Triggers

An event trigger is a special type of trigger that is not associated with a specific table. Instead, it is executed in response to specific user object events, such as table create/drop/alter.

Creating Event Triggers

The following is the syntax:

```
CREATE EVENT TRIGGER <name_of_the_trigger>
    ON event
    [WHEN <required_condition>]
    EXECUTE FUNCTION <name_of_the_function>();
```

Example: Log DDL Changes

Let's take an example where you want to log all DDL (Data Definition Language) statements executed on a PostgreSQL database. You can use an event trigger to capture all DDL events and log them to a separate table.

Create a table called ddl_log to store the log data:

```
CREATE TABLE ddl_log (
    event_type text,
    event_time timestamp,
    object_name text,
    statement text
);
```

This table records the type of event that occurred, the timestamp of the event, the schema and name of the object that was affected by the event, and the DDL statement that was executed.

Create a function to log the DDL events:

```
CREATE OR REPLACE FUNCTION log_ddl_event()
    RETURNS event_trigger AS $$
DECLARE
rec RECORD;
BEGIN

    rec := pg_event_trigger_ddl_commands();
        INSERT INTO ddl_log (event_type, event_time, object_name,
        statement)
        VALUES (tg_tag, current_timestamp, rec.object_identity, current_
        query());

END;
$$ LANGUAGE plpgsql;
```

Whenever a DDL event occurs on the database, the log_ddl_event function will be executed, and a new log entry will be inserted into the ddl_log table with the type of event that occurred, the timestamp of the event, the schema and name of the object that was affected by the event, and the DDL statement that was executed.

Create the event trigger to execute the function:

```
CREATE EVENT TRIGGER ddl_event_trigger ON ddl_command_end
EXECUTE PROCEDURE log_ddl_event();
```

This event trigger will execute the log_ddl_event function whenever a DDL event occurs on the database. The ON ddl_command_end clause specifies that the trigger should be executed after the DDL statement has been executed.

Now, whenever a DDL statement is executed on the database, a log entry will be created in the ddl_log table with the type of event that occurred, the timestamp of the event, the schema and name of the object that was affected by the event, and the DDL statement that was executed.

Let's try executing an ALTER on any table in the database and check the rows of the ddl_log table:

```
postgres=# ALTER TABLE employees ALTER COLUMN name TYPE TEXT;
ALTER TABLE
postgres=# SELECT * FROM ddl_log ;
-[ RECORD 1 ]----------------------------------------------------
event_type  | ALTER TABLE
event_time  | 2023-07-14 23:52:00.647656
object_name | public.employees
statement   | ALTER TABLE employees ALTER COLUMN name TYPE TEXT;
```

As you can see, ALTER details are updated in the ddl_log table.

Advantages of Triggers

Row-level triggers

- Row-level triggers allow for fine-grained control over data constraints and replication.

- They can be used to enforce complex business rules that cannot be enforced with constraints or indexes alone.

- They provide a simple way to maintain consistency across distributed systems.

Statement-level triggers

- Statement-level triggers provide a simple way to log changes to a table or database.

- They can be used to enforce database-wide constraints or replicate data across databases.

Event triggers

- Event triggers provide a simple way to respond to user object events, such as table creation, alter, or drop.

- They can be used to automate administrative tasks, such as creating table backups or performing maintenance tasks.

Disadvantages of Triggers

- Triggers cause some performance overhead. Make sure you measure the performance overhead before you implement a trigger on any table.

- Triggers can be complex and difficult to debug, especially when they involve complex logic or interactions with other triggers or functions.

- They can cause performance issues if they are poorly written or executed frequently, leading to slower query execution times or even database crashes.

- They can be disabled or circumvented, either intentionally or unintentionally, leading to data inconsistencies or security vulnerabilities.

DROP Triggers

You can drop row- and statement-level triggers using the DROP TRIGGER command. The following is the syntax:

```
DROP TRIGGER <trigger_name> ON <table_name>;
```

For more options, you can go through the DROP TRIGGER documentation.
You can drop the triggers created in one of the examples as follows:

```
DROP TRIGGER insert_customer_report ON customers;
```

However, to drop event triggers, you need to use the DROP EVENT TRIGGER command as follows:

```
DROP EVENT TRIGGER ddl_event_trigger;
```

Summary

In this chapter, we have discussed the types of triggers in PostgreSQL, their syntax and usage, as well as their advantages and disadvantages with real-world use cases. While triggers can be used for enforcing data constraints, replicating data, or logging changes, they should be used with caution, especially when dealing with complex logic or large datasets. Otherwise, the triggers will severely affect the database performance.

What's Next

In the next chapter, we will be covering some key features of transaction management in PL/pgSQL like the following:

- **Advanced Transaction Scenarios**: Explore more complex transaction management scenarios, including nested transactions and savepoints.

- **Exception Handling and Rollback**: Learn how to handle exceptions within transactions and perform controlled rollbacks when needed.

CHAPTER 16

Transaction Management

In the previous chapter, we talked about triggers in PostgreSQL and how to build trigger functions in PL/pgSQLPL/pgSQLreturn values/parameters. We covered different types of triggers with examples and use cases when to use each type of trigger. We explained advantages and disadvantages of triggers. In this chapter, we will cover transaction management in PL/pgSQL and how to write proper transactional code. By the end of this chapter, you will have a better understanding of how transactions work inside PL/pgSQL blocks and how to write transactional statements inside PL/pgSQL blocks that have exception handling.

Nested Transactions

PL/pgSQL allows us to run transactional control statements inside BEGIN/END blocks. However, the behavior of these transactions has its own internal implementation that is not exposed externally. Consider the following example:

```
postgres=# CREATE TABLE test(
    transaction_ids bigint
);
CREATE TABLE

postgres=# DO
$$
DECLARE
    v_cnt integer:=3;
BEGIN
    FOR i IN 1..v_cnt LOOP
      INSERT INTO test (transaction_ids) VALUES (txid_current());
```

© Baji Shaik and Dinesh Kumar Chemuduru 2023
B. Shaik and D. K. Chemuduru, *Procedural Programming with PostgreSQL PL/pgSQL*,
https://doi.org/10.1007/978-1-4842-9840-4_16

```
    END LOOP;
COMMIT;
END;
$$;
DO

postgres=# TABLE test;
 transaction_ids
-----------------
             756
             756
             756
(3 rows)
```

In the preceding example, we created a table called "test" to store the current transaction ID number. To retrieve the current transaction ID, we used PostgreSQL's "txid_current()" function, which returns the transaction in which the statements are being executed. From the preceding output, we can see that the INSERT statement was executed in a LOOP three times and recorded the same transaction ID 756 because the entire anonymous block was executed in a single transaction.

Now, change the anonymous code block to use COMMIT after each INSERT operation as follows, and see the table results:

```
postgres=# TRUNCATE test;
TRUNCATE TABLE

postgres=# DO
$$
DECLARE
    v_cnt integer:=3;
BEGIN
    FOR i IN 1..v_cnt LOOP
        INSERT INTO test (transaction_ids) VALUES (txid_current());
        COMMIT;
    END LOOP;
END;
$$;
DO
```

```
postgres=# TABLE test;
 transaction_ids
-----------------
             758
             759
             760
(3 rows)
```

In the preceding example, a different transaction ID was generated after each INSERT operation that was committed. This means that using COMMIT inside PL/pgSQL blocks will close the current transaction and create a new transaction. This makes sense as we have multiple COMMIT statements in a loop, which opens new transactions for each INSERT statement.

Now, let's run the same example inside a transaction and see the result:

```
postgres=# BEGIN WORK;
BEGIN

postgres=*# DO
 $$
DECLARE
     v_cnt integer:=3;
 BEGIN
     FOR i IN 1..v_cnt LOOP
     INSERT INTO test (transaction_ids) VALUES (txid_current());
     COMMIT;
     END LOOP;
 END;
 $$;

ERROR:  invalid transaction termination
CONTEXT:  PL/pgSQL function inline_code_block line 7 at COMMIT
postgres=!#
```

As demonstrated in the preceding example, an error occurred when dealing with nested transactions. To be specific, an explicit transaction was initiated using BEGIN WORK, and COMMIT was executed within that explicit transaction, which is not supported. Another potential circumstance that could result in the same error is when calling multiple procedures that are not written in PL/pgSQL.

Exception Handling

Exception handling is an essential part of transaction behavior. It allows us to handle errors that occur during the execution of a transaction. In PL/pgSQL, we can use the EXCEPTION block to catch and handle errors. This block is executed when an error occurs and provides the opportunity to perform certain actions, such as logging the error or rolling back the transaction. By using exception handling, we can ensure that our transactions are executed in a reliable, consistent, and safe manner. We discussed more about this in Chapter 14.

Now, let's discuss how transaction handling would work in the case of an exception being thrown:

```
postgres=# CREATE OR REPLACE PROCEDURE public.recon_order_payment()
LANGUAGE plpgsql
AS $procedure$
DECLARE
      v_rec RECORD;
BEGIN
      PERFORM 1/1;
      COMMIT;
      RAISE NOTICE 'before commit: %', txid_current();
      EXCEPTION
                WHEN OTHERS THEN
                RAISE NOTICE 'Got error : %', SQLERRM;
END;
$procedure$;

CREATE PROCEDURE
```

```
postgres=# CALL recon_order_payment();
NOTICE:  Got error : cannot commit while a subtransaction is active
CALL
```

In the previous code, there may be no obvious errors, but when attempting to execute the procedure, the following exception occurs: "cannot commit while a subtransaction is active." As a result, the execution of the CALL statement fails. Now, try to execute the same procedure without any EXCEPTION block and see the output:

```
postgres=# CREATE OR REPLACE PROCEDURE public.recon_order_payment()
LANGUAGE plpgsql
AS $procedure$
DECLARE
      v_rec RECORD;
BEGIN
      PERFORM 1/1;
      COMMIT;
      RAISE NOTICE 'before commit: %', txid_current();
END;
$procedure$;
CREATE PROCEDURE

postgres=# CALL recon_order_payment();
NOTICE:  before commit: 772
CALL
```

If we remove the EXCEPTION block from the previous PL/pgSQL procedure, the CALL statement can be executed successfully. This indicates that the presence of the EXCEPTION block, when there is a COMMIT statement, causes the "cannot commit while a subtransaction is active" error. To confirm this behavior, execute the preceding PL/pgSQL code with an EXCEPTION block but without a COMMIT statement, and observe the output:

```
postgres=# CREATE OR REPLACE PROCEDURE public.recon_order_payment()
LANGUAGE plpgsql
AS $procedure$
DECLARE
      v_rec RECORD;
```

```
BEGIN
      PERFORM 1/1;
      RAISE NOTICE 'before commit: %', txid_current();
      EXCEPTION
                WHEN OTHERS THEN
                RAISE NOTICE 'Got error : %', SQLERRM;
END;
$procedure$;

CREATE PROCEDURE

postgres=# CALL recon_order_payment();
NOTICE:   before commit: 774
CALL
```

The preceding output confirms that COMMIT and EXCEPTION blocks should not be in a single BEGIN END block in that order. The reason for this behavior is the way transactions are handled inside the PL/pgSQL blocks. Each BEGIN END block creates an implicit subtransaction with the help of SAVEPOINT. Consider the following sample PL/pgSQL template:

```
BEGIN
 --- Statements
<<COMMIT/ROLLBACK>>
EXCEPTION WHEN others THEN
  --- Handle exception
END
```

The preceding code implicitly gets converted into multiple subtransaction calls as follows:

```
BEGIN
  SAVEPOINT one;
  --- Statements
<<COMMIT/ROLLBACK>>
  RELEASE SAVEPOINT one;
```

```
EXCEPTION WHEN others THEN
  ROLLBACK TO SAVEPOINT one;
  --- Handle exception
END
```

In the preceding example, if an exception occurs while the savepoint is active, we either commit or roll back the transaction. This makes the ROLLBACK TO SAVEPOINT one command useless in case of an exception since we had already executed the COMMIT command in the previous step. This breaks the basic transaction principle where the transaction must be rolled back during an exception. This is the only reason PL/pgSQL blocks don't allow us to put the COMMIT/ROLLBACK prior to the EXCEPTION blocks.

Now, if we put COMMIT/ROLLBACK as the last executable statement of the procedure, it would work since it doesn't break the behavior. To demonstrate this, let us change the preceding PL/pgSQL code to issue COMMIT after the EXCEPTION block:

```
postgres=# CREATE OR REPLACE PROCEDURE public.recon_order_payment()
 LANGUAGE plpgsql
 AS $procedure$
 DECLARE
     v_rec RECORD;
 BEGIN
     PERFORM 1/1;
     RAISE NOTICE 'before commit: %', txid_current();
     EXCEPTION
             WHEN OTHERS THEN
             RAISE NOTICE 'Got error : %', SQLERRM;
     COMMIT;
 END;
 $procedure$;

CREATE PROCEDURE

postgres=# CALL  public.recon_order_payment();
NOTICE:  before commit: 777
CALL
```

Based on the preceding output, it is evident that if we use COMMIT/ROLLBACK as the last executable statement in the procedure, it will not throw any exceptions.

Summary

This chapter covered the behavior of transactions and exception handling in PL/pgSQL. It emphasizes the importance of understanding the implications of using `COMMIT` within PL/pgSQL blocks and how it affects transaction behavior. When COMMIT is used inside PL/pgSQL blocks, it closes the current transaction and creates a new transaction. This feature is useful for ensuring that transactions are executed in a reliable, consistent, and safe manner.

We also discuss the importance of exception handling in transaction behavior. It explains how the EXCEPTION block can be used to catch and handle errors that occur during the execution of a transaction. The documentation provides a detailed example of how exception handling can be used to ensure that transactions are executed in a reliable, consistent, and safe manner.

Finally, we highlighted the importance of ensuring that `COMMIT/ROLLBACK` is the last executable statement in the procedure to avoid the error "cannot commit while a subtransaction is active." By doing so, it ensures that the basic transaction principle is followed, where the transaction must be rolled back during an exception.

What's Next

In the next chapter, we will be covering some key features of aggregates in PL/pgSQL like the following:

- **Custom Aggregate Functions**: Learn how to create your own custom aggregate functions to perform complex calculations on data.

- **Parallel Aggregation**: Explore techniques for parallelizing aggregate computations to improve performance on large datasets.

- **State Transition Aggregates**: Discover how to create aggregates that maintain state across rows to perform advanced analytics.

CHAPTER 17

Aggregates

In the previous chapter, we discussed transaction management and how transactions work within an implicit or explicit transaction. This chapter covers the concepts of writing aggregates in PostgreSQL and demonstrates how to write a custom aggregate. We also discuss the core elements of an aggregate, such as the state transition function and final function.

Custom Aggregate

PL/pgSQL offers a wide range of developer-friendly features and capabilities to users. One of these features is the ability to create custom aggregates, which can perform specialized calculations on data. Custom aggregates can be created using the CREATE AGGREGATE statement, and they can incorporate user-defined functions to perform complex calculations.

Using custom aggregates can provide greater flexibility and control over the calculations performed on datasets in PostgreSQL. In contrast to standard aggregates like SUM, AVG, MAX, MIN, and COUNT, custom aggregates can be tailored to specific use cases and datasets. This can be particularly useful in scenarios where standard aggregates do not provide the necessary functionality or accuracy.

Custom aggregates can also be used in conjunction with the GROUP BY clause to perform calculations on subsets of data. Before creating custom aggregates, it is necessary to first create a set of functions that can help calculate the aggregated results over a group of selected rows. These functions are a part of the custom aggregate definition and are invoked implicitly whenever an aggregate function is called on the dataset.

© Baji Shaik and Dinesh Kumar Chemuduru 2023
B. Shaik and D. K. Chemuduru, *Procedural Programming with PostgreSQL PL/pgSQL*,
https://doi.org/10.1007/978-1-4842-9840-4_17

Simple Example

PostgreSQL supports several default data aggregate functions, including SUM, MAX, MIN, and AVG, which can be used with multiple data types. By utilizing these built-in aggregate functions, we can perform the aforementioned operations on several datasets. Consider the following example:

```
postgres=# CREATE TABLE test(t INT);
CREATE TABLE
postgres=# INSERT INTO test VALUES(generate_series(1, 10));
INSERT 0 10
postgres=# SELECT AVG(t) FROM test;
        avg
--------------------
 5.5000000000000000
(1 row)
```

The preceding example is quite simple. We created a table named "test," inserted ten records into it, and calculated the average of these ten values by computing the sum of all the values and dividing it by the number of values. Let's consider a moderately complex problem where we need to calculate the average rating of a product by including all possible rating elements, such as 1, 2, 3, 4, and 5. Now, let's go and create the data model for the product's rating and insert some random rating values as follows:

```
postgres=# CREATE TABLE products_rating(id INT, rating INT, CHECK (rating
BETWEEN 1 AND 5) );
CREATE TABLE

postgres=# INSERT INTO products_rating SELECT 1, floor(1 + (random() * (5 -
1 + 1)))::int FROM generate_series(1, 100);
INSERT 0 100

postgres=# SELECT * FROM products_rating LIMIT 5;
id | rating
----+--------
1 |      4
1 |      1
```

```
1 |      5
1 |      2
1 |      3
(5 rows)
```

As you can see in the preceding output, we have inserted 100 randomly generated product rating values into the table "products_rating". The next step is to display the number of ratings that we received for each value (1 through 5) for the product with an ID of 1. To do this, we can run the following query, which uses the COUNT and FILTER statements to convert the single "rating" column into five separate columns:

```
postgres=# SELECT COUNT( * ) FILTER (WHERE rating = 1) AS rating_1,
       COUNT( * ) FILTER (WHERE rating = 2) AS rating_2,
       COUNT( * ) FILTER (WHERE rating = 3) AS rating_3,
       COUNT( * ) FILTER (WHERE rating = 4) AS rating_4,
       COUNT( * ) FILTER (WHERE rating = 5) AS rating_5
FROM products_rating WHERE id = 1;
rating_1 | rating_2 | rating_3 | rating_4 | rating_5
---------+----------+----------+----------+---------
      16 |       21 |       26 |       17 |       20
(1 row)
```

As you can see in the preceding example, the SQL query for fetching product IDs and their corresponding rating values is readable and perfectly fine. However, we can simplify this query even further by using the concept of custom aggregates to abstract all of its COUNT() and FILTER functionality. Before implementing custom aggregates, it is important to discuss the concepts of state transition function and final function.

State Transition Function

The state transition function is a key concept in custom aggregates. It defines how the aggregate state is updated for each row in the group. This function is responsible for updating the aggregate state as new rows are added to the group. The final state of the aggregate is returned when the last row of the group has been processed.

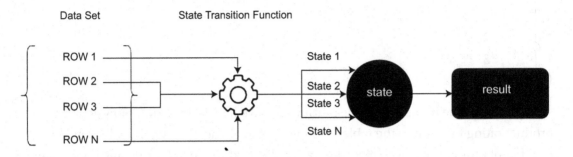

Consider the preceding pictorial representation, where we have a dataset with several rows. We also have a state transition function that gets executed for each row in the dataset and maintains its current state. This current state is reevaluated for each row as the state transition function processes them. Finally, when there are no more rows to process, the state transition function returns the final state as a result to the calling environment. Consider the following example, which demonstrates the default behavior of the max aggregate function:

```
postgres=# CREATE TABLE test(t INT);
CREATE TABLE
postgres=# INSERT INTO test VALUES (10), (15), (25), (55);
INSERT 0 4
postgres=# SELECT MAX(t) FROM test;
 max
-----
  55
(1 row)
```

In the preceding example, we created four records and used the max function to find the maximum among them. To accomplish this, there is a state transition function that executes for each row and stores the current state value. The sample pseudocode for this would look like the following:

```
initial_value = 0;
state = initial_value;

function state_trans_func_max(value):
        if (row.value > state)
                      state = row.value
      return state
```

```
# rows are (10, 15, 25, 55)
for row in rows:
        state_trans_func_max(row);

# Find maximum number
print(state);
```

In the preceding pseudocode, we created a transition function called state_trans_ func_max. This function is called for all rows and updates the current state value for each row. Now, let's represent the preceding example in the following diagram:

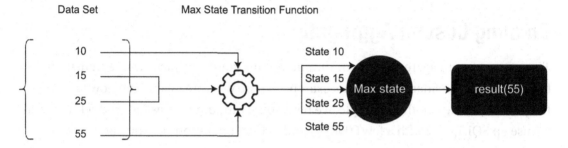

Final Function

The final function is another key concept in custom aggregates. It defines how the final value of the aggregate is calculated once all rows in the group have been processed. This function takes the final state of the aggregate as an argument and returns the final value of the aggregate. The final function is specified as part of the CREATE AGGREGATE statement, and it can be any user-defined function that takes the final state value as an argument and returns a value. By combining the state transition function and the final function, we can create powerful custom aggregates that can perform complex calculations on datasets. Consider the following simple AVG() aggregate as an example:

```
postgres=# CREATE TABLE test(t INT);
CREATE TABLE
postgres=# INSERT INTO test VALUES(generate_series(1, 10));
INSERT 0 10
postgres=# SELECT AVG(t) FROM test;
        avg
--------------------
 5.5000000000000000
(1 row)
```

In the preceding example, we used AVG() as an aggregate function, which implicitly performs the following two actions:

1. **State Transition Function**: To perform the sum of all values

2. **Final Function**: Result from the preceding state transition function and the total number of elements

Not all aggregate functions require a final function, but functions like avg and variance do require this final function. The final function performs the final calculation on the result obtained from the state transition function.

Creating Custom Aggregate

To create a custom aggregate, the minimum requirement is to have a state transition function. Let's consider the previous example where we were discussing how to display the product ratings. In this example, we have some random ratings for product ID 1, and we use an SQL query with a few COUNT() and FILTER operations on the data:

```
postgres=# SELECT COUNT( * ) FILTER (WHERE rating = 1) AS rating_1,
        COUNT( * ) FILTER (WHERE rating = 2) AS rating_2,
        COUNT( * ) FILTER (WHERE rating = 3) AS rating_3,
        COUNT( * ) FILTER (WHERE rating = 4) AS rating_4,
        COUNT( * ) FILTER (WHERE rating = 5) AS rating_5
FROM products_rating WHERE id = 1;
 rating_1 | rating_2 | rating_3 | rating_4 | rating_5
----------+----------+----------+----------+---------
 16       |       21 |       26 |       17 |       20
(1 row)
```

Now, let's abstract away all these internal details and write a simple SQL query as follows which gives the same result:

```
postgres=# SELECT (custom_rating_agg(p.*)).* FROM products_rating p
where id = 1;
 rating_1 | rating_2 | rating_3 | rating_4 | rating_5
----------+----------+----------+----------+---------
 16       |       21 |       26 |       17 |       20
(1 row)
```

The preceding query is much simpler than the previous COUNT() and FILTER() functions. To achieve this behavior, we need to start by creating the state transition function. When designing the state transition function, we must keep in mind that its return type should match the expected result of the SQL statement.

Create Type

Create a data type that holds the state of each row, as well as the return value of the state transition function:

```
postgres=# CREATE TYPE rating AS(
        rating_1 int,
        rating_2 int,
        rating_3 int,
        rating_4 int,
        rating_5 int
);
CREATE TYPE
```

Let's create a rating custom type as before, as it is matching the SQL result set.

Create State Transition Function

Create the state transition function which would be having two parameters as arguments: one is of the type rating, and the other one is of the type products_rating.

```
postgres=# CREATE OR REPLACE FUNCTION rating_agg_transfn(rollingState
rating, rollingValue products_rating)
RETURNS rating LANGUAGE plpgsql AS $$
 BEGIN
        IF rollingValue.rating =1 THEN
        rollingState.rating_1 := rollingState.rating_1 + 1;
        ELSIF rollingValue.rating =2 THEN
                rollingState.rating_2 := rollingState.rating_2 + 1;
        ELSIF rollingValue.rating =3 THEN
                rollingState.rating_3 := rollingState.rating_3 + 1;
        ELSIF rollingValue.rating =4 THEN
                rollingState.rating_4 := rollingState.rating_4 + 1;
```

```
        ELSIF rollingValue.rating =5 THEN
                rollingState.rating_5 := rollingState.rating_5 + 1;
        END IF;
        RETURN rollingState;
  END;
$$;
CREATE FUNCTION
```

The preceding function is used as part of a custom aggregation process. It accumulates and aggregates product ratings based on their values (which are assumed to be integers between 1 and 5). This function accepts two parameters:

1. **rollingState**: This is the state of the aggregation that's being updated as each product rating is processed. It's of the type `rating`.

2. **rollingValue**: This parameter represents the current product's rating that needs to be aggregated. It's of the type relation `products_rating`. This is the parameter which holds all the rows which we process on the table products_rating.

Inside the function, we put the **IF** statement to check the value of the rating given by **rollingValue**. Depending on the value, it increments the appropriate count in the **rollingState** state variable. Finally, the updated `rollingState` is returned as the result of the function, which will be used as the accumulating value for the aggregation process.

Create Aggregate

To create a custom aggregate, we first need a state transition function, which we have already created. Now, let's use the CREATE AGGREGATE to create the custom aggregate and specify the state transition function as follows:

```
postgres=# CREATE AGGREGATE custom_rating_agg(products_rating) (
    SFUNC = rating_agg_transfn,
    STYPE = rating,
    INITCOND = '(0,0,0,0,0)'
);
CREATE AGGREGATE
```

In the preceding CREATE AGGREGATE definition, the input value's parameter type is specified as products_rating. That is, we use this aggregate on the products_table. The SFUNC (state transition function) is specified as rating_agg_transfn, and the STYPE (state type) is specified as rating. Also, we specified the initial state value of all these rating members as 0.

Now, let's execute this aggregate on the products_table and see the results:

```
postgres=# SELECT custom_rating_agg(p.*) FROM products_rating p
where id = 1;
 custom_rating_agg
-------------------
 (16,21,26,17,20)
(1 row)
```

The preceding query result matches the SQL query that uses COUNT() and FILTER() aggregates. However, the result is displayed in a single row. If we need the result to be displayed in a multicolumn format, we need to rewrite the SQL query as follows:

```
postgres=#  SELECT (custom_rating_agg(p.*)).* FROM products_rating p;
rating_1 | rating_2 | rating_3 | rating_4 | rating_5
---------+----------+----------+----------+---------
16       |       21 |       26 |       17 |       20
(1 row)
```

Final Function

In the previous examples, we displayed individual ratings, and it would be nice if we also show the overall rating by considering the state transition function output. Now, let's write a final function which takes a state transition function input as an argument and returns all the ratings, including the final rating value:

```
postgres=# CREATE TYPE all_rating AS(
        rating_1 int,
        rating_2 int,
        rating_3 int,
        rating_4 int,
```

```
        rating_5 int,
        all_rating float
);
CREATE TYPE

postgres=# CREATE OR REPLACE FUNCTION final_func(rating) RETURNS all_
rating AS $$
SELECT $1.rating_1, $1.rating_2, $1.rating_3, $1.rating_4, $1.rating_5,
( 1* $1.rating_1 + 2*$1.rating_2 + 3*$1.rating_3 + 4*$1.rating_4 + 5*$1.
rating_5)::float / ($1.rating_1 + $1.rating_2 + $1.rating_3 + $1.rating_4 +
$1.rating_5) AS avg_rating;
$$ LANGUAGE SQL;
CREATE FUNCTION
```

In the preceding function, we return the rating values and also calculate the average rating of the product by adding some weights to each rating value. Now, drop the previous aggregate and re-create it with this function, which will be evaluated on the final result of the state transition function:

```
postgres=# DROP AGGREGATE custom_rating_agg(products_rating);
DROP AGGREGATE

postgres=# CREATE AGGREGATE custom_rating_agg(products_rating) (
    SFUNC = rating_agg_transfn,
    STYPE = rating,
    INITCOND = '(0,0,0,0,0)',
    FINALFUNC = final_func
);
CREATE AGGREGATE
```

Now, execute the aggregate on the table and see all the results at once:

```
postgres=# SELECT (custom_rating_agg(p.*)).* FROM products_rating p;
 rating_1 | rating_2 | rating_3 | rating_4 | rating_5 | all_rating
----------+----------+----------+----------+----------+-----------
       16 |       21 |       26 |       17 |       20 |       3.04
(1 row)
```

Summary

This chapter explained how to create custom aggregates in PostgreSQL using the `CREATE AGGREGATE` statement. Aggregates are useful for performing specialized calculations on datasets that standard aggregates cannot handle. Custom aggregates can be created using the `CREATE AGGREGATE` statement and can incorporate user-defined functions to perform complex calculations.

The chapter also discussed the concepts of state transition function and final function, which are key components of custom aggregate creation. The state transition function updates the aggregate state as new rows are added to the group, while the final function calculates the final value of the aggregate once all rows in the group have been processed.

In addition to these functions, PostgreSQL allows us to create moving aggregate functions that help in writing custom window functions. It also supports writing combined aggregate functions that help in processing the aggregates in parallel. Overall, custom aggregates provide greater flexibility and control over calculations on datasets in PostgreSQL.

What's Next

In the next chapter, we will be covering some key features of the LISTEN and NOTIFY commands like the following:

- **Real-Time Event Handling**: Dive into using the LISTEN and NOTIFY commands for building real-time event-driven applications.

- **Advanced Notification Scenarios**: Explore more complex use cases for LISTEN and NOTIFY, including custom payload and multiplexing.

- **Interprocess Communication**: Discover how to use LISTEN and NOTIFY for interprocess communication between different application components.

- **Error Handling and Reliability**: Learn how to handle notification errors and ensure reliable delivery of notifications.

- **Database Triggers and Notifications**: Explore combining database triggers with NOTIFY to achieve complex data synchronization scenarios.

CHAPTER 18

Listen and Notify

In the previous chapter, we discussed aggregate concepts, where we created custom aggregates to solve users' specific problems using state changes and final functions. In this chapter, we will talk about the LISTEN and NOTIFY commands, which act as interprocess communication between database connections. Essentially, two sessions communicate over a channel, with LISTEN looking for changes from the other session and NOTIFY sending messages to all listening channels.

PostgreSQL Listen and Notify is a powerful feature that can be used by developers to create real-time applications that are triggered by database events. This feature allows applications to send and receive asynchronous notifications, making it easy for developers to create applications that respond quickly to changes in the database. To use PostgreSQL Listen and Notify, an application simply needs to register to listen to one or more channels. When a message is sent to that channel, the application will receive a notification. These notifications can be used to trigger actions within the application, such as updating a user interface or sending a notification to a user.

Simple Example

To initiate a listen for incoming messages, we can use the LISTEN command. Within a single session, multiple channels can be invoked for incoming messages. When the session is closed, these listening channels will also be closed. The following is an example of opening channels for the LISTEN command:

```
postgres=# LISTEN tcn;
LISTEN
postgres=# LISTEN abcd;
LISTEN
postgres=# SELECT pg_listening_channels();
 pg_listening_channels
-----------------------
```

© Baji Shaik and Dinesh Kumar Chemuduru 2023
B. Shaik and D. K. Chemuduru, *Procedural Programming with PostgreSQL PL/pgSQL*,
https://doi.org/10.1007/978-1-4842-9840-4_18

```
tcn
abcd
(2 rows)
```

As seen in the preceding example, we can use the pg_listening_channels() function to retrieve all active listeners available in the current session. Consider the following example, which demonstrates the two sessions' interprocess communication. Table 18-1 describes this behavior.

Table 18-1. *Interprocess communication using LISTEN and NOTIFY*

Session 1	Session 2
postgres=# LISTEN listening; LISTEN	
	postgres=# NOTIFY listening, 'Hello world!'; NOTIFY
postgres=# LISTEN listening; LISTEN Asynchronous notification "listening" with payload "Hello world!" received from server process with PID 656.	

In the preceding example, we have two sessions. In session 1, we executed the LISTEN command, and in session 2, we executed the NOTIFY command. It is important to execute LISTEN first, as it establishes the communication channel for incoming messages from NOTIFY. This process works by using a built-in queue in the PostgreSQL database system. The queue has a default size of 8GB and is where all NOTIFY command messages are stored, along with the PID of the sender. The LISTEN session retrieves messages from this queue and then processes accordingly. To track the size of this queue, we can use the function "pg_notification_queue_usage()", which displays the percentage of the queue that has unprocessed entries.

We used the "psql" client tool to demonstrate the LISTEN and NOTIFY behaviors. However, the "psql" client tool does not provide a polling mechanism on the listening channel. Therefore, in the preceding example, we needed to execute an additional LISTEN statement to print the messages received from the NOTIFY command. This example can also be demonstrated at the application level. Thanks to language-specific drivers with built-in polling mechanisms over the channel, there is no need to run the same command multiple times, as is necessary with "psql."

Build Polling in psql

The purpose of a database client tool is to send requests to the database server and print the response or error. One example of such a tool is "psql," which allows us to send SQL or utility commands to the database server and wait for a response. To build polling in "psql," we need to emulate the behavior of an application that polls the server for incoming notifications and print messages. To achieve this kind of emulation, we need to rely on an extension called "dblink," which provides the polling mechanism for notification channels.

The dblink extension provides the flexibility to connect to a remote database from a local database and execute a set of commands on the remote database system, returning the result set to the local database. This can be useful for applications that need to access data from multiple databases or perform operations on remote databases. To use dblink, the extension needs to be enabled in the system and the appropriate permissions need to be granted to the user.

Now, we can create the dblink extension in the system and use the dblink_get_notify function to poll the database server:

```
postgres=# CREATE EXTENSION dblink;
CREATE EXTENSION

postgres=# \df dblink_get_notify
List of functions
-[ RECORD 1 ]-------+------------------------------------------------------------
Schema              | public
Name                | dblink_get_notify
Result data type    | SETOF record
Argument data types | conname text, OUT notify_name text, OUT be_pid
                      integer, OUT extra text
Type                | func
-[ RECORD 2 ]-------+------------------------------------------------------------
Schema              | public
```

```
Name                   | dblink_get_notify
Result data type       | SETOF record
Argument data types    | OUT notify_name text, OUT be_pid integer, OUT
                             extra text
Type                   | func
```

Let's write an anonymous PL/pgSQL block using the dblink_get_notify function. This function establishes a new connection to the database with the help of the dblink extension and listens for incoming changes. Table 18-2 describes this behavior.

Table 18-2. *LISTEN continuously and print NOTIFY using* dblink_get_notify

Session 1	Session 2

postgres=# DO
$$
DECLARE
v_rec RECORD;
BEGIN
PERFORM dblink_connect('host=127.0.0.1
dbname=postgres password=postgres
user=postgres');
PERFORM dblink_exec('LISTEN test_channel');
 	
WHILE true LOOP
FOR v_rec IN (SELECT * FROM dblink_get_
notify()) LOOP
RAISE NOTICE 'Got record %', v_rec.extra;
END LOOP;
END LOOP;
END;
$$;
 	
..... Waiting for the incoming messages	

	postgres=# NOTIFY test_ channel, 'Hello world!'; NOTIFY

(continued)

Table 18-2. (*continued*)

Session 1	Session 2
NOTICE: Got record Hello world!	
	postgres=# NOTIFY test_ channel, 'This is second message'; NOTIFY
NOTICE: Got record This is second message	

As you can see, session 1 enters into the listening state and prints the messages whenever it receives a message over the channel from session 2. As mentioned earlier, we imitate the app polling mechanism using the dblink function dblink_get_notify. Let's use this as an example to create a live stream of event notifications for a table that undergoes frequent modifications from the application. Consider the following example, which has a table named test and an AFTER trigger that forms the payload in the form of JSON and sends it to the listeners:

```
postgres=# CREATE TABLE test(
id INT PRIMARY KEY,
name VARCHAR(100) NOT NULL);
CREATE TABLE

postgres=# CREATE OR REPLACE FUNCTION test_trg_func() RETURNS TRIGGER AS $$
BEGIN

    IF TG_OP = 'INSERT' THEN
        PERFORM pg_notify('test', (row_to_json(NEW)::jsonb||'{"OP":
        "INSERT"}'::jsonb)::text);
        RETURN NEW;

    ELSIF TG_OP = 'UPDATE' THEN
        PERFORM pg_notify('test', (row_to_json(OLD)::jsonb||'{"OP":
        "UPDATE OLD"}'::jsonb)::text);
        PERFORM pg_notify('test', (row_to_json(NEW)::jsonb||'{"OP":
        "UPDATE NEW"}'::jsonb)::text);
        RETURN NEW;
```

```
    ELSE
        PERFORM pg_notify('test', (row_to_json(OLD)::jsonb||
        '{"OP": "DELETE"}'::jsonb)::text);
        RETURN OLD;

    END IF;
END;
$$ LANGUAGE plpgsql;
CREATE FUNCTION

postgres=# CREATE TRIGGER test_trg AFTER INSERT OR UPDATE OR DELETE ON test
FOREACH ROW EXECUTE PROCEDURE test_trg_func();
CREATE TRIGGER
```

As shown in the preceding example, we created a table called test and a trigger function called test_trg_func() that is attached to the test_trg trigger. The function converts rows into JSON format and sends that data as a payload to the notifiers. Table 18-3 describes this behavior.

Table 18-3. *LISTEN and NOTIFY with a table trigger*

Session 1	Session 2
postgres=# DO	
$$	
DECLARE	
v_rec RECORD;	
BEGIN	
PERFORM dblink_connect('host=127.0.0.1	
dbname=postgres password=postgres	
user=postgres');	
PERFORM dblink_exec('LISTEN test');	
WHILE true LOOP	
FOR v_rec IN (SELECT * FROM dblink_get_	
notify()) LOOP	
RAISE NOTICE 'Got record %', v_rec.extra;	
END LOOP;	
END LOOP;	
END;	
$$;	
..... Waiting for the incoming messages	
	postgres=# INSERT INTO test
	VALUES (1, 'test');
	INSERT 0 1
NOTICE: Got record {"OP": "INSERT", "id": 1,	
"name": "test"}	
	postgres=# UPDATE test SET
	name='test 123' WHERE id=1;
	UPDATE 1

(continued)

Table 18-3. (*continued*)

Session 1	Session 2
NOTICE: Got record {"OP": "UPDATE OLD", "id": 1, "name": "test"} NOTICE: Got record {"OP": "UPDATE NEW", "id": 1, "name": "test 123"}	
	postgres=# DELETE FROM test; DELETE 1
NOTICE: Got record {"OP": "DELETE", "id": 1, "name": "test 123"}	

In the preceding example, we are able to capture any changes made to the test table via the listen and notify mechanism. This means that DML operations performed on the table will be notified to different sessions. We can also receive these notify messages on multiple sessions, where a single notify will send the message to all active listen sessions.

TCN Extension

TCN is a trusted extension in PostgreSQL that provides a single function called triggered_change_notification. In contrast to the previous example, which sends the entire inserted/updated or deleted record as a payload to the listeners, this extension only sends the key value details along with the table name and operation (INSERT, UPDATE, and DELETE) codes. By default, this function sends a notification to the tcn channel. However, you can specify a different channel by providing its name as an argument to the function.

Consider the following example:

```
postgres=# CREATE EXTENSION tcn;
CREATE EXTENSION

postgres=# CREATE TABLE test(id int primary key, name text);
CREATE TABLE

postgres=# CREATE TRIGGER test_tcn_trg AFTER INSERT OR UPDATE OR DELETE ON
test FOREACH ROW EXECUTE FUNCTION triggered_change_notification();
CREATE TRIGGER
```

To perform the following actions, follow the same process as in the previous example and conduct two sessions. Table 18-4 describes this behavior.

Table 18-4. *TCN extension demo for LISTEN and NOTIFY*

Session 1	Session 2

`postgres=# DO`
`$$`
`DECLARE`
`v_rec RECORD;`
`BEGIN`
`PERFORM dblink_connect('host=127.0.0.1`
`dbname=postgres password=postgres`
`user=postgres');`
`PERFORM dblink_exec('LISTEN tcn');`
`WHILE true LOOP`
`FOR v_rec IN (SELECT * FROM dblink_`
`get_notify()) LOOP`
`RAISE NOTICE 'Got record %', v_rec.extra;`
`END LOOP;`
`END LOOP;`
`END;`
`$$;`
 	
`... waiting for the incoming changes`	

	`postgres=# INSERT INTO test`
	`VALUES(1, 'test');`
	`INSERT 0 1`

`NOTICE: Got record "test",I,"id"='1'`	

	`postgres=# UPDATE test SET`
	`name='abcd' WHERE id=1;`
	`UPDATE 1`

`NOTICE: Got record "test",U,"id"='1'`	

The preceding output indicates that the listener was able to capture the DML operations on key columns that occurred during session 2.

Summary

The PostgreSQL Listen and Notify feature enables developers to create real-time applications that respond quickly to changes in the database. We have covered the LISTEN and NOTIFY commands which establish communication channels between database connections, and the TCN extension provides a function that sends notifications to the "tcn" channel, which includes only key value details along with the table name and operation codes. This feature simplifies the process of creating real-time applications and allows developers to quickly set up a communication channel between a database and an application.

What's Next

In the next chapter, we will be covering some key extensions that help with PL/pgSQL like the following:

- **PL/pgSQL Extensions**: Explore advanced extensions for PL/pgSQL, such as plprofiler and plpgsql-check extensions.

- **Integrating Extensions**: Learn how to integrate these extensions with your PL/pgSQL code to enhance functionality.

- **Extensions and Performance**: Dive into considerations for extension performance and optimization within PL/pgSQL functions.

- **Extensions for Complex Operations**: Explore extensions that provide specialized functionality for advanced data manipulation and analysis.

CHAPTER 19

PL/pgSQL Essential Extensions

In the previous chapter, we talked about the LISTEN and NOTIFY commands for building real-time event-driven applications and learned to handle notification errors to ensure reliable delivery of notifications. In this chapter, we will discuss the extensions that help with PL/pgSQL programming. We will cover a few extensions like `plpgsql_check` which will help to compile PL/pgSQL functions or procedures in syntactical and symmetrical way and `plprofiler` which will help to troubleshoot slow-running functions.

plprofiler Extension

`plprofiler` is an extension for PostgreSQL that allows you to measure the performance of PL/pgSQL functions through profiling. Profiling involves measuring the execution time of a function and identifying any areas that may be causing performance issues. With `plprofiler`, you can gather information about the function's runtime, the number of calls made to different parts of the code, and more.

Using `plprofiler`, you can identify which parts of your PL/pgSQL function are taking the most time, providing valuable insights for optimization. This tool is particularly helpful when working with complex PL/pgSQL code that requires performance tuning.

293

© Baji Shaik and Dinesh Kumar Chemuduru 2023
B. Shaik and D. K. Chemuduru, *Procedural Programming with PostgreSQL PL/pgSQL*,
https://doi.org/10.1007/978-1-4842-9840-4_19

Here are some use cases where plprofiler can be used:

1. **Identifying Slow-Running Functions in a Web Application**: Let's say you have a web application that uses PostgreSQL as the back-end database, and you've noticed that the application is running slow. By using `plprofiler`, you can profile the performance of the PL/pgSQL functions that are being called by the web application and identify which functions are taking the most time to execute. This can help you optimize your code and improve overall performance.

2. **Analyzing Performance Across Different Versions of a Function**: If you make changes to a PL/pgSQL function, you can use `plprofiler` to compare the performance of the function before and after the changes. This can help you understand the impact of your changes on performance and optimize the function accordingly.

3. **Identifying Performance Bottlenecks in Complex Functions**: If you have a complex PL/pgSQL function that's causing performance issues, you can use `plprofiler` to identify which parts of the function are causing the most problems. By analyzing the performance data generated by `plprofiler`, you can focus your optimization efforts on the areas of the function that are causing the most performance issues.

4. **Debugging Complex Functions**: When you have a complex PL/pgSQL function that is not working as expected, `plprofiler` can help you understand the flow of execution through the function. By analyzing the performance data, you can identify which parts of the function are causing issues and debug them more effectively.

To use `plprofiler`, you must first install the extension and enable it for specific functions you want to profile. During function execution, `plprofiler` collects data, which you can later analyze to understand how the function performs.

Installation

To install the `plprofiler` extension, you can follow two ways – install from the source or install it from the RPMs (RPM Package Manager).

You can follow these steps to install using source code:

1. Retrieve the Git repository and place it within the "contrib" directory of your PostgreSQL installation:

    ```
    git clone https://github.com/bigsql/plprofiler.git
    ```

2. Go to the `contrib` location and install:

    ```
    cd contrib/plprofiler
    make install
    ```

3. In case plprofiler was cloned to a location outside the "contrib" directory, you can make use of the subsequent commands:

    ```
    cd plprofiler
    USE_PGXS=1 make install
    ```

4. In either situation, you will install the plprofiler-client component using setup.py. For a pristine and separated environment, it's strongly advised to make use of Python virtual environments:

    ```
    cd python-plprofiler
    python ./setup.py install
    ```

5. To engage with the database, the client requires the psycopg2 database connector. Given that the plprofiler client was pip-installed in this setup, it's recommended to run the subsequent command:

    ```
    pip install psycopg2-binary
    ```

6. Modify the shared_preload_libraries parameter within the postgresql.conf file, then proceed to restart PostgreSQL:

    ```
    shared_preload_libraries='plprofiler'
    ```

7. Connect to the database and create an extension using the following command:

```
CREATE EXTENSION plprofiler;
```

You can follow these steps to install using RPMs:

1. Download the required RPMs from the repository. For example, you can download from the following location for RHEL 9 and PostgreSQL 15:

```
https://download.postgresql.org/pub/repos/yum/15/redhat/
rhel-9-x86_64/
```

You can look at this location based on your PostgreSQL and OS version: `https://yum.postgresql.org/packages/#pg15`.

2. Run the RPMs using the following command:

```
rpm -ivh <downloaded_rpms>
```

3. For Ubuntu, you can run the following command:

```
sudo apg-get update
sudo pip3.5 install plprofiler
```

4. Update the shared_preload_libraries parameter in postgresql.conf file and restart the PostgreSQL:

```
shared_preload_libraries='plprofiler'
```

5. Connect to the database and create an extension using the following command:

```
CREATE EXTENSION plprofiler;
```

Usage

To use `plprofiler`, you need to instrument your PL/pgSQL function with the `profiler` function. Let's take an example of the following function:

```
CREATE OR REPLACE FUNCTION slow_function() RETURNS VOID AS $$
BEGIN
    PERFORM pg_sleep(0.01);
```

```
    PERFORM pg_sleep(0.1);
    PERFORM pg_sleep(1);
    PERFORM pg_sleep(2);
END;
$$ LANGUAGE plpgsql;
```

The function contains four PERFORM statements that pause for a certain amount of time using the pg_sleep() function. These pauses simulate work being done in the function. The function does not return any values, as its return type is VOID.

Let's run the function and see the execution times:

```
postgres=# select slow_function();
 slow_function
---------------

(1 row)

Time: 3113.062 ms (00:03.113)
```

It ran little over 3 secs. Now generate an explain plan to see what is slow inside this function:

```
postgres=# explain analyze select slow_function();
                                    QUERY PLAN
--------------------------------------------------------------------------------
 Result  (cost=0.00..0.26 rows=1 width=4) (actual time=3113.642..3113.644
 rows=1 loops=1)
 Planning Time: 0.019 ms
 Execution Time: 3113.662 ms
(3 rows)
```

As you can see, the explain plan of the function does not show what's exactly slow inside the function. This is where plprofiler helps us.

Let's run the plprofiler report for the function using the following command:

```
$ plprofiler run --command " SELECT slow_function()" --output /tmp/slow_
function.html
```

This will generate the report that looks something like this:

PL Profiler Report for current

PL/pgSQL Call Graph

PL Profiler Report for current

public.slow_function() oid=16460

List of functions detailed below

- public.slow_function() oid=16460

All 1 functions (by self_time)

Function public.slow_function() oid=16460 (hide)

self_time = 3,113,996 μs
total_time = 3,113,996 μs

public.slow_function ()
  RETURNS void

Line	exec_count	total_time	longest_time	Source Code
0		13,113,996 μs (100.00%)	3,113,996 μs	-- Function Totals
1		0 μs (0.00%)	0 μs	
2		0 μs (0.00%)	0 μs	DECLARE
3		0 μs (0.00%)	0 μs	i INTEGER;
4		13,113,991 μs (100.00%)	3,113,991 μs	BEGIN
5		0 μs (0.00%)	0 μs	--FOR i IN 1..5 LOOP
6	1	10,235 μs (0.33%)	10,235 μs	PERFORM pg_sleep(0.01);
7	1	100,262 μs (3.22%)	100,262 μs	PERFORM pg_sleep(0.1);
8	1	1,001,262 μs (32.15%)	1,001,262 μs	PERFORM pg_sleep(1);
9		12,002,220 μs (64.30%)	2,002,220 μs	PERFORM pg_sleep(2);
10		0 μs (0.00%)	0 μs	--END LOOP;
11		0 μs (0.00%)	0 μs	END;
12		0 μs (0.00%)	0 μs	

This report shows the total time spent in the function (in milliseconds) for each line of code in the function. The report clearly shows that the pg_sleep(2) function accounted for most of the time.

Let's look at another example where we can troubleshoot the function and fix it.

Create two tables: orders and order_items. The orders table has columns id and total, and the order_items table has columns id, order_id, price, and quantity:

```
CREATE TABLE orders (
  id SERIAL,
  total DECIMAL
);
```

```
CREATE TABLE order_items (
  id SERIAL,
  order_id INTEGER,
  price DECIMAL,
  quantity INTEGER
);
```

Here's an example PL/pgSQL function that calculates the total for a given order by calculating the subtotal of all order items, adding the tax, and then updating the order total:

```
CREATE OR REPLACE FUNCTION calculate_order_totals(orderid INTEGER) RETURNS
VOID AS $$
DECLARE
  v_subtotal DECIMAL;
  v_tax DECIMAL;
  v_total DECIMAL;
BEGIN
  -- calculate the subtotal
  SELECT SUM(price * quantity) INTO v_subtotal FROM order_items WHERE
  order_id = $1;

  -- calculate the tax
  SELECT v_subtotal * 0.1 INTO v_tax;

  -- calculate the total
  SELECT v_subtotal + v_tax INTO v_total;

  -- update the order total
  UPDATE orders SET total = total + v_total WHERE id = $1;
END;
$$ LANGUAGE plpgsql;
```

To test this function with plprofiler, you can create some sample data in the orders and order_items tables:

```
INSERT INTO orders VALUES (generate_series(1,10000000), 0);
INSERT INTO order_items  (order_id, price, quantity) VALUES (generate_
series(1,10000000), round(random()::numeric,4)*100, round(random()::numer
ic*10,2));
postgres=# select * from order_items limit 10;
 id | order_id |  price  | quantity
----+----------+---------+----------
  1 |        1 | 30.6300 |        1
  2 |        2 | 49.2200 |        7
  3 |        3 | 80.7100 |        3
  4 |        4 | 76.2300 |        5
  5 |        5 | 53.3300 |        4
  6 |        6 | 55.4400 |        4
```

```
    7 |          7 |  55.2800 |              8
    8 |          8 |  51.9000 |              3
    9 |          9 |  52.6400 |              7
   10 |         10 |   7.4300 |              3
(10 rows)
```

Time: 0.346 ms

Let us run the `plprofiler` report for this function:

```
plprofiler run --command " SELECT calculate_order_totals(500)" --output ~/
Documents/calc_orders_before.html
```

```
 SELECT calculate_order_totals(500)
-- row1:
  calculate_order_totals:
[current]
----

(1 rows)
SELECT 1 (0.838 seconds)
```

Let's look at the report generated – `calc_orders_before.html`:

PL Profiler Report for current

PL/pgSQL Call Graph

PL Profiler Report for current

public.calculate_order_totals() oid=70707

List of functions detailed below

- public.calculate_order_totals() oid=70707

All 1 functions (by self_time)

Function public.calculate_order_totals() oid=70707 (hide)

self_time = 836,601 μs
total_time = 836,601 μs

public.calculate_order_totals (orderid integer)
RETURNS void

Line	exec_count	total_time	longest_time	Source Code
0		836,601 μs (100.00%)	836,601 μs	-- Function Totals
1	0	0 μs (0.00%)	0 μs	
2	0	0 μs (0.00%)	0 μs	DECLARE
3	0	0 μs (0.00%)	0 μs	v_subtotal DECIMAL;
4	0	0 μs (0.00%)	0 μs	v_tax DECIMAL;
5	0	0 μs (0.00%)	0 μs	v_total DECIMAL;
6	1	836,596 μs (100.00%)	836,596 μs	BEGIN
7	0	0 μs (0.00%)	0 μs	-- calculate the subtotal
8	1	254,413 μs (30.41%)	254,413 μs	SELECT SUM(price * quantity) INTO v_subtotal FROM order_items WHERE order_id = $1;
9	0	0 μs (0.00%)	0 μs	
10	0	0 μs (0.00%)	0 μs	-- calculate the tax
11	1	120 μs (0.01%)	120 μs	SELECT v_subtotal * 0.1 INTO v_tax;
12	0	0 μs (0.00%)	0 μs	
13	0	0 μs (0.00%)	0 μs	-- calculate the total
14	1	46 μs (0.01%)	46 μs	SELECT v_subtotal + v_tax INTO v_total;
15	0	0 μs (0.00%)	0 μs	
16	0	0 μs (0.00%)	0 μs	-- update the order total
17	1	582,013 μs (69.57%)	582,013 μs	UPDATE orders SET total = total + v_total WHERE id = $1;
18	0	0 μs (0.00%)	0 μs	END;
19	0	0 μs (0.00%)	0 μs	

As the report says, the total execution time of the function is 836 ms in which SELECT took 254 ms and UPDATE took 582 ms. If you try to generate an explain analyze plan of both the SQLs:

```
postgres=# explain analyze SELECT SUM(price * quantity) FROM order_items
WHERE order_id = 100;
                                QUERY PLAN
---------------------------------------------------------------------------
 Aggregate  (cost=116777.77..116777.78 rows=1 width=32) (actual
time=1020.964..1023.719 rows=1 loops=1)
    ->  Gather  (cost=1000.00..116777.76 rows=1 width=10) (actual
        time=57.376..1023.692 rows=1 loops=1)
        Workers Planned: 2
        Workers Launched: 2
        ->  Parallel Seq Scan on order_items  (cost=0.00..115777.66 rows=1
            width=10) (actual time=692.880..1014.015 rows=0 loops=3)
            Filter: (order_id = 100)
            Rows Removed by Filter: 3333333
 Planning Time: 0.242 ms
 Execution Time: 1023.779 ms
(9 rows)

Time: 1024.597 ms (00:01.025)
postgres=#
postgres=#
postgres=# begin;
BEGIN
Time: 0.095 ms
postgres=*# explain analyze update orders set total =1000 where id=100;
                                QUERY PLAN
---------------------------------------------------------------------------
 Update on orders  (cost=0.00..169248.60 rows=0 width=0) (actual
time=791.527..791.527 rows=0 loops=1)
    ->  Seq Scan on orders  (cost=0.00..169248.60 rows=1 width=38)
        (actual time=1.345..791.495 rows=1 loops=1)
        Filter: (id = 100)
        Rows Removed by Filter: 9999999
```

```
 Planning Time: 0.144 ms
 Execution Time: 791.649 ms
(6 rows)

Time: 792.049 ms
postgres=*# rollback;
ROLLBACK
Time: 0.137 ms
postgres=#
```

Both plans show a full table scan. Let's try to fix and generate a new report. If you think of a design prospective, both tables are missing primary keys on id columns. order_id of the order_items table should be referred to the id of the orders table as they both refer to the same order ids. Also, the first SELECT is running based on the order_id column, so create an index on that column.

```
postgres=# alter table orders add primary key (id);
ALTER TABLE
Time: 4915.782 ms (00:04.916)
postgres=# alter table order_items add primary key (id);
ALTER TABLE
Time: 5519.565 ms (00:05.520)
postgres=# alter table order_items add constraint fk_orders FOREIGN KEY
(order_id) REFERENCES orders(id);
ALTER TABLE
Time: 7436.968 ms (00:07.437)
postgres=# create index idx_ord_items_ord_id on order_items (order_id);
CREATE INDEX
Time: 5107.908 ms (00:05.108)
postgres=# analyze orders;
ANALYZE
Time: 243.553 ms
postgres=# analyze order_items ;
ANALYZE
```

Now try to run the plans and see what happens:

```
postgres=# explain analyze SELECT SUM(price * quantity) FROM order_items
WHERE order_id = 100;
                                QUERY PLAN
--------------------------------------------------------------------------
 Aggregate  (cost=8.46..8.47 rows=1 width=32) (actual time=0.034..0.034
 rows=1 loops=1)
   ->  Index Scan using idx_ord_items_ord_id on order_items
       (cost=0.43..8.45 rows=1 width=10) (actual time=0.024..0.025 rows=1
       loops=1)
         Index Cond: (order_id = 100)
 Planning Time: 0.391 ms
 Execution Time: 0.052 ms
(5 rows)

Time: 0.739 ms
postgres=# begin;
BEGIN
Time: 0.099 ms
postgres=*# explain analyze update orders set total =1000 where id=100;
                                QUERY PLAN
--------------------------------------------------------------------------
 Update on orders  (cost=0.43..8.45 rows=0 width=0) (actual
 time=0.065..0.066 rows=0 loops=1)
   ->  Index Scan using orders_pkey on orders  (cost=0.43..8.45 rows=1
       width=38) (actual time=0.012..0.013 rows=1 loops=1)
         Index Cond: (id = 100)
 Planning Time: 0.260 ms
 Execution Time: 1.026 ms
(5 rows)

Time: 1.567 ms
postgres=*# rollback;
ROLLBACK
```

As you can see, it picked up index scans, and query timings are much improved. Let's generate the report:

```
plprofiler run --command " SELECT calculate_order_totals(600)" --output ~/
Documents/calc_orders_after.html
 SELECT calculate_order_totals(600)
-- row1:
  calculate_order_totals:
----
(1 rows)
SELECT 1 (0.002 seconds)
```

Look at the report:

PL Profiler Report for current

PL/pgSQL Call Graph

PL Profiler Report for current

public.calculate_order_totals() oid=70707

List of functions detailed below

- public.calculate_order_totals() oid=70707

All 1 functions (by self_time)

Function public.calculate_order_totals() oid=70707 (hide)

self_time = 1,556 μs
total_time = 1,556 μs

public.calculate_order_totals (orderid integer)
    RETURNS void

Line	exec_count	total_time	longest_time	Source Code
0		1,556 μs (100.00%)	1,556 μs	-- Function Totals
1	0	0 μs (0.00%)	0 μs	
2	0	0 μs (0.00%)	0 μs	DECLARE
3	0	0 μs (0.00%)	0 μs	v_subtotal DECIMAL;
4	0	0 μs (0.00%)	0 μs	v_tax DECIMAL;
5	0	0 μs (0.00%)	0 μs	v_total DECIMAL;
6		1,552 μs (99.74%)	1,552 μs	BEGIN
7	0	0 μs (0.00%)	0 μs	-- calculate the subtotal
8	1	935 μs (60.09%)	935 μs	SELECT SUM(price * quantity) INTO v_subtotal FROM order_items WHERE order_id = $1;
9	0	0 μs (0.00%)	0 μs	
10	0	0 μs (0.00%)	0 μs	-- calculate the tax
11	1	49 μs (3.15%)	49 μs	SELECT v_subtotal * 0.1 INTO v_tax;
12	0	0 μs (0.00%)	0 μs	
13	0	0 μs (0.00%)	0 μs	-- calculate the total
14	1	34 μs (2.19%)	34 μs	SELECT v_subtotal + v_tax INTO v_total;
15	0	0 μs (0.00%)	0 μs	
16	0	0 μs (0.00%)	0 μs	-- update the order total
17	1	531 μs (34.13%)	531 μs	UPDATE orders SET total = total + v_total WHERE id = $1;
18	0	0 μs (0.00%)	0 μs	END;
19	0	0 μs (0.00%)	0 μs	

As you can see, the function took 1.5 ms in which SELECT is 0.9 ms and UPDATE took 0.6 ms.

Overall, plprofiler is a nice developer tool that can help you optimize the performance of your PL/pgSQL functions and improve the overall performance of your PostgreSQL database. By providing detailed performance information about functions, it can help identify performance bottlenecks and areas for optimization. With its functions for analyzing and visualizing performance data, it is a must-have for any developer working with PL/pgSQL.

plpgsql_check Extension

plpgsql_check is a PostgreSQL extension designed to enhance the development and debugging process of PL/pgSQL functions. It offers a collection of features that help developers identify potential issues, optimize code, and ensure reliable behavior of PL/pgSQL functions. The extension performs static analysis on PL/pgSQL code, which means it examines the code without executing it, identifying issues that might not be apparent during a simple visual review.

plpgsql_check can detect syntax errors, variable misuse, unused variables, incorrect parameter handling, and more, helping developers catch mistakes before running the code. It provides insights into code coverage, showing which parts of a PL/pgSQL function are executed during testing, aiding in verifying test comprehensiveness. The extension offers an interface for annotating code with special comments that influence its behavior during analysis, allowing developers to customize checks for their specific needs.

plpgsql_check is particularly useful in complex systems where PL/pgSQL functions play a significant role in business logic or data manipulation. By detecting potential problems early in the development cycle, plpgsql_check helps reduce the likelihood of bugs making their way into production environments. It can be integrated into continuous integration and deployment pipelines, ensuring that PL/pgSQL code quality is maintained throughout the software development life cycle.

Installation

You can follow these steps to install using source code:

1. Retrieve the Git repository and place it within the "contrib" directory of your PostgreSQL installation:

   ```
   git clone https://github.com/okbob/plpgsql_check.git
   ```

2. Go to the contrib location and install:

   ```
   cd contrib/plpgsql_check
   make
   make install
   ```

3.   To install the plpgsql_check extension, run the following
     command in your PostgreSQL database:

```
CREATE EXTENSION plpgsql_check;
```

Usage

You can use the plpgsql_check_function function to check the errors in your functions:

```
SELECT plpgsql_check_function('<function>', <different_options>);
```

This will return a table with information about any errors in the function. If there are
no errors, the table will be empty.

Let's look at a couple of examples where one is with error and one without errors:

```
CREATE OR REPLACE FUNCTION public.variable_example()
RETURNS void
LANGUAGE plpgsql
AS $function$
DECLARE
  x INT := 10;
BEGIN
  RAISE NOTICE 'x: %', x;
END;
$function$;
```

There is nothing wrong with the preceding example. Let's execute the plpgsql_check
function:

```
postgres=# SELECT plpgsql_check_function('public.variable_example');
 plpgsql_check_function
------------------------
(0 rows)

Time: 0.477 ms
postgres=#
```

It does not return anything, which means no errors or warnings as expected.

Let's take another example:

```
CREATE OR REPLACE FUNCTION public.variable_example()
RETURNS void
LANGUAGE plpgsql
AS $function$
DECLARE
  x INT := 10;
  y INT;
BEGIN
  RAISE NOTICE 'x: %', x;
END;
$function$;
```

In the preceding example, the variable y is defined but not used. Let's run the plpgsql_check function:

```
postgres=# SELECT plpgsql_check_function('public.variable_example');
          plpgsql_check_function
-------------------------------------------------
 warning:00000:4:DECLARE:unused variable "y"
(1 row)

Time: 0.590 ms
postgres=#
```

It shows a warning that y is not used.

The "plpgsql_check" extension can help in finding errors up front, providing an opportunity to fix unknown errors before they become problematic. Consider the following simple example:

```
postgres=#  CREATE OR REPLACE FUNCTION test_func() RETURNS void AS $$
BEGIN
PERFORM function_which_does_not_exist();
END;
$$ LANGUAGE plpgsql;
CREATE FUNCTION
```

In the preceding example, we created a function called test_func, and from inside we are trying to invoke a function which does not exist in the database at all. The function definition was created, but got an error when we tried to execute the function test_func. See the invocation as follows:

```
postgres=# SELECT test_func();
ERROR:  function function_which_does_not_exist() does not exist
LINE 1: SELECT function_which_does_not_exist()
               ^
HINT:  No function matches the given name and argument types. You might
need to add explicit type casts.
QUERY:  SELECT function_which_does_not_exist()
CONTEXT:  PL/pgSQL function test_func() line 3 at PERFORM
```

Having a linter for PL/pgSQL functions that provides detailed information about the function definition up front would be helpful. The plpgsql_check extension can perform this linting against the given function definition and print error messages. Try this extension on the preceding function to see the report we get:

```
postgres=# SELECT * FROM plpgsql_check_function_tb('test_func()');
[ RECORD 1 ]
functionid | test_func
lineno     | 3
statement  | PERFORM
sqlstate   | 42883
message    | function function_which_does_not_exist() does not exist
detail     |
hint       | No function matches the given name and argument types. You
             might need to add explicit type casts.
level      | error
position   | 8
query      | SELECT function_which_does_not_exist()
context    |
```

As you can see in the preceding output, this extension is complaining about a function that does not exist. Invoking this method will result in an error. The plpgsql_check extension is a valuable asset to developers. It helps in identifying errors that can only be caught during execution.

Summary

In this chapter, we talked about the extensions that help with PL/pgSQL programming. We covered the plpgsql_check extension which really helps to compile your functions to check if there are any identified potential issues, unused variables, and other code-related problems. We have also explained the plprofiler extension which allows you to profile the execution of PL/pgSQL functions. Profiling is the process of measuring the performance of a function to identify potential bottlenecks and optimize its execution.

Index

A, B

Aggregates
  rollingState/rollingValue, 278
  AVG() function, 275
  COUNT()/FILTER() operations,
      276, 277
  COUNT/FILTER statements, 273
  CREATE AGGREGATE, 278, 279
  data type, 277
  final function, 275, 276, 279, 280
  flexibility/control statement, 271
  GROUP BY clause, 271
  key features, 270
  pictorial representation, 274
  state_trans_func_max, 275
  state transition function, 273–275,
      277, 278
  SUM, MAX, MIN, and AVG, 272, 273
Arrays
  append elements, 93, 94
  declaration, 53
  dims function, 95
  FOR loop, 54
  iterate, 91, 92
  key features, 85
  length function, 89–91
  merge, 94
  multidimensional arrays, 94–96
  one/zero-based index, 88, 89
  remove duplicate elements, 92, 93
  single- and multidimensional arrays, 87

source code, 57, 58
square brackets, 53

C

Casting consistency
  castcontext, 154
  castfunc, 154
  castmethod, 156
  casttarget, 154
  conversion function, 163
  CREATE CAST command, 160
  data types, 163–165
  implicit type casting, 155
  JSONB, 165–167
  key features, 149
  pg_cast, 157, 158, 160
  pg_cast catalog table, 153
  pg_class table, 152
  regclass, 151
  temperature values, 161–163
  explicit type casting, 155, 156
Control statements, 59
  CASE statement, 66–68, 81
  complex control statements, 84
  IF/ELSE statement
      cascading statement, 65, 66
      conditional flow, 62–65
      ORDER BY clause, 63
      SELECT statement, 64
  key features, 61
  meaningful variable names, 84

© Baji Shaik and Dinesh Kumar Chemuduru 2023
B. Shaik and D. K. Chemuduru, *Procedural Programming with PostgreSQL PL/pgSQL*,
https://doi.org/10.1007/978-1-4842-9840-4

Control statements (*cont.*)
   principles, 84
   testing process, 84
   users/transactions, 78–81
Cursors
   attributes, 115
   code block, 114
   definition, 113
   FOUND attribute, 117, 118
   ISOPEN attribute, 115–117
   key features, 112
   monitor, 122, 123
   NOTFOUND attribute, 119, 120
   RAISE NOTICE statement, 119
   refcursors, 128–130
   ROWCOUNT attribute, 120, 121
   SCROLL keyword
      BEGIN WORK, 125
      declaration, 123, 124
      FETCH NEXT, 125
      NO SCROLL, 125–127
      WITH HOLD, 127, 128
   SQL interface, 113, 114
   test_refcursor() function, 129

D

Data Definition Language (DDL), 258, 259
Data types
   base types, 32
   code values, 31
   composite type, 33, 34
   declaration variables, 28, 29
   domain types, 35, 36
   multirange, 40, 41
   primitive data types, 28
   pseudo data types, 37
   pseudo-types, 27

   range, 38–40
   strings, 43
   supports base types, 30, 31
Dynamic SQL
   build complex queries, 173, 174
   column selection, 176–178
   considerations, 178–181
   definition, 169
   EXECUTE statement, 169
   index creation, 175, 176
   injection, 179
   parameterized queries, 179
   performance optimization, 180
   query statement, 170, 171
   quoting and escaping functions, 179
   sanitization/validation, 179
   security, 180
   table creation, 171–173
   use cases, 171

E

Exception handling
   advantages, 238
   assertions, 234
   attributes, 232
   BEGIN/END statements, 226–230
   constraint violations, 225
   data type mismatch errors, 225
   disadvantages, 239
   error messages, 232
   foreign key violations, 225
   FOUND, 223, 224
   GET call stack, 235, 236
   GET DIAGNOSTICS, 219–223
   GET STACKED DIAGNOSTICS
      statement, 237, 238
   key features, 217

object not found errors, 225

RAISE statement, 231, 232

RAISE NOTICE statement, 237

rethrow exception, 233, 234

SQLSTATE and SQLERRM, 229

syntax errors, 225

transaction

COMMIT/EXCEPTION blocks, 268

EXCEPTION block, 267

handle errors, 266

ROLLBACK/COMMIT, 269

thrown, 266

F, G

Functions

calling function, 184

categories, 185

definition, 183, 184

immutable, 186

pi() function, 185

STABLE functions, 188–191

VOLATILE functions, 191–194

H

Handling exceptions, *see* Exception
handling

I

Iterative statements

ARRAY, 76

CONTINUE statement, 70

EXIT statement, 70

features, 68

FOREACH, 77

FOR statement, 74–77

LOOP statement, 69–72

SLICE option, 77

WHILE statement, 72, 73

J, K

JavaScript Object Notation (JSON)

advantages, 104

built-in functions, 111

configuration data, 101

definition, 97

disadvantages, 104

flexible schema, 100

-> and ->> operators, 98

#>/#>> operator, 99

indexing data, 109, 110

INSERT statement, 97

JSONB, 165–167

key features, 96

metadata, 101

NoSQL-like data, 103

PL/pgSQL function, 105–109

SELECT statement, 98

user preferences, 102

L, M

LISTEN/NOTIFY commands, 283

dblink extension, 285

incoming messages, 283–285

interprocess communication, 284

key features, 281

psql extension, 285–290

test_trg_func(), 288

triggered_change_notification,
290, 291

N

NOTIFY, *see* LISTEN/NOTIFY commands
Numerical data types
    binary representation, 51
    bitwise operator, 51
    financial/scientific calculations, 51
    floating-point numbers, 52
    scientific/complex calculations, 51
    smallint data type, 50
    source code, 55, 56
    types, 50

O

Operators, 131
    advantages, 148
    arithmetic operators, 133
    benefits, 142
    bitwise operators, 134
    case-sensitive, 140–142
    comparison operators, 133
    concatenation, 138
    CREATE OPERATOR command, 135
    cust_opr schema, 139, 142
    data classification, 146–148
    data type math, 142, 143
    dates, 144–146
    disadvantages, 149
    equality/inequality, 136–140
    integers, 133
    integer value, 144
    interval data type, 145
    key features, 130
    logical operators, 134
    set operators, 134
    source code, 131, 132
    symbol/keyword, 131

    syntax, 135
    text operators, 134

P, Q

PL/pgSQL
    aggregates, 270, 271
    anonymous/named code
        blocks, 1
    arrays, 85
    block-structured language, 6
        anonymous/unnamed
            blocks, 6–10
        BEGIN ... END block, 8
        Hello World message, 8
        named blocks, 10, 11
        nested block, 9
    casting consistency, 151–167
    control statements, 59, 61–85
    cursors, 112–129
    data types, 25, 27–41
    dynamic SQL, 168–181
    exception handling, 217
    execution flow, 5–7
    extensions, 292, 293
    features, 1
    functions/procedures, 181, 183
    handling arrays, 87–96
    handling exceptions, 219
    installation process, 2–4
    JSON strings, 96, 97
    key features, 12
    LISTEN and NOTIFY commands,
        281, 283
    operators, 130–135
    return values/parameters, 199, 201
    stored procedures/functions, 2
    strings, numbers and arrays, 41, 43–58

transaction management, 262, 263

triggers, 240, 241

variables (*see* Variables, PostgreSQL)

plpgsql_check extension

    development/debugging process, 305

    error messages, 306–308

    installation, 305

    test_func, 308

    usage, 306

plprofiler extension

    calc_orders_before.html, 300

    debugging, 294

    installation, 295, 296

    order_items table, 298, 299

    PERFORM statements, 297

    performance/optimization, 294

    profiling, 293, 294

    report format, 298

    run option, 300

    SELECT statement, 301–304

    slow_function(), 297

    web application, 294

PostgreSQL, *see* PL/pgSQL

Procedures

    COMMIT/ROLLBACK operations, 195

    design/implementation, 198

    function (*see* Functions)

    log_message() method, 197

    LOOP/control statements, 194

    query creation, 194

    temporary function, 196, 197

    VARIADIC function, 197–199

R

Return values/parameters

    advantages/disadvantages, 203

    data type, 210

difference matrix, 206

INOUT parameter type, 216

integer parameters, 202

methods, 206

NEXT, 209

OUT parameters, 205, 214, 215

QUERY statement, 211

query statement, 202

RECORD type, 211, 212

RETURN statement, 203

RETURNS keyword, 201

SELECT statement, 207

SETOF/TABLE syntax, 212–214

SETOF, 204, 210

SQL statement, 213

TABLE, 205, 206, 208

S

Strings

    benchmarking disk, 44

    char(n) data type, 44

    concatenation operator (||), 43, 54, 55

    data types, 43

    format() function, 46–48

    NULL, 47–49

    table insert, 45

Structured Query Language (SQL)

    dynamic SQL, 169–181

    See also PL/pgSQL

T, U

Transaction management, 263

    COMMIT statements, 265

    exception handling, 266–269

    features, 262

    nested transactions, 263–266

triggered_change_notification (TCN), 290, 291

Triggers

advantages, 260

BEFORE/AFTER keywords, 242

CREATE TRIGGER command, 242, 243

definition, 241

disadvantages, 261

DROP TRIGGER command, 261

events, 258

ALTER, 260

creation, 258

log DDL, 258–260

INSERT table, 245

INSTEAD OF, 253, 254

key features, 240

last_modified column, 245

PRIMARY KEY/FOREIGN KEY, 243

referential integrity table, 243

row-level

BEFORE/AFTER, 248, 249

creation, 246

data constraint, 246, 247

events, 249

nested invocations, 249, 250

replicate data tables, 250–254

statement-level, 254

DML operation, 256

FOREACH ROW clause, 254–258

INSERT/UPDATE/DELETE statements, 255

order_log table, 255, 257

TG_OP arguments, 257

table creation, 244

V, W, X, Y, Z

Variables, PostgreSQL

ALIAS

array variables, 21

CURSOR keyword, 23, 24

record, 22, 23

reference/short-length variables, 18, 19

scalar, 20, 21

BEGIN...END block, 16

constant variables, 17

declaration section, 13–15

scope declaration, 15–17

Printed in the United States
by Baker & Taylor Publisher Services